Psychology AS

The Exam Companion

Mike Cardwell

•

Cara Flanagan

Nelson Thornes

a Wolters Kluwer business

First edition 2004

Revised edition published in 2005 by:
Nelson Thornes Ltd
Delta Place
27 Bath Road
CHELTENHAM
GL53 7TH
United Kingdom

06 07 08 09 / 10 9 8 7 6 5 4 3 2

A catalogue record for this book is available from the British Library

ISBN 978 0 7487 9475 1

Page make-up by GreenGate Publishing Services, Tonbridge

Printed in Croatia by Zrinski

Contents

COGNITIVE PSYCHOLOGY: HUMAN MEMORY

DEVELOPMENTAL PSYCHOLOGY: ATTACHMENTS IN DEVELOPMENT

PHYSIOLOGICAL PSYCHOLOGY: STRESS

INDIVIDUAL DIFFERENCES: ABNORMALITY

SOCIAL PSYCHOLOGY: SOCIAL INFLUENCE

RESEARCH METHODS

Introduction

The aim of this book is to provide a bank of exam-style questions for students taking the AQA (A) AS level examination, with comments on how to answer them. We hope to provide a comprehensive set of possible questions that could be asked. We can do this because the questions for the exam are written according to a set of rules as outlined on the next few pages. Of course there never can be a guarantee that we have identified *all* the possible questions but this resource should enable you to turn your knowledge of psychology into successful examination performance by providing questions and answers and in addition giving advice on how to answer the questions.

The book is divided into five modules: cognitive psychology, developmental psychology, physiological psychology, individual differences, and social psychology. The sixth module in the specification, research methods, is covered throughout the book and there is also a separate chapter with research methods exam-style questions and answers. Each module is divided into three sections and each section is again divided into topics (as few as one topic in some cases or as many as five).

Each **topic** is covered on a *double-paged spread.*

On the left-hand side you will find:

On the right-hand side you will find:

- A list of exam questions, each with a comment. The comment might be a suggestion about what to include in your answer or it might be an indication about where students typically go wrong.
- An example of an **A01/A02** question (more about this later) for that topic, with guidance about how you might structure your answer.
- A few research methods questions to build up your understanding of this area of the specification.

Examples of 'model' answers to all the questions.

We don't like the phrase 'model answers' because it suggests that they are the 'right answer'. There are no right answers in psychology. For each question there are many possible answers and we are providing only one example of an answer that would receive full marks. We have also provided answers to a range of A01/A02 questions. In some cases we have provided a complete answer, in others we have started the process and left you to finish it.

At the end of each section is a **review** feature, with an exam question complete with student answers and examiner's comments. The question relates to the topics covered in the section. You can answer it yourself, compare your answer with the student's efforts, and *learn* from what the examiner has to say about the sample answer.

In order to answer the questions in this book, you can use three sources of information: your teacher, your textbooks and the Internet.

This Exam Companion is based on material in *Psychology AS: The Complete Companion Revised Edition.*

AQA A AS examination 'rules': The exam

There are three unit exams:

Unit 1: Cognitive Psychology and Developmental Psychology

Unit 2: Physiological Psychology and Individual Differences

Unit 3: Social Psychology and Research Methods

Research methods is different (we will describe it later).

Each unit contains **two** sections.

Each of the unit exams is **one** hour in duration.

You have to answer **two** questions in one hour, selecting one question from each section (and there are two questions in each section).

Each question is divided into **three** parts.

Part (a) is worth 6 marks and is an **AO1** question.

Part (b) is the same.

Part (c) is worth 18 marks: 6 marks **AO1** and 12 marks **AO2**.

*What is **AO1** and **AO2**? Look at the next page...*

This is what a specification entry looks like:

Cognitive psychology: Human memory

a Short-term memory and long-term memory

Research into the nature and structure of short-term memory (STM) and long-term memory (LTM) (e.g. encoding, capacity and duration). The multi-store model of memory (Atkinson and Shiffrin) and at least one alternative to this (e.g. working memory: Baddeley and Hitch, levels of processing: Craik and Lockhart).

b Remembering and forgetting

Explanations of forgetting in short-term memory (e.g. decay and displacement). Explanations of forgetting in long-term memory (e.g. retrieval failure and interference). The role of emotional factors in memory, including flashbulb memories and repression (e.g. Freud).

Critical issue: Eyewitness testimony

Research into reconstructive memory (e.g. Bartlett). Memory research into eyewitness testimony (e.g. Loftus), including the role of leading questions.

This is what exam questions drawn from this part of the specification might look like:

SECTION A – Cognitive Psychology

Answer **one** question from this Section. You should attempt all parts of the question you choose.

1   **Total for this question:**   **30 marks**

     (a) Describe **three** differences between short-term memory and long-term memory.
            (2 marks + 2 marks + 2 marks)

     (b) Outline findings of research into reconstructive memory.   *(6 marks)*

     (c) Outline and evaluate the multi-store model of memory.   *(18 marks)*

2   **Total for this question:**   **30 marks**

     (a) Describe **two** explanations for forgetting in short-term memory.
            (3 marks + 3 marks)

     (b) Describe the procedures and findings of **one** study of the nature of long-term memory.   *(6 marks)*

     (c) 'Eyewitness testimony is extremely unreliable.'
     Consider psychological research into eyewitness testimony.   *(18 marks)*

SECTION B – Developmental Psychology

Answer **one** question from this Section. You should attempt all parts of the question you choose.

1   **Total for this question:**   **30 marks**

     (a) Explain what is meant by secure and insecure attachments.
            (3 marks + 3 marks)

     (b) Outline Bowlby's maternal deprivation hypothesis.   *(6 marks)*

     (c) Assess the extent to which research (theories **and/or** studies) supports the view that day care has negative effects on children's cognitive development.
            (18 marks)

2   **Total for this question:**   **30 marks**

     (a) Describe **two** effects of privation.
            (3 marks + 3 marks)

     (b) Describe the findings of **one** study of individual differences in attachment and give **one** criticism of this study.
            (3 marks + 3 marks)

     (c) To what extent are there cross-cultural variations in attachment?   *(18 marks)*

All three parts of each question *may* be on the same sub-section or may be drawn from more than one sub-section.

Across the two questions all sub-sections of the content will be sampled.

Note how closely the wording of the exam questions matches the wording of the specification. The wording of the specification dictates the wording of exam questions and therefore should guide your revision.

AQA A AS examination 'rules': How the questions are set

Don't be put off by this terminology. It is simply a formal way of distinguishing between the three different types of skill that the examination will test.

Examples
Anything that is given as an example (such as Freud) cannot be required as part of a question.

Questions are only set using the wording of the specification.

Including
Questions can be asked on Bowlby's maternal deprivation hypothesis because this is named and included in the specification.

Knowledge has two components:
Knowing the facts (A01).
Knowing the value of the facts (A02).

This objective is used for research methods questions only.

Questions are set with three **assessment objectives** in mind:

Assessment objective 1 (AO1)
Knowledge and understanding of psychology.

Assessment objective 2 (AO2)
Analysis and evaluation of psychology.

Assessment objective 3 (AO3)
To design, conduct and report psychological investigations.

In each question there will be 18 **AO1** marks and 12 **AO2** marks.
Parts (a) and (b) of each question are description (**AO1**) only. Part (c) is **AO1** + **AO2**.

Types of AO1 questions

You will only be asked to define 'key terms'. These are listed on page xi.

Criticisms can be positive or negative

Definitions
What is meant by the following terms … (2 marks + 2 marks + 2 marks) or (3 marks + 3 marks)
Describe **two** differences between … (3 marks + 3 marks)

APFCC (aims, procedures, findings, conclusions and criticisms)
Describe the aims and conclusions of **one** study of xxx … (6 marks)
Describe the procedures and findings of **one** study of xxx … (6 marks)
Describe the findings of **one** study of xxx and give **one** criticism of this study. (3 marks + 3 marks)

Note that APFCC questions will only be set on certain topics (see the table on page xi) whereas you could be asked about findings or conclusions in relation to any part of the specification.

Factors, effects and ways
Describe **two** factors that influence … (3 marks + 3 marks)
Describe **two** effects of … (3 marks + 3 marks)
Outline **two** ways that … (3 marks + 3 marks)

You might also be asked to give a criticism of the explanation or theory.

Research findings or conclusions
Outline the findings of research into … (6 marks)
Briefly describe the conclusions of research into … (6 marks)

Theories or explanations
Describe/outline **one** theory of … (6 marks)
Describe **one/two** explanations of … (6 marks) or (3 marks + 3 marks)

Types of AO1/AO2 questions

Question possibilities include:
To what extent …
Consider how psychologists have justified …
Outline and evaluate research (theories **and/or** studies) of …
Outline … and consider the strengths and weaknesses …

In the **AO1/AO2** part of the question students are asked to put their psychology into action.

The AO1/AO2 question will *sometimes* be preceded by a **quotation** which aims to offer some ideas about where to start the answer and/or what to discuss.

A useful tip is to read the quotation after reading the question, otherwise you might try to answer the quotation instead of the question. The quotation is intended to give you ideas.

How your answers are marked

AO1 (assessment objective 1)

AO1 questions are worth 2, 3 or 6 marks. When examiners assess this assessment objective they use one of the mark schemes shown on the right. The 'partial performance' criterion is applied when you are asked to provide more than one of something (such as aims and conclusions of a study) but you only cover one.

2 marks	The answer is both **accurate** and **detailed**.
1 mark	The answer is **basic, lacking detail, muddled** and/or **flawed**.
0 marks	The answer is **inappropriate** or **incorrect**.

3 marks	6–5 marks	The answer is both **accurate** and **detailed**.
2 marks	4–3 marks	The answer is **limited**. It is generally **accurate** but **less detailed**. (Partial performance is **accurate** and **detailed**).
1 mark	2–1 marks	The answer is **basic, lacking detail, muddled** and/or **flawed**. (Partial performance is **limited**, **generally accurate** but **less detailed**).
0 marks	0 marks	The answer is **inappropriate** or **incorrect**.

AO2 (assessment objective 2)

Commentary. *It is sometimes appropriate to offer your own comment upon a piece of research. The more that your comments are informed, the more you will receive credit. Simply saying 'It was a good study' lacks information whereas 'This was a good study because it was a well-controlled laboratory experiment' is an informed comment.*

Analysis. *This means breaking your answer down into its constituent parts. Once you have read the question you need to analyse what you should put in your response. You might identify certain key arguments, studies, examples, and so on.*

Effective use of material. *There is a crucial difference between describing theories, studies, and so on, and using them to make a point. The descriptive material must be used effectively – you must say what the study contributes to the topic being discussed or what a theory implies.*

This assessment objective is only applied in the part (c) questions. There are three things the examiner looks for when deciding what mark to award: commentary, analysis and effective use of material, as shown in the table.

Marks	Commentary	Analysis	Effective use of material
12–11	There is an **informed** commentary	**Reasonably thorough analysis** of the relevant psychological studies/methods	Material has been used in an **effective** manner
10–9	Reasonable	Slightly limited	Effective
8–7	Reasonable	Limited	Reasonably effective
6–5	Basic	Limited	Reasonably effective
4–3	Superficial	Rudimentary	Minimal interpretation
2–1	Just discernible	Weak and muddled	Mainly irrelevant
0	Absent	Wholly irrelevant	Wholly irrelevant

AO3 (assessment objective 3)

Most of the research methods questions are assessed using this third objective. Out of 30 marks, 21 marks are assessed in terms of **AO3**. A further 3 marks are **AO1** and the remaining 6 marks are **AO2**. The marking allocation is generally the same as the one used for AO1, i.e. accuracy and detail are important.

Improving exam performance: A few key pieces of advice

If the question says 'Describe how psychologists deal with ethical issues', you must think carefully about what is 'demanded'. This does not mean, for example, noting that the question is about ethical issues and then writing everything you know about ethical issues. You are required to write about how psychologists deal with ethical issues, and therefore you should restrict your answer to describing ways of dealing with the issues rather than the issues themselves.

When a person feels anxious they are best at recalling knowledge they understand well. The rest becomes fragmentary.

1 **In an exam it is harder to access information you have learned by rote.**

4 **Spend time thinking about the demands of the question.**

If you are likely to forget rote-learned material when anxious, it is critical that you don't simply learn facts for the exam. You need to understand them.

One way to achieve this is by deep processing, something you should know from your study of memory and the levels of processing approach. The study below illustrates this.

2 **Deeply process material as often as possible!**

5 **Focus on the requirements of the question.**

If you are asked to describe the findings of a study then you get no marks for mentioning conclusions or criticisms. Sometimes candidates who write less get more marks because what they write is exactly to the point.

3 **Time management is crucial.**

A psychologist asked participants to sort a pack of 52 cards, each with a word on it. The instructions were to sort the cards into whatever categories the participants chose. Once the first sort was completed, the cards were collected in and then handed back to the participants with the same instructions. The participants were asked to repeat the sorts until two consecutive sorts were almost the same. Then they were asked to write down as many words as they could remember. Not surprisingly they did rather well, and the more categories a participant had used the more words they recalled.

Why? Because in sorting the cards the words were processed in a meaningful way, and this caused the words to become lodged in memory. No participant tried to memorise the words, the words simply became part of that person's knowledge. This is the way we acquire most of what we know. And you can apply this to your study and recall of psychology. Engage in active processing and you will remember things effortlessly.

[This study was by Mandler, 1967]

In the examination you should write no more and no less than is indicated by the marks for the question. In the AQA (A) AS exam there are 30 marks for each question and you have 30 minutes to answer the question. This means there is a mark a minute. If a question is worth 6 marks you should spend no more than 6 minutes on your answer. This 6 minutes includes thinking as well as writing time.
Spend some time thinking about the demands of each question before choosing which ones to answer.

Many research methods questions require the answer to be in context.

6 **Research methods questions are different.**

Some research methods questions include the phrase 'in this study'. This means that you must set your answer in the context of the study or at least make some reference to the study described in the examination question.

Thus, when asked to describe one disadvantage of using an independent groups design in this study, the answer 'Participant variables are not controlled' would receive 1 out of 2 marks (because no context is given), whereas the answer 'Participant variables, such as susceptibility to alcohol, are not controlled' would received the full 2 marks (if the study was about susceptibility to alcohol).

These questions are not given 'positive marking'.

In this part of the exam, candidates are only credited for their first answer. If you are asked for 'one advantage of a laboratory experiment' and you describe two advantages ('They are artificial and tend to produce demand characteristics, where a participant responds to the experimenter's cues') then you will only receive credit for the first answer even when the second answer is better.

Where candidates go wrong

AO1 questions: Detail

The main difference between a good answer and a weak answer is *detail*.

An answer that gets 3 marks out of 3 marks is more detailed than one that receives 1 mark.

Consider the answers on the right, to the question:

Explain what is meant by majority influence. *(3 marks)*

These will assist your explanation. It is not sufficient to say 'for example, when you do the same as all your friends'.

Answer 1 Majority influence is when the majority in a group influence the behaviour of other members of the group. For example, in Asch's study one true participant went along with other members of the group when asked to judge the length of the line even though he knew the answer was wrong. It is likely that the change of opinion was only public.

Answers 1 and 2 are both accurate and detailed, worth 3 marks. Answer 3 is lacking detail and muddled, worth 1 mark.

Answer 2 Majority influence is when the behaviour or attitudes of an individual are altered due to group pressure. An example would be when you say you liked a new song because all your friends say it's great.

Answer 3 Majority influence is where the majority influence the rest of the group even if they don't want to be influenced.

How can you provide more detail?

- Provide examples.
- Refer to relevant psychological studies.
- Use technical terms.

Don't just say 'For example, Asch's study'. You need to provide some relevant details of this study.

Display your psychological knowledge by using psychological language (technical terms). This gives precision to your answer.

AO2 skills

AO2 skills: Commentary, analysis and effective use of material

Part (c) of each question is worth 18 marks: 6 marks **AO1** and 12 marks **AO2**. **AO1** is description and **AO2** is evaluation which consists of commentary, analysis and effective use of material.

Commentary

It is sometimes appropriate to offer your own comment on a piece of research. For example, you might say, 'This study suggests that children who experience early privation do suffer permanent emotional damage'. The more that your comments are *informed*, the more you will receive credit. Simply saying 'There are weaknesses in this theory' lacks information, whereas 'There are weaknesses in this theory, for example, it doesn't account for different kinds of LTM' is an informed comment.

Analysis: breaking something down into its constituent parts

When you are asked a question it is important to identify various components of the question and of your answer. Such components provide your answer with *structure*. You might decide on a plan for your answer such as four points you wish to make or four studies you wish to discuss. Each of these would be one paragraph of about 80 words (⅓ AO1 and ⅔ AO2), making an essay of 320 words. A mini-essay of this length is enough for an excellent response.

Effective use of material

Often we have a vague idea of what material might form an appropriate response. For example, if you are asked about ethical issues in social influence research, you might choose to write about Milgram's classic study. However, just describing the procedures of this study leaves the examiner with the task of teasing out what the ethical issues were. You must *use the material effectively* and actually state what it is you think you are demonstrating. For example, you might say, 'The prods that were used in the experiment made participants feel they didn't have the right to withdraw. *This shows that* the study lacked ethics'.

Evaluation means 'to establish the value' of a theory, study or whatever. At advanced level you are expected to go beyond knowing something and show that you have an opinion about its value.

There are many ways to establish 'value'.

Positive evaluation/criticism, such as

- Reference to studies that support the research cited.
- Applications of the research which demonstrate its usefulness.
- Citing strengths of the methodology, as in a highly controlled experiment.

Negative evaluation/criticism, such as

- Poor ecological validity (findings apply to particular settings only).
- Poor population validity (may use only American male students).
- Poor internal validity (study may have confounding variables).

Key terms and key studies

Cognitive psychology: Memory			Key Studies
Eyewitness testimony	Memory	Short-term memory	The nature of STM
Flashbulb memories	Multi-store model		The nature of LTM
Forgetting	Reconstructive memory		Reconstructive memory
Long-term memory	Repression		The role of leading questions
Developmental psychology: Attachment			
Attachment	Deprivation	Social development	Individual differences in attachment
Cognitive development	Insecure attachment		Cross-cultural differences in attachment
Cross-cultural variation	Privation		Effects of deprivation
Day care	Secure attachment		The effects of privation
Physiological psychology: Stress			
Cardiovascular disorders	Physiological approaches to stress management	Workplace stressor	Stress and cardiovascular disorders
General adaptation syndrome	Psychological approaches to stress management Stress		Stress and the immune system
Immune system	Stress management		Life changes
Life changes	Stressor		Workplace stressors
Individual differences: Abnormality			
Abnormality	Deviation from ideal mental health	Failure to function adequately	Biological explanation of eating disorders
Anorexia nervosa	Deviation from social norms	Statistical infrequency	Psychological explanation of eating disorders
Bulimia nervosa	Eating disorders		
Social psychology: Social influence			
Conformity (majority influence)	Informed consent	Protection of participants from psychological harm	Conformity (majority influence)
Deception	Internal validity	Social influence	Minority influence
Ethical issues	Minority influence		Obedience to authority
Experimental validity	Obedience to authority		

Cognitive psychology is one area of psychology. Cognitive psychologists believe that human behaviour can be best explained if we first understand the mental processes that underlie behaviour. It is, therefore, the study of how people learn, structure, store and use knowledge – essentially how people *think* about the world around them.

This module is divided into

Short-term memory and long-term memory

The nature and structure of short-term memory (STM)

The nature and structure of long-term memory (LTM)

The multi-store model of memory

Alternative models of memory

End of section review

Remembering and forgetting

Forgetting in short-term memory

Forgetting in long-term memory

Emotional factors in memory

End of section review

Critical issue: Eyewitness testimony

Reconstructive memory

Research into eyewitness testimony

End of section review

COGNITIVE PSYCHOLOGY: HUMAN MEMORY

DEVELOPMENTAL PSYCHOLOGY: ATTACHMENTS IN DEVELOPMENT

PHYSIOLOGICAL PSYCHOLOGY: STRESS

INDIVIDUAL DIFFERENCES: ABNORMALITY

SOCIAL PSYCHOLOGY: SOCIAL INFLUENCE

RESEARCH METHODS

The nature and structure of short-term memory (STM)

Specification extract

Research into the nature and structure of short-term memory (STM) (e.g. encoding, capacity and duration).

At most you need 4 marks' worth of material for the procedures and then less for findings (or vice versa). These questions do not require a balance, so you could write twice as much on procedures as findings and still get full marks.

Take care when writing about conclusions – if you include any *findings* they won't receive credit.

There are three things to do: 1. name the criticism (e.g. a lack of ecological validity), 2. explain this (what is 'ecological validity'?) and 3. set your criticism in context (why is a lack of ecological validity true in this study?). This is the **three-point rule**.

You can either report many findings from one study or look at many different studies. However, you should make sure you focus only on findings.

Very important note: The inclusion of research methods questions follows the order that these are done in *Psychology AS: The Complete Companion*.

a) What is meant by the 'aims' of a study?

b) Many studies use the single blind technique. What is this?

c) Did the main study you describe here use single blind?

d) What is double blind? Why is it sometimes necessary to use a double blind design?

e) What is participant reactivity?

f) What are standardised instructions? Why are they used?

You need to identify what to write for AO1 (6 marks in every question) and what might constitute AO2 (12 marks). In this question you need to evaluate research into the nature and structure of STM (AO2 content) and therefore the AO1 must be some brief description of this research.

AO1 questions

1. Describe the procedures and findings of **one** study into the nature of STM.   *(6 marks)*

2. Describe the aims and conclusions of **one** study into the nature of STM.   *(6 marks)*

3. Give **two** criticisms of this study.   *(3 marks + 3 marks)*

4. Outline findings of research into the nature of STM.
                                     (6 marks)

AO1/AO2 question

Consider what research (studies **and/or** theories) has told us about the nature and structure of short-term memory (STM).   *(18 marks)*

Possible plan

	AO1 Describe research (write about 100–150 words in total)	AO2 Give strengths and/or limitations (write about 200–250 words *in total*)
Study/theory 1		
Study/theory 2		
Study/theory 3		

1 A study on the nature of STM: Peterson and Peterson (1959). The procedures were that each participant was given a nonsense trigram (e.g. WRT) and a three-digit number. The participant had to count backwards from this number until told to stop and say what the trigram was. Each participant was given two practice trials followed by eight trials. On each trial the retention interval was different: 3, 6, 9, 12, 15 or 18 seconds. The findings were that participants remembered about 90% when there was only a 3 second interval and about 2% when there was an 18 second interval. After 18 seconds recall tailed off slowly.

Notice that an example can be used to increase the detail of the answer. If you refer to a study as an example, you should explain how it illustrates your point. You should not simply say 'For example the study by Bahrick et al.', but might say 'For example, Bahrick et al. found that people could name the photographs of people they were at high school with up to 48 years later.'

2 A study on the nature of STM: Peterson and Peterson (1959). The aims were to conduct a systematic and controlled study; to look at the duration of immediate or short-term memory; and to do this when verbal rehearsal is prevented.
We can conclude from this study that information remains in STM for less than 18 seconds if verbal rehearsal is prevented. The findings also show that most information has disappeared within a few seconds. This allows us to assess the duration of STM and conclude that STM and LTM are distinctly different kinds of memory.

3 **Criticism 1:** A particular kind of memory was tested in this experiment, as in many memory experiments (called episodic memory). Other kinds of memory may behave somewhat differently. This means that this study lacks ecological validity (cannot be easily applied to other settings).
Criticism 2: The participants in this study were students. It is quite likely that they have rather different memories than people of other age groups. This means that the study lacked population validity.

4 Peterson and Peterson found that participants correctly recalled 90% of the trigrams they were given when the retention interval was 3 seconds, about 50% after 6 seconds of counting backwards and about 2% when there was an 18 second interval. After 18 seconds recall tailed off slowly.
Sebrechts *et al.* found that participants could remember words if asked to recall them immediately after they heard them but that recall dropped to almost zero after 4 seconds.

There are no marks for creative writing, just record the findings.

research methods A

a) Aims are a statement of what the researcher(s) intend to find out. This may refer to a hypothesis or it may refer to a previous study which the researcher is attempting to support or challenge.

b) Single blind technique is a form of research design where the participants do not know the aims of the study, to prevent the participant trying to alter their behaviour to please (or annoy) the experimenter.

c) In Peterson and Peterson's study, participants weren't told the aims of the study but they weren't deceived and as they were psychology students it is likely that they would guess what it was about.

d) Double blind is when neither the participant nor the experimenter knows the aims of the study. If an experimenter knows the aims, he/she may inadvertently give cues about how to behave (in this case the person conducting the study, the experimenter, is not the same as the person who has designed and is directing the study).

e) Participant reactivity refers to the fact that participants react to cues in the experimental situation and adjust their behaviour.

f) A set of instructions used for each participant. They must always be the same otherwise differences between participants might be due to the use of different instructions.

Describe a study	Give strengths and/or limitations
Peterson and Peterson used the Brown–Peterson technique (recalling trigrams) to show that information has all but disappeared from STM after about 20 seconds.	The use of a controlled technique enables precise measurement of human behaviour. This study lacked population validity because it was just students. Psychology students may also have guessed the purpose of the study. It is quite likely that they have rather different memories than people of other age groups. This means that the study lacked population validity.
Baddeley (1966) tested STM recall and found that participants with an acoustically similar word list recalled about 55% if STM was tested but this was over 70% when LTM was tested. The reverse was true for semantically similar words. STM recall was good (75%) whereas it was poor when LTM was tested (about 55%).	A strength of this study is that it demonstrates how STM and LTM are different. A limitation is that many memory experiments relate to one *particular* kind of memory. Most memory experiments, like this one, are concerned with semantic memory and the findings don't necessarily apply to other kinds of memory such as episodic and procedural memory.
Jacobs found that participants could recall more digits than letters. The average span for digits was 9.3 items whereas it was 7.3 for letters. Jacobs also found that recall increased steadily with age; he found that 8 year olds could remember an average of 6.6 digits whereas the mean for 19 year olds was 8.6 digits.	One strength is that other studies have produced findings that confirm the original study, for example Miller suggested that the capacity of memory was 7 ± 2. This suggests that the original finding was right (or valid), although later research has refined the original findings. A limitation is that in other studies it has been shown that there are individual differences in digit span. Some people only can recall 4 items whereas others can cope with 10 or more. This suggests that performance may be affected by factors other than the capacity of STM.

COGNITIVE PSYCHOLOGY: HUMAN MEMORY

The nature and structure of long-term memory (LTM)

Specification extract

Research into the nature and structure of long-term memory (LTM) (e.g. encoding, capacity and duration).

a) *What is research?*

b) *What is the difference between a finding and a conclusion?*

In a psychological study the researchers found that older participants could recall, on average, 60% of a word list whereas younger participants could recall 85%.

c) *What might you conclude from these findings?*

d) *Suggest **one** reason why this conclusion might be wrong.*

For 'key studies' you need to know details of aims, procedures, findings, conclusions and criticisms (APFCC). You can be asked for one or two of these APFCC in any question. A list of all the APFCC studies is given on page xi.

This question makes life easy because you don't have to distinguish between findings and conclusions – they are both creditworthy.

State the criticism, and explain why it is an issue in the context of this particular study.

You can write about the findings of one study, or can describe the findings from several different studies.

Make sure you outline conclusions and not findings. What do the findings *show*?

This question makes it easy to identify the **AO1** and **AO2** components. For 6 marks (about 6 minutes' worth of writing) you should outline research. 'Research' can be a study or a theory/explanation. In this case it is likely that you would describe a few studies. For the **AO2** component of your answer you need to evaluate the research you have described. This could consist of positive and/or negative criticisms, such as methodological problems (was the study conducted in an artificial environment or did it use artificial stimulus materials?) or useful applications of the findings.

AO1 questions

1. Describe the aims and procedures of **one** study into the nature of LTM. *(6 marks)*

2. Describe the findings and conclusions of **one** study into the nature of LTM. *(6 marks)*

3. Give **two** criticisms of this study. *(3 marks + 3 marks)*

4. Outline findings of research into the nature of LTM. *(6 marks)*

5. Outline conclusions of research into the nature of LTM. *(6 marks)*

AO1/AO2 question

Outline and evaluate research (theories **and/or** studies) into the duration of memory. *(18 marks)*

Possible plan

	AO1 Outline procedures/ findings/ conclusions	**AO2** Criticism 1	**AO2** Criticism 2
Study 1			
Study 2			
And so on			

1 A study on the nature of LTM: Bahrick *et al.* (1975). The aim was to investigate very long-term memory in a natural setting where the things to be remembered were of personal significance. The study also aimed to compare verbal and visual LTM. The procedure was to test nearly 400 participants aged 17 to 74, who were given a free-recall test and asked to list all the names that they could remember of individuals in their graduating class, a photo recognition test consisting of 50 photos, some of which were from the participant's high-school yearbook and a name recognition test for ex-school friends.

> *The aims and procedures don't have to be of the same length, but you should try for more than just a very brief statement of aims.*

research methods A

2 A study on the nature of LTM: Bahrick *et al.* (1975). The findings were that those participants who were tested within 15 years of graduation were about 90% accurate in identifying faces and names in a recognition test. After 48 years, this declined to about 80% for names and 70% for photos. After 15 years, free recall was only about 60% accurate, dropping to 30% after 48 years. The conclusions were that there is evidence of VLTM (very long-term memory) up to 57 years after graduation, though there is some loss of memory over time. Recognition was better than recall, which suggests that in real life our memories contain a vast amount of information but we are not always able to recall it.

3 **Criticism 1:** This is a much better way to test memory than the more usual laboratory studies. Studies carried out in the laboratory have found much larger retention losses over long periods than was found in this study. This means that this study is more true to life and can be used to build up a more valid theory.
Criticism 2: It is possible that the reason why participants had better recall for the people they knew in high school than when memories are tested in laboratory settings was because they regularly rehearsed this knowledge. They might have even seen ex-classmates regularly.

> *Criticism should be sufficiently elaborated to gain the full 3 marks. Remember to include some mention of the consequences of a particular criticism.*

4 Bahrick *et al.* (1975) found that those participants who were tested within 15 years of graduation were about 90% accurate in identifying faces and names in a recognition test. After 48 years, this declined to about 80% for names and 70% for photos. After 15 years, free recall was only about 60% accurate, dropping to 30% after 48 years. Shepard (1967) found that participants showed almost perfect recognition of about 600 memorable pictures when shown them an hour later. Four months later they were still able to recognise 50% of the photographs.

5 We can conclude from Bahrick *et al.* (1975) that there is evidence of VLTM up to 57 years after graduation, though there is some loss of memory over time. Recognition was better than recall, which suggests that in real life our memories contain a vast amount of information but we are not always able to recall it. This is supported by the research by Shepard (1967). The findings of this study suggest that recall may be almost perfect in the mid-term (after one hour) but even after a few days it is fairly good (50% recall).

> *It is easy to slip into a description of findings when asked for conclusions. One way to avoid this is to briefly state findings and then state what the findings show or what we can conclude from them, as has been done here.*

a) Scientists aim to produce answers to questions about behaviour that are better than commonsense. They do this by conducting well-controlled studies.

b) A finding is what was found out. It consists of pieces of factual information such as percentage of correct answers. A conclusion is some kind of interpretation of the facts – the researcher's opinion, based on the facts.

> If you write about 'participants' instead of 'people' this would be a finding and not a conclusion.

c) We might conclude from this finding that older people have poorer recall of words than younger people.

d) This conclusion may be wrong because of differences in motivation. Younger people may be more competitive and therefore try harder to recall as many words as they can. Older people may not be as motivated to do well in the task and so perform relatively poorly.

AO1 Outline study	AO2 Criticism 1	AO2 Criticism 2
Bahrick *et al.* (1975) looked at the duration of LTM and tested nearly 400 participants aged 17 to 74 on their recall of classmates using yearbook photos. They found that after 48 years people could recall 80% of their names.	This is a much better way to test memory than the more usual laboratory studies and suggests that in the real world people can remember more than has been found in many laboratory studies.	It is possible that the reason why participants had better recall for the people they knew in high school than when memories were tested in laboratory settings was because they might even have seen ex-classmates regularly.
Baddeley (1966) tested STM recall and found that participants with an acoustically similar word list recalled about 55% if STM was tested but this was over 70% when LTM was tested. The reverse was true for semantically similar words. STM recall was good (75%) whereas it was poor when LTM was tested (about 55%).	A strength of this study is that it demonstrates how STM and LTM are different. This shows that words in STM tend to be remembered in terms of their sounds (i.e. acoustically) rather than their meaning (i.e. semantically), but that in LTM words tend to be coded in terms of their meaning (i.e. semantically).	A strength of this study is that it demonstrates how STM and LTM are different. A limitation is that many memory experiments relate to one *particular* kind of memory. Most memory experiments, like this one, are concerned with semantic memory and the findings don't necessarily apply to other kinds of memory such as episodic and procedural memory.
Waganaar and Groeneweg (1990) interviewed people who had been imprisoned in concentration camps during the Second World War. Thirty years on their recall was still good for certain details, such as the name of the camp commandant.	However they had forgotten many other details. This raises the question of why some memories are enduring while others aren't. It may be that we do remember a lot of things but just can't *recall* them.	The emotional nature of these memories means that one might explain their duration in terms of emotional factors. This means we cannot generalise these findings to all long-term memory.

The multi-store model of memory

Specification extract

The multi-store model of memory (Atkinson and Shiffrin).

research methods Q

a) What is experimental control?

b) Why is control needed?

In an experiment on memory, participants were shown a list of long or short nonsense syllables to see if the length of the syllable affected recall. After 10 minutes they were asked to recall the nonsense syllables.

c) What was the IV in this study?

d) What was the DV?

e) Name one other factor that might have varied in this study.

f) How could you have controlled this variable?

This is usually an easy question for candidates; in fact, so easy that they tend to write too much for the 2 marks available for each component. You simply want to name the difference and give a piece of detail, e.g. state that the STM and LTM use different codes *and* that these codes are acoustic in the case of STM and semantic in the case of LTM. Saying capacity of STM is 7±2 is worth about 1 mark. If the question awarded 3 marks for each difference, you would need to provide further detail of each difference, such as making reference to research support.

The temptation is to draw a diagram of the model. A diagram alone demonstrates knowledge but not understanding. For the understanding part, you need to add a description of how the boxes relate to each other. In other words, you need to describe the *processes* involved with the model.

For this question (unlike question 2) you just want to give a brief outline of the model and focus on the *concept* more than the structure of the model.

You could just write about the findings from one study, or you might include findings from a variety of studies. Either way you want details of about four or five findings.

Strictly speaking you couldn't be asked this question (or number 6) because strengths and limitations are not specified in the specification. You *could* be asked to describe two criticisms of the multi-store model as an AO1 question and could be asked to evaluate the multi-store model as an AO1/AO2 question. In an AO1/AO2 question it is useful to be familiar with strengths and limitations so you can give a balanced evaluation of the model.

This question may throw you slightly. It does not require any description of the multi-store model. It requires a description of *criticisms* of the model, such as those you provided in your answers to questions 5 and 6 above. For each criticism you must outline it then consider whether this criticism is valid. For example, you might suggest that the multi-store model is well supported by experimental research and then cite one or two studies to support this statement. You might further mention research that doesn't support the model, as a further means of evaluating the criticisms. And what do you conclude about this particular criticism? Was it fair or not? The question says 'some criticisms' as a cue to remind you that you do not need to list *all* the criticisms you know. Restrict yourself to a few and evaluate each thoroughly. You receive AO1 marks for accuracy and detail, not a lengthy list with little detail.

AO1 questions

1. Outline **three** differences between short-term memory and long-term memory. *(2 marks + 2 marks + 2 marks)*

2. Outline the main features of the multi-store model of memory. *(6 marks)*

3. What is the multi-store model of memory? *(3 marks)*

4. Outline research findings that support the multi-store model. *(6 marks)*

5. Describe **two** strengths of the multi-store model of memory. *(3 marks + 3 marks)*

6. Describe **two** limitations of the multi-store model of memory. *(3 marks + 3 marks)*

AO1/AO2 question

Outline some criticisms of the multi-store model of memory and consider to what extent these criticisms are fair. *(18 marks)*

Possible plan

	AO1 Outline the criticism	**AO2** Provide evidence to support the criticism	**AO2** Provide evidence to challenge the criticism	**AO2** What can you conclude about this criticism? (Is it fair?)
Criticism 1				
Criticism 2				
Criticism 3				

1 STM has a very limited duration whereas LTM has potentially unlimited duration.

STM has a very limited capacity whereas LTM has potentially unlimited capacity.

Information in STM is encoded acoustically, whereas information in LTM is encoded semantically.

2 Atkinson and Shiffrin (1968) claimed that memory is comprised of three different stores. The sensory stores are constantly receiving information but most of this receives no attention. This incoming data remains in the sensory store for a very brief period. If a person's attention is focused on the sensory store, the data is then transferred to STM.

It is worth practising the art of précis. You should be able to summarise models such as this in a concise yet informative way.

The second step is moving information from STM to LTM. Atkinson and Shiffrin said that this happens through rehearsal. They proposed a direct relationship between rehearsal in STM and the strength of the long-term memory – the more the information is rehearsed, the better it is remembered.

3 The multi-store model of memory is a description of how memory works in terms of three 'stores' – sensory memory, STM (limited capacity, short duration) and LTM (potentially unlimited capacity and duration). Attention and rehearsal explain how data is transferred.

This is a précis of your précis, even more challenging!

4 Sperling (1960) found that when asked to report a complete grid of digits and letters, participants' recall was poorer than when asked to give one row only, showing that information decays rapidly in the sensory store. Glanzer and Cunitz (1966) found that participants tend to remember the words from the start of the list (rehearsed and in LTM) and from the end of the list (still in STM) but are

There's no penalty for mentioning conclusions (Sperling's study showed that information decays rapidly) but you should avoid spending time writing descriptions of procedures that will gain no credit.

less good at recalling words in the middle. Research has found that different areas of the brain are active in STM and LTM, with the prefrontal cortex active during STM tasks and the hippocampus active when long-term memory is engaged.

5 **Strength 1:** Studies on duration, capacity and encoding have tended to support the distinction proposed by Atkinson and Shiffrin. For example, Baddeley found that STM uses an acoustic code whereas LTM uses a semantic code.

research methods **A**

a) Using techniques to ensure that confounding variables are eliminated.

b) Confounding variables might otherwise affect the outcome of an investigation because they act as additional IVs.

c) The length of the nonsense syllable (long or short).

d) The number of words recalled.

e) The amount of time each participant was allowed to read the nonsense syllables.

f) By using a computer program that showed each nonsense syllable for the same amount of time.

Strength 2: The existence of separate stores is further supported by the use of brain-scanning techniques, which have shown that the prefrontal cortex is active when individuals are working on a task in STM whereas the hippocampus is active when LTM is engaged.

Having research support is a strength of any model, so don't be afraid to state this.

6 **Limitation 1:** Despite the research support, the multi-store model is probably an oversimplification of memory processes. The multi-store model just proposes one long-term store whereas research suggests several different forms of LTM (e.g. episodic, semantic and procedural memory).

*Remember the **three-point rule** for criticisms.*

Limitation 2: The multi-store model proposes one mechanism for how data is stored in LTM – rehearsal. It is unlikely that rehearsal is the only way that information finds its way into LTM. Flashbulb memories, for example, are extremely long-lasting, without any form of rehearsal taking place.

AO1 Outline the criticism	AO2 Provide evidence to support the criticism	AO2 Provide evidence to challenge the criticism	AO2 What can you conclude about this criticism? (Is it fair?)
Many research studies show that there are three distinctly different memory stores, therefore the model makes good sense. The idea of STM and LTM continues to provide a framework that psychologists find useful for describing and understanding memory.	Research has found that the prefrontal cortex is active when individuals are working on a task in immediate memory (Beardsley, 1997) whereas the hippocampus is active when long-term memory is engaged (Squire *et al.*, 1992).	Baddeley and Hitch (1974) proposed an alternative model to explain short-term memory. They felt that STM was not just one store but a number of different stores.	In a study of brain-damaged patients, one (LH) performed better on spatial tasks than those involving visual imagery. This supports the working memory rather than the multi-store model because it suggests separate visual and spatial systems rather than one unitary short-term memory.
There are lots of different kinds of long-term memory (e.g. episodic memory and procedural memory) and this model doesn't include them.	The multi-store model proposes one mechanism for how data is stored in LTM – rehearsal. Flashbulb memories, for example, are extremely long-lasting, without any form of rehearsal taking place.	Evidence from other studies suggests that flashbulb memories are not a special long-lasting type of memory, and contain many distortions.	The multi-store model is probably an oversimplification of memory processes. Despite Atkinson and Shiffrin's claim, it is unlikely that rehearsal is the only way that information finds its way into LTM.

Alternative models of memory

research methods

Q

a) List **three** kinds of experimental design.

b) For each design describe **one** advantage and **one** disadvantage.

c) What are 'order effects'?

d) Describe **two** kinds of order effect.

e) What are 'participant variables'?

f) Identify **two** participant variables that often cause problems in research.

g) What design was used in Craik and Tulving's (1975) experiment?

h) State **one** advantage and **one** disadvantage of the design **in the context of this study**.

i) If you were to conduct the same study as an independent measures design, how would you do this?

Possible plan

1/3 of the answer (A01)	2/3 of the answer (A02)	Elaborate the strength/ limitation (A02)
Describe one feature of the model	Present a strength or limitation of this feature	Elaborate the strength/limitation
Describe another feature	Present a strength or limitation of this feature	Elaborate the strength/limitation
Describe a third feature	Present a strength or limitation of this feature	Elaborate the strength/limitation

The specification gives two examples of alternatives to the multi-store model: the working memory model and the levels of processing model. You could use either of these, or any other that you have studied. If you describe the levels of processing approach, beware as previous examiners' reports say that candidates find this model difficult. Candidates seem to just know the basic assumptions and can offer no further detail. Don't try to fill up your answer by giving criticisms. These will not attract any credit.

This is not a legitimate question because the levels of processing model is only given as an example in the specification. However, *assuming* that this is the model that you have studied, this is an opportunity to practise writing a brief account. What you have to do is select the three most important points. Doing this will help you understand the approach more clearly.

If you haven't studied the levels of processing approach, outline findings related to the alternative model that you have studied.

Again this is not a legitimate question, but if you have studied this model, you should be able to describe two strengths. Strengths might be a description of a study that supports the model, or an application of the model, or the fact that it can explain certain findings that can't be explained by the multi-store model.

Candidates often know a criticism, such as 'the model is circular', but can't explain this any further and therefore get few marks. You could try to explain what is circular about the model and why this is a limitation.

Be sure to divide your time appropriately when answering this question. Spend 1/3 of your time describing the model you have selected and 2/3 of the time giving strengths and/or limitations of this model. For high marks you need to do more than just list the criticisms. Remember the three-point rule: name it, explain it and explain why it is a criticism in this context.

A01 questions

1. Outline **one** model of memory that is an alternative to the multi-store model. *(6 marks)*

2. What is the levels of processing model? *(3 marks)*

3. Outline research findings that support the levels of processing approach. *(6 marks)*

4. Describe **two** strengths of the levels of processing approach. *(3 marks + 3 marks)*

5. Describe **two** limitations of the levels of processing approach. *(3 marks + 3 marks)*

A01/A02 question

Briefly describe **one** alternative to the multi-store model of memory and consider the strengths and/or limitations of this model. *(18 marks)*

8

1 The working memory model (Baddeley and Hitch, 1976) has three separate components. The central executive acts as an attentional system, allocating attention to different inputs and monitoring the operation of the other components. The phonological loop is a limited-capacity system that is subdivided into the articulatory control system, where information is rehearsed subvocally in speech-based form, and the phonological store, which holds speech input for a brief period (1½–2 seconds). The visuospatial sketchpad deals with visual information, which either comes direct from the senses, or is retrieved from long-term memory.

This is a difficult model to summarise, so prepare both a 6 mark version (as here) and a 3 mark version.

2 Craik and Lockhart (1972) suggested that during the encoding process, some information is processed more deeply than others. Information that is more likely to be recalled later is simply that which has been processed more deeply during this process.

Notice that the answer to question 2 is shorter than for question 1, reflecting the marks available.

3 Craik and Tulving (1975) found that participants remembered most words from a deeply processed list (analysis of meaning) and least from a list that had been subjected to shallow processing (physical structure only). Mandler (1967) found that organising material during encoding made it more memorable during later recall. Participants who had used the most categories remembered the most words, and recall was poorest for those who had used the fewest. Eysenck and Eysenck (1980) found that participants who were asked to say words in a distinctive way, for example saying all the letters of 'comb', later had better recall of those words than those who were not asked to do this.

Three of the studies given in The Complete Companion have been used here. This has given the answer both breadth and depth.

4 **Strength 1:** Research support for the model comes from Craik and Tulving (1975), who found that participants remembered most words from a list that had been processed for meaning and least from those that had simply been processed for their structure. This showed that deeper processing led to enhanced memory, a key assumption of the model.
Strength 2: Later research has clarified the objective meaning of 'depth' to include organisation, distinctiveness, elaboration and effort. Research by Eysenck and Eysenck (1980), for example, provided evidence for the importance of elaboration as an aspect of deeper processing, showing that this led to enhanced later recall of material that had been elaborated during initial presentation.

5 **Limitation 1:** Many psychologists question the idea of 'depth'. If something is better remembered, this is taken as an indication that it has been more deeply processed, which is then taken to be the reason for the better retention of that information. This is a circular argument.
Limitation 2: Morris *et al.* (1977) asked participants not simply to recall the words but to recall words that rhymed with words on the original list. The words that were best remembered were not the ones that had been deeply processed but those that had been phonemically processed. This shows that there are other explanations for memory, not just depth of processing.

As with all limitations and criticisms, elaboration is necessary for the full 3 marks.

research methods
A

a) Repeated measures design, matched participants and independent groups design.

b) Repeated measures: advantage – good control for participant variables; disadvantage – prone to order effects (e.g. boredom, practice).

Matched participants: advantage – overcomes order effects because different participants in each condition; disadvantage – matching is difficult and never totally successful.

Independent groups: advantage – avoids order effects because different participants in each condition; disadvantage – lacks control of participant variables which may influence the outcome (DV).

c) Participants may perform differently on two or more conditions in an experiment simply because of the order in which they do them.

d) Participants may become bored because they have to do the same (or a similar) task twice. They may also get better because of practice.

e) Participant variables are personal characteristics that participants bring to the experiment that might influence the outcome of the DV if not controlled.

f) Common participant variables are age and gender.

g) Repeated measures design.

h) Advantage: It uses only one-third the number of participants than would be necessary in an independent groups design.

Disadvantage: because each participant was given 60 words to remember in total, this would have increased the likelihood of them becoming bored.

i) It would be necessary to allocate participants to each of the three conditions (shallow, phonemic and deep processing) and compare the three groups of participants.

Describe one feature of the model (AO1)	Present a strength or limitation of this feature (AO2)	Elaborate the strength/limitation (AO2)
Craik and Lockhart (1972) suggested that enduring memories are created by the *processing* that you do rather than through rehearsal.	Research support for the model comes from Craik and Tulving (1975), who found that participants remembered most words from a list that had been processed for meaning and least from those that had simply been processed for their structure.	This showed that deeper processing led to enhanced memory, a key assumption of the model.
They suggested that during the encoding process, some information is processed more deeply than others.	Many psychologists question the idea of 'depth'. If something is better remembered, this is taken as an indication that it has been more deeply processed, which is then taken to be the reason for the better retention of that information.	This is a circular argument. It is assumed that what is best remembered has been most deeply processed.
Information that is more likely to be recalled later is simply that which has been processed more deeply during this process.	Morris *et al.* (1977) asked participants not to simply recall the words but to recall words that rhymed with words on the original list. The words that were best remembered were not the ones that had been deeply processed but those that had been phonemically processed.	This shows that there are other explanations for memory, not just depth of processing.
'Depth' may be achieved through semantic analysis but also can be due to organisation or distinctiveness or elaboration.	Various studies have demonstrated this.	For example, Eysenck and Eysenck (1980) found higher recall when participants had to say words in a distinctive way, for example saying all the letters of 'comb'.

End of section review

Sample exam question

a. Describe the procedures of **one** study on the nature of long-term memory and give **one** criticism of this study. *(3 marks + 3 marks)*

b. Describe findings from research into the nature and structure of short-term memory (STM). *(6 marks)*

c. Outline and evaluate the multi-store model of memory. *(18 marks)*

See page viii for an explanation of how questions are marked.

Student answer	Examiner's comments
(a) Bahrick *et al.* conducted a study where participants were asked to list the names of all the students they could remember from their high school class. This was free recall. They were also given a recognition test where they were shown 50 photos, some of which were from the participant's high school yearbook. Altogether there were nearly 400 participants aged 17 to 74.	Notice how the answer focuses exclusively on the procedures of this study. It is not a description of all of the procedures in this study but enough for the 3 available marks.
One criticism of this study is a positive one: that it was testing memory in a real-life setting (asking to recall people rather than meaningless pictures or words) and therefore has mundane realism and high ecological validity. This means that we can generalise the findings to other settings.	The criticism is also worth three marks as it is accurate and detailed – the three-point rule has been followed – name it, justify it and answer the question 'so what'. = **3 + 3 marks**.
(b) One study (Peterson and Peterson) found that participants remembered almost all of the trigrams when there was a a 3 second interval between seeing the trigram and recall, but if there was an 18 second interval recall fell to 2%. This shows that short-term memory has a very short duration.	Two findings from one study have been described in detail but this is not enough for the full six marks. The final sentence relates to conclusions and thus gains no credit. = **3 marks**.
(c) The multi-store model suggests that information is first of all processed in sensory memory (SM). It is then stored in short-term memory (STM). If it is rehearsed, the memory will be stored in long-term memory (LTM). If it is not rehearsed, it will not be stored in long-term memory and will disappear. This model was developed by Atkinson and Shiffrin.

This model is good because it has lots of research supporting it. The research on encoding shows that there is a difference between STM and LTM. STM uses an acoustic code and LTM uses a semantic code. Though one study found that STM doesn't always use an acoustic code, it depends on how memory is tested. If you ask someone to recall what something looked like then they use a visual code.

But there is evidence to show that they are different in duration. LTM definitely lasts longer.

One way to criticise this model is by comparing it with other explanations. One other explanation is the levels of processing approach. This was by Craik and Lockhart, who said that we remember those things that we process deeply. This model is good because it deals with active processing, whereas the multi-store model suggests memory is just a passive process. Bartlett's reconstruction model showed that it is active not passive. The multi-store model can't explain why words that are deeply processed become more memorable. Nor can it explain different kinds of memory such as memory for riding a bicycle.

On the whole it has been an important and useful model. [260 words] | Always provide plenty of AO2 (evaluation) but you must also ensure sufficient AO1 material. Here there is only a brief description of the multi-store model. It's not 'muddled or flawed' and thus worth more than 2 marks but is also not 'accurate and detailed', thus **3 marks for AO1**.

The commentary is reasonably effective or even 'effective'. Each point is introduced as commentary (e.g. 'One way to criticise the model ...'). A number of studies and other points are made (= 'slightly limited') but it is a shame that these are not linked to particular researchers. This means the commentary cannot be described as 'informed'. Overall **9 marks for AO2**, a **total of 12 marks**. |
| | Total for whole question is **21 marks**, equivalent to a Grade A. |

This module is divided into

Short-term memory and long-term memory

The nature and structure of short-term memory (STM)

The nature and structure of long-term memory (LTM)

The multi-store model of memory

Alternative models of memory

End of section review

Remembering and forgetting

Forgetting in short-term memory

Forgetting in long-term memory

Emotional factors in memory

End of section review

Critical issue: Eyewitness testimony

Reconstructive memory

Research into eyewitness testimony

End of section review

COGNITIVE PSYCHOLOGY:
HUMAN MEMORY

DEVELOPMENTAL PSYCHOLOGY:
ATTACHMENTS IN DEVELOPMENT

PHYSIOLOGICAL PSYCHOLOGY:
STRESS

INDIVIDUAL DIFFERENCES:
ABNORMALITY

SOCIAL PSYCHOLOGY:
SOCIAL INFLUENCE

RESEARCH
METHODS

COGNITIVE PSYCHOLOGY: HUMAN MEMORY

Forgetting in short-term memory

Specification extract
Explanations of forgetting in short-term memory (e.g. decay and displacement).

research methods Q

a) Name one experimental study of forgetting in short-term memory.

b) Identify the IV and DV in this experiment.

c) Did this study use an independent measures design or a repeated measures design?

d) State **one** advantage and **one** disadvantage of the design **in the context of this study**.

e) Can you think of a way that participant reactivity might have affected the outcome of this study?

The fact that there are 3 marks indicates that it might be advisable to have three different things to say. Don't just try to say the same thing using different words.

Decay and displacement are the most likely alternatives but candidates tend to find it difficult to have enough to say about decay for 3 marks let alone for 6 marks. It may be necessary to amplify your answer by referring to research studies. Don't try to include a second explanation to fill out your answer. You will only receive marks for one explanation.

Don't make the mistake of overlooking the 'short-term memory' bit – easy to do this, especially in an examination.

Remember that criticisms can be positive.

Make sure that your criticisms are relevant to the explanation. It may help to 'fill out' your criticism by referring to research support.

You will gain no marks if you describe an activity that you did in class to investigate forgetting in short-term memory. The findings must be from identifiable studies.

You need 6 marks' worth of conclusions. These may come from one study or a number of different studies.

Decay and displacement are again the most likely answers to select.

AO1 questions

1. Explain what is meant by forgetting. *(3 marks)*

2. Describe **one** explanation of forgetting in short-term memory. *(6 marks)*

3. Outline **two** explanations of forgetting in short-term memory. *(3 marks + 3 marks)*

4. Give **two** criticisms of explanation 1. *(3 marks + 3 marks)*

5. Give **two** criticisms of explanation 2. *(3 marks + 3 marks)*

6. Outline findings of research into forgetting in short-term memory. *(6 marks)*

7. Outline conclusions of research into forgetting in short-term memory. *(6 marks)*

8. Describe **two** factors that influence forgetting in short-term memory. *(3 marks + 3 marks)*

AO1/AO2 question

Outline **two** explanations of forgetting in STM and decide which one is better. Present evidence to support your decision. *(18 marks)*

Possible plan

	Outline of the explanation (AO1)	Criticisms (AO2)	Evidence that supports or challenges this explanation (AO2)
Explanation 1			
Explanation 2			
Conclusion about which explanation is best			

This question is not in the style used in the examination but is a useful way to test your understanding of the explanations presented above. Select any two explanations and decide which one you think is best. Having made a decision, you now need to explain the decision based on psychological evidence (you should *always* make your answers psychologically informed). You may, of course, decide the two explanations are equally good (or bad).

1 Forgetting is the inability to recall or recognise something that has previously been learned. This may be due to a lack of availability, as in the case of decay, or may be due to a lack of accessibility, as in the case of cue-dependent forgetting.

> There is sufficient elaboration to turn this from a 2 mark definition to a 3 mark explanation.

research methods **A**

a) Peterson and Peterson (1959).

2 One way to think about memory is in terms of a *memory trace* (or engram). This refers to the physical representation of information in the brain. In decay theory it is suggested that a memory trace is maintained in STM only so long as it is rehearsed. The memory trace simply disappears or decays if it is no longer rehearsed. This would explain the results from the Peterson and Peterson experiment (1959). No rehearsal was permitted and the information had disappeared from STM after 18 seconds at the most.

b) The IV was the retention interval. The DV was whether or not a trigram was remembered after that interval.

3 **Explanation 1:** In decay theory it is suggested that a memory trace is maintained in STM only so long as it is subject to rehearsal. The memory trace simply disappears or decays if it is no longer rehearsed.
Explanation 2: The displacement explanation is that a new set of information physically overwrites an older set. This happens because STM is a limited capacity store. When it is full and more information is presented then all that can happen is displacement – by overwriting.

> These are very concise explanations. Can you add a third statement to explanation 1 to ensure full marks?

c) Peterson and Peterson used a repeated measures design.

d) Advantage: the possibility that participant variables (such as age) might interfere with the accurate investigation of the effects of retention interval on recall was removed by using the same participants for all three retention intervals.

4 **Criticism 1:** One problem with the decay explanation is that we cannot be sure that decay really has taken place. It is possible that the first information was simply pushed out or displaced. In the case of the Peterson and Peterson experiment, the digits that the participants were counting might have *displaced* the original trigrams.
Criticism 2: Decay theory does have some research support. Reitman (1974) found that after a 15 second interval, participants' recall for five words dropped by 24%. This is evidence for decay, except that we can't be entirely certain that new information had not entered STM.

Disadvantage: as participants became more used to trying to remember nonsense trigrams, they may have learned techniques (such as having the three consonants represent three related words) that would improve their performance, thus there would be an order effect operating (i.e. practice).

5 **Criticism 1:** Waugh and Norman (1965) found that if a serial probe came near the end of a word list, recall was good (over 80%) but if the probe was early in the list, recall was poor (less than 20%). This supports displacement theory because forgetting must be due to the fact that subsequent numbers increasingly displaced earlier numbers.
Criticism 2: Shallice (1967) also used the serial probe technique and found that forgetting was less if the numbers were presented faster (suggesting decay), but found a stronger effect for moving the position of the probe. This suggests that displacement and decay explain forgetting in STM *but* that displacement is more important.

> In order to turn these research studies into positive criticisms, it was necessary to add the last sentence in each. This made sure the material was used *critically*.

e) It is possible that participants might have tried harder to remember the trigrams, because they were aware they were taking part in an experiment, and therefore likely to be evaluated.

6 Peterson and Peterson (1959) found that participants recalled only 2% of nonsense trigrams when the retention interval was 18 seconds or longer. Waugh and Norman (1965) found that if a serial probe came near the end of a word list, recall was good (over 80%) but if the probe was early in the list, recall was poor (less than 20%). Shallice (1967) also used the serial probe technique and found that forgetting was less if the numbers were presented faster (suggesting decay), but found a stronger effect for moving the position of the probe.

7 We can conclude from the Peterson and Peterson study that information remains in STM for less than 18 seconds if verbal rehearsal is prevented. In fact, much information disappeared within a few seconds. The Waugh and Norman study shows that forgetting must be due to displacement because the earlier the probe, the more was forgotten. Shallice (1967) concluded that both displacement and decay explain forgetting in STM but that displacement is more important because if the numbers were speeded up then recall was better to a limited degree.

8 See answer to question 3.

Outline of the explanation (AO1)	Criticisms (AO2)	Evidence that supports (or challenges) this explanation (AO2)
In decay theory it is suggested that a memory trace is maintained in STM only so long as it is subject to rehearsal. The memory trace simply disappears or decays if it is no longer rehearsed.	One problem with the decay explanation is that we cannot be sure that decay really has taken place. It is possible that the first information was simply pushed out or displaced. In the case of the Peterson and Peterson experiment, the digits that the participants were counting might have *displaced* the original trigrams.	Decay theory does have some research support. Reitman (1974) found that after a 15-second interval participants' recall for five words dropped by 24%, which is evidence for decay, except that we can't be entirely certain that new information had not entered STM.
The displacement explanation is that a new set of information physically overwrites an older set. This happens because STM is a limited capacity store. When it is full and more information is presented then all that can happen is displacement – by overwriting.	Waugh and Norman (1965) found that if a serial probe came near the end of a word list, recall was good (over 80%) but if the probe was early in the list, recall was poor (less than 20%). This supports displacement theory because forgetting must be due to the fact that subsequent numbers increasingly displaced earlier numbers.	Shallice (1967) also used the serial probe technique and found that forgetting was less if the numbers were presented faster (suggesting decay), but found a stronger effect for moving the position of the probe.
Conclusion: Shallice's finding suggests that displacement and decay explain forgetting in STM *but* that displacement is more important.		

Forgetting in long-term memory

Specification extract

Explanations of forgetting in long-term memory (e.g. retrieval failure and interference).

research methods **Q**

a) What is the difference between an extraneous variable and a confounding variable?

b) Explain what is meant by a hypothesis.

c) What is the difference between the aims of a study and the hypothesis?

A study on memory aimed to find out whether people recalled more just before eating lunch or just after.

d) Write a suitable directional hypothesis for this study.

e) Write a suitable non-directional hypothesis for this study.

f) Explain why you would choose to use a directional rather than a non-directional hypothesis.

You can use a research study to assist your explanation but make sure you relate the study to the explanation.

You can use repression as an explanation of forgetting in long-term memory.

Many candidates use alternative explanations of forgetting as an effective evaluation, but some candidates simply state that there are alternative explanations and offer no further elaboration. They get very little credit.

Another way to criticise an explanation is to consider how much research evidence exists or how difficult it is to collect research evidence.

Ensure that your findings do relate to long-term memory (and forgetting).

Make sure you outline conclusions and not findings. Any sentence that starts with 'The findings suggest that ...' is going to be a conclusion.

Which of the following could be appropriate factors: decay, displacement, emotion, motivation, interference, importance repression, retrieval cues?

Your task is to describe a minimum of one explanation and then consider relevant research evidence with a view to deciding whether or not research does support your chosen explanation. In order to do this well, you should include evidence for and against.
Don't stray from forgetting in long-term memory unless you can make the material relevant.

AO1 questions

1. Describe **one** explanation of forgetting in long-term memory. *(6 marks)*

2. Outline **two** explanations of forgetting in long-term memory. *(3 marks + 3 marks)*

3. Give **two** criticisms of explanation 1. *(3 marks + 3 marks)*

4. Give **two** criticisms of explanation 2. *(3 marks + 3 marks)*

5. Outline findings of research into forgetting in long-term memory. *(6 marks)*

6. Outline conclusions of research into forgetting in long-term memory. *(6 marks)*

7. Describe **two** factors that influence forgetting in long-term memory. *(3 marks + 3 marks)*

AO1/AO2 question

Outline **one or more** explanations of forgetting in long-term memory and consider to what extent these are supported by psychological research. *(18 marks)*

Possible plan

	Describe the explanation (A01)	Present evidence that supports the explanation (A02)	Present evidence that challenges the explanation (A02)	What do you conclude about the explanation? (A02)
Explanation 1				
Explanation 2				
And if you still have time, explanation 3				

1 Retrieval failure is the failure to find an item of information because we have insufficient clues or cues. The context where initial learning takes place or the mood we were in may act as a cue later. After learning material in one place and then attempting to recall it in another, we do not have the benefit of the familiar location acting as a cue, therefore we are less likely to recall the material. Lack of internal cues (e.g. not being in the same psychological state during encoding and recall) will also limit the amount of information we are able to recall.

2 **Explanation 1:** Retrieval failure is the failure to find an item of information because we have insufficient clues or cues. The context where initial learning takes place or the mood we were in may act as a cue later. Lack of these cues will lead to greater forgetting.

Although there is no formal marking rule, three accurate sentences should get the full 3 marks for each explanation.

Explanation 2: Interference refers to the tendency for one memory to 'interfere with' the accurate retrieval of another (similar) memory. Proactive interference is when past material interferes with attempts to learn similar new material, causing us to forget new material. Retroactive interference is when current learning interferes with material already learned, causing us to forget the material already learned.

3 **Criticism 1:** Research tends to support the importance of retrieval cues; for example, Miles and Hardman (1998) found that people who learned a list of words while exercising on a static bicycle then remembered them better when exercising again than while at rest.

Before putting pen to paper, it is wise to ask yourself 'why is this material good or bad for the explanation?'

Criticism 2: Many of the studies used to support cue-dependent forgetting are laboratory-based and therefore represent a more artificial test of memory that is not very much like everyday memory. As a result, cue-dependent recall may not apply to some aspects of how we use memory in everyday life (e.g. procedural memory).

4 **Criticism 1:** Interference does cause forgetting but only when the same stimulus is paired with two different responses. These conditions are rare in everyday life and therefore interference only explains a limited range of situations where material has been forgotten.

Criticism 2: Tulving and Pstoka (1971) found that when participants in a memory test were given cued recall, the previous effects of interference disappeared. This shows that interference effects may simply mask what is actually in memory, i.e. the information is there but cannot be retrieved.

5 Jenkins and Dallenbach (1924) found that participants who stayed awake in the period between learning and recall recalled less than if they had been asleep (because of displacement).

In the examples in this book the dates are given for studies. You would not lose marks if you did not include dates. They are an 'extra' detail. It is more important to know the other details, such as the findings, of any study.

Abernethy (1940) found that participants tested by a different instructor in a different room forgot more than those who were tested by the same instructor and in the same room as when they had originally learned the material. Miles and Hardman (1998) found that people who learned a list of words while exercising on a static bicycle then remembered them better when exercising again than while at rest.

6 We can conclude from the Jenkins and Dallenbach (1924) study that displacement explains forgetting because at night there was no displacement and little forgetting. In the Abernethy (1940) study, the fact that participants forgot more in the absence of familiar external cues shows that forgetting in LTM is cue-dependent. We can conclude from the Miles and Hardman study that internal cues (in this case the physiological arousal caused by exercise) are also encoded with the material being learned, and the absence of these cues during retrieval increases the likelihood that this material will be hard to retrieve (forgotten).

It is more difficult than it may appear to write effective answers to questions such as this. You need to 'frame' your conclusions without having your answer 'hijacked' by a description of the study's findings.

7 See answer to question 2.

research methods **A**

a) The difference between an extraneous variable and a confounding variable is that whereas the former **might** affect the DV, the latter **does** affect the DV.

b) A hypothesis is a clear statement, made at the beginning of an investigation, which aims to predict or explain events.

c) The aims set out the intentions of what will be studied whereas the hypothesis states the researcher's expectations in a way that can be tested (the variables are operationalised).

d) Participants recall more words when tested before eating lunch than when tested after eating lunch.

e) There is a difference in the number of words recalled from a word list just before eating lunch and just after eating lunch.

f) A directional hypothesis would be chosen if we had evidence from past research or experience that suggests this is the likely direction of the results.

Describe the explanation	Present evidence that supports the explanation	Present evidence that challenges the explanation	What do you conclude about the explanation?
Retrieval failure is the failure to find an item of information because we have insufficient clues or cues.	Research tends to support the importance of retrieval cues, for example Miles and Hardman (1998) found that people who learned a list of words while exercising on a static bicycle remembered them better when exercising again than while at rest.	Penfield (1958) stimulated the temporal lobes of patients to test retrieval of otherwise forgotten memories. Only 40 of 520 patients could retrieve real memories and most of these resembled dreams rather than memories.	We can conclude from the Miles and Hardman study that internal cues are also encoded with the material being learned, and the absence of these cues during retrieval increases the likelihood that this material will be forgotten.
Interference refers to the tendency for one memory to 'interfere with' the accurate retrieval of another (similar) memory. Proactive interference – past learning interferes with current attempts to learn something. Retroactive interference – current attempts to learn something interfere with past learning.	Support for interference theory comes from Jenkins and Dallenbach (1924), who found that after learning lists of nonsense syllables, participants' recall was much better when the intervening time had been filled primarily with sleep rather than a comparable period of being awake.	Tulving and Pstoka (1971) found that when participants in a memory test were given cued recall the previous effects of interference disappeared. This shows that interference effects may simply mask what is actually in memory, i.e. the information is there but cannot be retrieved.	Interference does cause forgetting but only when the same stimulus is paired with two different responses. These conditions are rare in everyday life and therefore interference only explains a limited range of situations where material has been forgotten.

Emotional factors in memory

Specification extract

The role of emotional factors in memory, including flashbulb memories and repression (e.g. Freud).

research methods **Q**

a) What is meant by the term 'confederate' in a research study?

b) Why do psychologists use confederates in their research?

c) What is the difference between a structured and an unstructured interview?

In a study of repressed memory, participants were interviewed about their early childhood. The interview record was compared to reports recorded during each individual's childhood.

d) Give **one** advantage and **one** disadvantage of using the interview method in the context of this study.

e) What is a quasi-experiment?

You can give examples to help your explanation but make sure they are appropriate. Is a memory of Princess Diana an example of a flashbulb memory? The answer is no. If you do not understand why then you should reread your notes on flashbulb memories.

Candidates often make the mistake of writing about flashbulb memories in general rather than the findings of an identifiable study. You've been warned.

Don't tell anecdotes about cases of flashbulb memories. These will get no credit.

Make sure you restrict yourself to 3 marks' worth. You might want to impress the examiner by writing all you know about repression but the examiner can only give you 3 marks. Practise writing responses of the right length so you don't waste valuable examination time.

'Findings' can come from one study or several studies.

Remember the **three-point rule**.

Remember research can be a study or an explanation of flashbulb memories.

Do you think there is such a thing as a flashbulb memory? If your answer is yes then you should be able to provide *some* evidence to support this belief. The same applies if your answer is no. This question does not make it clear what is AO1 and what is AO2. AO1 credit will be given for description of research and AO2 for effective use of such research in order to determine whether or not flashbulb memories are real, or just the same as ordinary memories. Part of your commentary may concern the validity of the research examined. For example, you might look at methodological limitations of natural experiments.

AO1 questions

1. Explain what is meant by flashbulb memories.
   (3 marks)

2. Outline findings of research into flashbulb memories.
   (6 marks)

3. Outline conclusions of research into flashbulb memories. *(6 marks)*

4. Explain what is meant by repression. *(3 marks)*

5. Outline findings of research into repression.
   (6 marks)

6. Outline conclusions of research into repression.
   (6 marks)

7. Give **two** criticisms of research into repression.
   (3 marks + 3 marks)

AO1/AO2 question

To what extent does research (theory **and/or** studies) provide support for the existence of flashbulb memories? *(18 marks)*

Possible plan

	Description of research **(AO1)**	Commentary on research (e.g. method-ological issues) **(AO2)**	What does the research tell us about flashbulb memories? **(AO2)**
Research 1			
Research 2			
Research 3			

1 A flashbulb memory is a special kind of memory where an individual has a detailed and enduring recollection of the context in which they first heard about a personally important event. Flashbulb memories tend to be memories of events (i.e. *episodic* memories) rather than memory for facts (i.e. *semantic* memories).

2 Brown and Kulik found that 14 of the black respondents and only 1 of the white respondents reported an FB for the assassination of Malcolm X (a black militant), whereas 25 of the white respondents and 20 of the black respondents reported an FB for the assassination of Robert Kennedy (a white politician). Schmolck *et al.* (2000) investigated the events surrounding the verdict in the O.J. Simpson murder trial and found that the quality of the recollections after 15 months (11% contained major distortions) was strikingly different from the quality of the recollections after 32 months (over 40% contained major distortions).

These are wordy studies to describe, so practise being concise yet informative.

3 Brown and Kulik's discovery of a race effect in FBs supports the view that 'consequentiality' is important. People have FBs for events that are of personal consequence because they are more emotionally important. Brown and Kulik also concluded that the more unexpected or surprising an event, the greater its emotional charge. Wright's (1993) interviews with people after the Hillsborough football disaster led him to conclude that most people reconstructed their memories, blending real experiences with accounts by other people and the media. Schmolck *et al.* (2000) concluded from their study of FBs after the O.J. Simpson verdict announcement that flashbulb memories do decay and are not enduringly accurate.

4 Repression is a way of dealing with memories for traumatic events so that the anxiety created by the memory does not have to be experienced. A repressed memory, therefore, is the memory of a traumatic event placed beyond conscious awareness, into the unconscious mind.

5 Williams (1994) found that over one-third (38%) of the women they interviewed did not show any recall for the earlier sexual abuse. Of those who did recall the abuse, 16% reported that they had, at one time, not been able to recall these incidents but had 'recovered' the memory. Williams also found that abuse that occurred at an earlier age was more likely to be forgotten. Bradley and Baddeley (1990) tested the effects of emotion on recall, and found that participants had more difficulty recalling emotionally charged words. However, this effect didn't occur if there was a long delay before testing recall. Some participants were tested after 28 days and they remembered the emotional associations better than those tested quite soon after initial learning.

6 In the Williams (1994) study, the sample mainly consisted of poor urban women, 86% of whom were African–American. The fact that this was a very narrow sample means that we might not be justified in generalising these findings to all people. A review of 60 years of experimental tests of repression (Holmes, 1990) led to the conclusion that there is no evidence that unequivocally supports the role of repression in forgetting. This therefore weakens the case for repression as a major cause of forgetting in long-term memory.

7 The findings from Williams' (1994) study suggest that having no memory of child sexual abuse is relatively common, which supports the idea that recovery of memories is possible, because some individuals have forgotten real incidents. Further, the fact that some individuals said they had recovered their early memories shows that recovery does occur. Both findings support the notion of repression in relation to painful memories. The findings from Bradley and Baddeley's study suggest that anxiety and arousal depresses short-term recall but enhances long-term recall. Alternatively it may be that anxiety/arousal initially causes repression but this disappears over time.

Nor does this question require findings! Notice how findings are used to provide conclusions.

research methods **A**

a) In many psychology experiments it is necessary to have someone who appears to be an ordinary person or another participant but in fact is working with the experimenter and has been told carefully how to behave. This person is called a confederate.

b) Having confederates in a study means that the experimenter can introduce changes in the behaviour of other members of the group in order to study the effect of those changes on the participant.

c) In a structured interview all the questions are predetermined and the interviewer tries hard to stick strictly to his/her script, whereas in an unstructured interview the interviewer starts with a few questions but then creates new questions in response to the answers given by the participant.

d) Advantage: the information collected can be very revealing because the questions have been shaped to the interviewee. This produces 'rich' data that can be corroborated by reports recorded during the individual's childhood.

Disadvantage: it is possible that participants would not want to tell the interviewers about any earlier abuse as they want to present themselves in a 'good light' and give 'socially desirable' answers (the social desirability bias).

e) A quasi-experiment is a type of experiment where the experimenter does not directly manipulate the IV. The IV varies naturally such as has been manipulated in a study of the effects of TV programmes watched where the experimenter makes use of divisions that already exist (e.g. male and female).

Description of research (AO1)	Commentary on research (AO2)	What does the research tell us about flashbulb memories? (AO2)
Brown and Kulik found that 14 of the black respondents and only 1 of the white respondents reported an FB for the assassination of Malcolm X whereas 25 of the white respondents and 20 of the black respondents reported an FB for the assassination of Robert Kennedy.	Participants may have responded to demand characteristics. For example the list of names may have prompted participants to think they did recall the context when they first heard about the event. There was also no way to find out if they were being truthful.	It would be unreasonable to conclude from this one study that emotion enhances recall. Other research shows that anxiety may lead to repressed memory.
Wright *et al.* (1993) interviewed people after the Hillsborough football disaster. After five months most people had rather vague memories of the event.	Very few studies have addressed the issue of gender differences in flashbulb memories. Wright *et al.* discovered that men reported having clearer memories of the Hillsborough disaster even though they thought that it was less important and less emotional than women did.	Wright concluded that most people reconstructed their memories, blending experiences with accounts by other real people and the media.
Schmolck *et al.* (2000) investigated the events surrounding the verdict in the O.J. Simpson murder trial and found that the quality of the recollections after 32 months was strikingly different from the quality of the recollections after 15 months.	The researchers showed that despite there being a lot of distortion in the participants' memories, they were still really confident about the accuracy of their memories.	This evidence suggests that flashbulb memories do decay and are not enduringly accurate, but people remain confident about them.

End of section review

Sample exam question

a. Describe **two** factors that influence forgetting in STM. *(3 marks + 3 marks)*

b. Describe the findings of **one** study that has investigated forgetting in LTM and give **one** criticism of this study. *(3 marks + 3 marks)*

c. 'Research on repression indicates that emotional factors have a negative effect on recall whereas research on flashbulb memories indicates the opposite.' Consider what psychological research (theories **and/or** studies) can tell us about the effect of emotional factors on memory. *(18 marks)*

See page viii for an explanation o how questions a marked.

Student answer	Examiner's comments
(a) Decay can influence forgetting in short-term memory. The memory trace simply disappears when it is not rehearsed. A second factor is displacement. Short-term memory has a limited capacity so that information that is stored there is displaced when there is no more room.	Two factors have been identified and each described in some detail. The second is slightly better but neither has quite enough detail for the full 3 marks, thus **2 + 2 marks**.
(b) One study that investigated forgetting in long-term memory was the study where participants were given cues. The study found that when participants were given cues they could recall information better than when they didn't have any cues. The closer the cues were to the original information the better memory was. One criticism of this study is that it was artificial because it was in a laboratory. This means that we can't generalise to all human behaviour.	The researchers' names have not been provided (Tulving and Psotka, 1971) but there is sufficient information to allow one to identify that it is this study. Two findings have been provided but neither is detailed, so 2 marks for this part. An appropriate criticism has been identified and some justification of the criticism is given plus an explanation of why it is a criticism. However, this is not quite enough for 3 marks as the details are not linked specifically to this study – the same statements could be provided for any laboratory study. Total for this question = **2 + 2 marks**.
(c) Studies of repression show that emotion may cause you to forget things. One study was done where women were interviewed about experiences earlier in their lives. The researchers also had records of the same women when they were younger. These records were of child abuse. A lot of the women were not able to recall being abused. This shows that unpleasant memories were repressed. One criticism of this study was that it may be that the women just didn't want to tell the interviewers about what had happened to them when they were younger. They could remember the abuse but didn't want to say. Another study of repression was done by Bradley and Baddeley. They found that emotionally charged words were not recalled when participants gave immediate recall but if there was a long delay before testing then emotionally charged words were recalled just as well as other words. This suggests that anxiety/arousal may initially cause repression but this disappears over time. One problem with studies of repression is that it may not really be repression but something called 'inhibited recall'. Freud's idea of repression was that emotionally upsetting information is actually not accessible. On the other hand, studies of flashbulb memory suggest that high emotion makes it more likely that you can recall things, such as what you were doing at the time you heard about Princess Diana's death. Research studies haven't been very successful at finding that flashbulb memories are that much better than other kinds of memories. It may just be that you repeat them again and again and this is why you remember them. On the whole it seems that emotional factors have a negative effect on memory. [281 words]	The AO1 requirement is to describe research. Two studies have been described accurately and with some detail but not enough for the top band, so the **AO1 mark would be 4**. The candidate has achieved a reasonable balance of AO1 and AO2 material, providing significantly more AO2 as is appropriate given the mark split for AO1 and AO2. There is well explained criticism of the first study, a reasonably effective analysis of the concept of repression versus inhibited recall and then a useful contrast with flashbulb memories. The second sentence on flashbulb memories has not been made relevant. The essay ends with a weak conclusion. Overall the commentary is 'limited' and 'reasonably effective', closer to reasonable rather than basic, thus **8 marks for AO2**, a **total of 12 marks**. Total for whole question is **20 marks**, equivalent to a Grade A.

COGNITIVE PSYCHOLOGY: HUMAN MEMORY

DEVELOPMENTAL PSYCHOLOGY: ATTACHMENTS IN DEVELOPMENT

PHYSIOLOGICAL PSYCHOLOGY: STRESS

INDIVIDUAL DIFFERENCES: ABNORMALITY

SOCIAL PSYCHOLOGY: SOCIAL INFLUENCE

RESEARCH METHODS

This module is divided into

Short-term memory and long-term memory

The nature and structure of short-term memory (STM)

The nature and structure of long-term memory (LTM)

The multi-store model of memory

Alternative models of memory

End of section review

Remembering and forgetting

Forgetting in short-term memory

Forgetting in long-term memory

Emotional factors in memory

End of section review

Critical issue: Eyewitness testimony

Reconstructive memory

Research into eyewitness testimony

End of section review

Reconstructive memory

Some candidates try to explain reconstructive memory with reference to reconstructions on programmes like *Crimewatch*. Such definitions rarely gain any marks. A good tip is to remember to mention 'schema' when explaining reconstructed memory. You can also refer to Bartlett's work.

Candidates often cannot resist including procedures even when they are not required. It is hard to discuss a study without some reference to the procedures but you don't have to include them, even though it may read better with them, and you will get no marks for including them.

Make sure that your conclusions are conclusions and are not findings.

Often candidates produce rather formulaic criticisms, such as saying 'This study lacks ecological validity' as if this was true of every study. *Why* did the study lack ecological validity? Make sure you contextualise and justify each criticism.

Could you get full marks if you only describe findings from Bartlett's study? Yes, if you provide 6 marks' worth of detail.

How could you use the report of the findings of Bartlett's study and make them into conclusions?

This is an expanded version of question 1. 'Research' refers to theory and/or studies.

Don't forget to contextualise your criticisms.

Which of the following factors might be suitable: culture, emotion, knowing the topic, time of day? You can elaborate your answer by referring to research findings.

Are memories reconstructed or are they just reproduced? What do you think? The second half of this question essentially asks you to reflect on this. You must use psychological evidence to support your view. You will not receive credit for a *description* of any research – AO1 credit is only for an outline of the concept of reconstructive memory. A useful tip is to identify the study and then say what it shows (state the conclusions). This demonstrates your skills of analysis.

Specification extract
Research into reconstructive memory (e.g. Bartlett).

research methods Q

a) Explain what is meant by ecological validity.
b) Which of the following best describes ecological validity?
   – Being able to apply findings to real life.
   – Being able to apply findings from one setting to another.
A psychologist conducted a laboratory experiment giving participants a story to read. Two weeks later she asked them to return and recall as much of the story as possible. She found that recall was very accurate.
c) Is this study high or low in terms of ecological validity?
d) Explain your answer.

AO1 questions

1. What is meant by reconstructive memory?
   (3 marks)

2. Describe the aims and findings of **one** study that has investigated reconstructive memory. *(6 marks)*

3. Describe the procedures and conclusions of **one** study of reconstructive memory.
   (6 marks)

4. Give **two** criticisms of this study. *(3 marks + 3 marks)*

5. Outline findings of research into reconstructive memory.
   (6 marks)

6. Outline conclusions of research into reconstructive memory. *(6 marks)*

7. Describe research into reconstructive memory (e.g. Bartlett). *(6 marks)*

8. Give **two** criticisms of this research.
   (3 marks + 3 marks)

9. Describe **two** factors that influence reconstructive memory.
   (3 marks + 3 marks)

Possible plan

AO1 1/3 of your time	AO2 2/3 of your time	
Outline the model of reconstructive memory	Identify studies (or theories) that support this model	What are the conclusions from each study? Is the study flawed in any way?
	Identify studies that challenge this model	What are the conclusions from each study?
	What do you conclude overall?	

AO1/AO2 question

Outline the concept of reconstructive memory and consider to what extent memory is 'reconstructive'.
(18 marks)

1 Reconstructive memory refers to the fact that fragments of stored information are reassembled during recall, and the gaps are filled in by our expectations and beliefs to produce a coherent narrative.

At about 30 words, this is just about right for a 3 mark 'explanation'.

2 A study of reconstructive memory (Bartlett, 1932).
Aims: To investigate how memory is reconstructed when recall is repeated over a period of weeks and months. In particular to see how cultural expectations affect memory and lead to predictable distortions.

There is probably more material than necessary on findings but this balances the somewhat limited information on aims.

Findings: Bartlett found that participants remembered different parts of stories and that they interpreted them within their own frames of reference (cultural expectations), changing the facts to make them fit. He found that the story was transformed in a number of different ways. It was shortened, mainly by omissions, and the phraseology was changed to language and concepts from the participant's own culture. For example, participants used the word 'boats' instead of 'canoes'.

3 A study of reconstructive memory (Bartlett, 1932).
Procedures: Bartlett showed a story, 'The War of the Ghosts', to a participant and asked them to repeat it back shortly thereafter and then repeatedly over weeks, months and years.
A key feature of the stimulus material was that it belonged to a culture that was exceedingly different to that of the participants.

Describing stimulus materials is part of the procedures. It is difficult to write about conclusions without also mentioning findings, but if you separate them in your revision, then you will find this task much easier.

Conclusions: Bartlett concluded that all of these transformations had the effect of making the material easier to remember. Individuals remembered the meaning and tried to sketch out the story using invented details. This reconstructed version of events is easier to remember and therefore becomes our memory for the event.

4 **Criticism 1:** This was not a very well-controlled study. The participants were not given very specific instructions and therefore some of the distortions may have resulted from conscious guessing rather than gaps in memory. Gauld and Stephenson (1967) found that when accurate recall was stressed at the outset, then errors fell by almost half.
Criticism 2: The study lacks relevance to real life. It may be that these findings don't hold up under more naturalistic conditions. Wynn and Logie (1998) tested students' recall of real-life events over a six-month period. Recall was relatively accurate and little transformation took place, suggesting that there was very little use of reconstruction in real-life situations.

5 Bartlett (1932) found that participants remembered different parts of stories and that they interpreted them within their own frames of reference (cultural expectations), changing the facts to make them fit. He found that the story was transformed in a number of different ways. It was shortened, mainly by omissions, and the phraseology was changed to language and concepts from the participant's own culture. For example, participants used the word 'boats' instead of 'canoes'. Cohen (1981) found that when participants were asked to recall things about a woman previously described either as a librarian or a waitress, they tended to recall things in line with the stereotype of a librarian or a waitress.

6 Bartlett (1932) concluded that the transformations found in his study had the effect of making the material easier to remember. Individuals remembered the meaning and tried to sketch out the story using invented details. This reconstructed version of events is easier to remember and therefore becomes

research methods **A**

a) *Ecological validity refers to the ability to generalise an experimental effect **beyond** the particular setting in which it is demonstrated.*

b) *Being able to apply research findings from one setting to another.*

c) *This study appears to be high in ecological validity.*

d) *Although the study was carried out in a laboratory, its findings were confirmed in another setting, this time a real-life one.*

our memory for the event. Cohen's study (1981) showed that people remember things in line with their existing stereotype. They failed to recall that this waitress liked reading because that was inconsistent with their stereotype. This is known as the confirmatory bias.

7 Bartlett proposed that memory is an *active* process. We store fragments of information and when we need to recall something, we reconstruct these fragments into a meaningful whole. This reconstruction leads to inaccuracy. Most importantly our past experience, beliefs and expectations shape the way we reconstruct memory. Past experiences are stored as schema. Schema are influenced by cultural expectations as well as personal experiences.

8 **Criticism 1:** There is considerable research support for the effect of schema on memory. Bartlett's studies support this idea of reconstructive memory. These studies show that schema do affect memory processes. Bartlett made an important contribution to our understanding of memory as an active and unreliable process.

Criticisms can be both positive and negative. In this answer, there is one of each.

Criticism 2: Contrary to Bartlett's claims, memory can be very accurate. For example, in situations that are personally important or distinctive we do remember considerable and accurate detail. In such instances memory can be quite passive.

9 **Factor 1:** Stereotypes are fairly simplistic schema that we have about a particular class or group of people. In order to maintain relative simplicity in our social world, as well as being able to predict the behaviour of those around us, we may resort to commonly held stereotypes when reconstructing a memory.
Factor 2: The way in which a witness is interviewed has been shown to influence *what* they recall – the more leading or suggestive the questions, the lower the accuracy. Interviewers may unintentionally communicate their expectations in various ways (e.g. tone of voice). Such expectations are found to affect the reconstruction of a memory and may distort a witness's version of an event.

	A01	A02
Outline of the concept of reconstructive memory (see answer to question 7).	For example, Bartlett (1932) and Cohen (1981) – see answer to question 5.	For example, Bartlett (1932) and Cohen (1981) – see answer to question 6. Criticisms of Bartlett study – see answer to question 4.
	Wynn and Logie (1998) tested students' recall of real-life events over a six-month period. Recall was relatively accurate and little transformation took place.	This suggests that there was very little use of reconstruction in real-life situations.
	Bartlett concluded that much human memory is influenced by factors which are social in origin and which may be obscured by laboratory methods because of the artificial nature of the material used in such experiments.	

Research into eyewitness testimony

Specification extract

Memory research into eyewitness testimony (e.g. Loftus), including the role of leading questions.

research methods Q

a) What is the difference between an experimental group and a control group in an experiment?

In a study to investigate the effects of emotion on recall, one group (group 1) were shown a distressing photograph and asked to recall details; another group (group 2) were shown a non-distressing picture.

b) Identify the IV and DV in this study.

c) Which group was the experimental group?

d) Which group was the control group?

e) Explain what is meant by a measure of central tendency.

f) Name **three** measures of central tendency.

g) For each measure of central tendency, state **one** advantage and **one** disadvantage.

The word 'explain' is intended to remind you that you should do more than *define* the term, you should *explain* it. A definition provides the meaning of a word; an explanation also includes more detail in order to make the definition clear or understandable.

A common failing is that candidates do not describe one identifiable study but, instead, combine the details of several different studies and as a result receive few, if any, marks.

Sometimes candidates find it difficult to think of enough to write about the aims of the study – what was it that the researcher wanted to test (the hypothesis)? What theory was being investigated?

Some candidates have been known to suggest that Loftus' study was flawed because it used misleading questions! They appear to have missed the point of the study.

You can base your whole answer on findings from Loftus' research, and/or include findings from other researchers. You may even be able to write 6 marks' worth on the findings from Loftus and Palmer's study alone.

This is one of those questions that, strictly speaking, is not on the specification but could be asked because it is integral with the content of the specification.

AO1 content will be the description of psychological research relating to eyewitness testimony. AO2 content will be commentary on this research. This commentary might include criticisms (strengths and/or limitations) of the studies themselves, and should include discussion of whether the research does or doesn't indicate that eyewitness testimony is accurate.

Possible plan

	Description of study (**AO1**)	Strengths and/or limitations of the study (**AO2**)	Conclusion regarding the accuracy of eyewitness testimony (**AO2**)	Evidence that contrasts with this (**AO2**)
Study 1				
Study 2				
Study 3				

AO1 questions

1. Explain what is meant by eyewitness testimony.
   (3 marks)

2. Describe the procedures and findings of **one** study of eyewitness testimony.
   (6 marks)

3. Describe the aims and conclusions of **one** study of eyewitness testimony.
   (6 marks)

4. Give **two** criticisms of the study that you have described above. *(3 marks + 3 marks)*

5. Outline findings of research into eyewitness testimony.
   (6 marks)

6. Describe **two** factors that influence the accuracy of eyewitness testimony.
   (3 marks + 3 marks)

AO1/AO2 question

'Eyewitness testimony may be all the evidence that is available in a trial but it is notoriously unreliable.' Consider what psychological research can tell us about the accuracy of eyewitness testimony. *(18 marks)*

1 Eyewitness testimony refers to the evidence provided in court by a person who witnessed a crime, with a view to identifying the perpetrator of the crime. The accuracy of eyewitness recall may be affected during initial encoding, subsequent storage and eventual retrieval.

2 A study on eyewitness testimony (Loftus and Palmer, 1974).
Procedure: Forty-five students were shown films of different traffic accidents. After each film they were given a questionnaire to describe the accident and then answer a series of specific questions about it. One group were given the question 'About how fast were the cars going when they hit each other?' The other five groups were given the verbs *smashed, collided, bumped* or *contacted* in place of the word *hit*.
Findings: The speed estimate was calculated for each group. The group given the verb 'smashed' estimated a higher speed than the other groups (about 41 mph). The group given the word 'contacted' estimated the lowest speed (about 30 mph).

> *Knowing one of Loftus' studies as a study of EWT gives you the added bonus of being able to use it in questions such as question 5.*

3 A study on eyewitness testimony (Loftus and Palmer, 1974).
Aims: The general aim of this study was to investigate the accuracy of memory after witnessing a car accident. In particular, it was to see if leading questions distort the accuracy of an eyewitness's immediate recall.
Conclusions: This study shows that the form of question can have a significant effect on a witness's answer to the question. In other words, leading questions can affect the accuracy of memory. It is possible that such post-event information causes the information to be altered before it is stored so that memory is permanently affected.

4 **Criticism 1:** A laboratory experiment may not represent real life as people don't take the experiment seriously and/or they are not emotionally aroused in the way that they would be in a real accident. Foster *et al.* (1994) found that if participants thought they were watching a real-life robbery and thought that their responses would influence the trial, their identification of a robber was more accurate.
Criticism 2: The design of an experiment leads to certain inevitable responses from participants. Participants look for cues because they are uncertain about what is expected of them (demand characteristics). As a result, they would be especially receptive to certain features of the experiment, such as leading questions, thus making any conclusions invalid.

> *Although general methodological criticisms are fine, remember to put them into the context of the question when answering.*

5 Loftus and Palmer (1974) found that participants' estimates of the speed of cars in accidents varied according to the verb used in the question. Those given the verb 'smashed' estimated a higher speed (about 41 mph) than the other groups. When participants returned to the lab one week later, they again gave higher speed estimates in the 'smashed' condition, and when questioned they were more likely to report having seen broken glass. Christianson and Hubinette (1993) found that emotional arousal can enhance the accuracy of memory. Witnesses who had been threatened in some way were more accurate in their recall and remembered more details than those who had been onlookers and less emotionally aroused.

research methods **A**

a) In an independent groups design, the experimental group are those participants who receive the experimental treatment (the IV), whereas the control group are those participants who receive no treatment, and whose responses act as a baseline.

b) The IV was the emotional content of the photograph (distressing or non-distressing). The DV was the subsequent recall of details of the photograph.

c) Group 1 was the experimental group.

d) Group 2 was the control group.

e) Measures of central tendency inform us about the central or typical values in a set of scores.

f) Three measures of central tendency are the mean, median and mode.

g) The mean makes use of all the values of all the data, but can be misrepresentative if there are extreme values.

The median is not affected by extreme scores, but is not as 'sensitive' as the mean.

The mode is useful when the data is in categories, but is not as useful when there are several modes.

6 **Factor 1:** Kind of characteristic. Research on the accuracy of eyewitness testimony has shown that witnesses generally remember some characteristics better than others. Kebbel and Wagstaff (1999) found that witnesses were normally very accurate when describing a person's sex, racial background, style of clothing and hair colour, but less accurate when describing things such as age, height and overall build.
Factor 2: Arousal. Many researchers believe that the effects of arousal on eyewitness testimony are *curvilinear*. This means that *small to medium* increases in arousal may increase the accuracy of memory, but *high* levels interfere with accuracy.

Description of study (AO1)	Strengths and/or limitations of the study (AO2)	Conclusion regarding the accuracy of eyewitness testimony (AO2)	Evidence that contrasts with this (AO2)
Loftus and Palmer (1974) found that participants' estimates of the speed of cars in accidents varied according to the verb used in the question. Those given the verb 'smashed' estimated a higher speed (about 41 mph) than the other groups.	A laboratory experiment may not represent real life as people don't take the experiment seriously and/or they are not emotionally aroused in the way that they would be in a real accident.	This study shows that the form of question can have a significant effect on a witness's answer to the question. In other words, leading questions can affect the accuracy of memory.	Foster *et al.* (1994) found that if participants thought they were watching a real-life robbery and thought that their responses would influence the trial, their identification of a robber was more accurate.
Repeat treatment for study 2.			
Repeat treatment (if time allows) for study 3.			

End of section review

Sample exam question

a. Explain what is meant by the terms memory and forgetting. *(3 marks + 3 marks)*

b. Describe the procedures and findings of **one** study of short-term memory. *(6 marks)*

c. Outline and evaluate psychological research (theories **and/or** studies) related to eyewitness testimony. *(18 marks)*

See page viii for an explanation of how questions are marked.

Student answer	Examiner's comments
(a) Memory is the act of storing things for a long time. Forgetting is when you can't bring something into conscious awareness. It may be that the material is not available, i.e. it was never stored in memory or is no longer stored, or it may be that the material is not accessible as in cue-dependent forgetting.	You can expect to be asked to explain certain key terms and these are two of them. The first definition really deserves very little credit but it isn't wrong. The second answer is detailed and accurate so **1 + 3 marks**.
(b) One study of encoding was done by Baddeley. He looked at the effects of encoding on short-term memory because past research had found that people encoded material in short-term memory in terms of the way the words sounded (an acoustic code). In Baddeley's experiment, participants were divided into four groups. The groups either had acoustically similar or acoustically dissimilar words, or words that were semantically similar or dissimilar. They were then asked either to recall the words immediately or after an interval (to test long-term memory). Baddeley found that when words had to be recalled immediately, participants were most confused when the words were acoustically similar. When words had to be recalled after an interval, there were more confusions for semantically similar words. This shows that there are differences in the way information is coded in STM and LTM.	An appropriate and identifiable study has been presented. The procedures are described in good detail and there are a reasonable range of findings, though these are less detailed. They are also not entirely clear. In what way were participants confused and what does this tell us about forgetting? The second sentence relates to aims and the final sentence relates to conclusions; neither would receive any credit. There is no requirement that procedures and findings are given in the same detail. Overall the answer would gain **5 marks**.
(c) Loftus and Palmer did a study of eyewitness testimony. They showed a film of a car accident to participants and then asked them how fast the car was travelling. They asked about speed using different words such as 'hit' or 'smashed'. They found that participants who were asked the question with the word 'smashed' gave the highest speed estimate. This shows that leading questions can affect recall which is important for eyewitness testimony.

However, there were problems with this study. It was conducted with students and it was done in a laboratory.

Another study of eyewitness testimony was Bartlett's study of 'The War of the Ghosts'. Participants heard this story and then were asked to repeat it over and over again. Each time Bartlett wrote down what they recalled. He found that participants' recall was distorted by their schema. This can be applied to eyewitness testimony because people recall the details of a crime scene in a way that is affected by their schema. However, another study found that people's recall was actually much more accurate when they had to recall things from real life. [185 words] | Two studies have been described but the second one, on 'The War of the Ghosts', might not be creditworthy as it does not relate directly to EWT. However, the candidate has made the link explicit and thus saves the day. A third study is mentioned in the final paragraph but there is too little detail for this to gain credit. Fortunately the first study is well detailed thus **5 marks for AO1** (rather than 6 marks because there is some temptation to describe the AO1 as 'limited').
There is almost no commentary bar the last sentence of the first paragraph and the second paragraph. Overall it is marginally better than 'just discernible' so **3 marks for AO2**, a **total of 8 marks**. |
| | Total for whole question is **17 marks**, equivalent to a Grade B. |

COGNITIVE PSYCHOLOGY: HUMAN MEMORY

DEVELOPMENTAL PSYCHOLOGY: ATTACHMENTS IN DEVELOPMENT

PHYSIOLOGICAL PSYCHOLOGY: STRESS

INDIVIDUAL DIFFERENCES: ABNORMALITY

SOCIAL PSYCHOLOGY: SOCIAL INFLUENCE

RESEARCH METHODS

MODULE 2

DEVELOPMENTAL PSYCHOLOGY: ATTACHMENTS IN DEVELOPMENT

Developmental psychology is concerned with how children and adults change as they get older. Developmental psychology looks at various influences on development, such as the influences of parents, peers and other people around you. These are all environmental influences (called **nurture**). Changes also happen as a consequence of **nature**. 'Nature' refers to biological factors such as genes.

This module is divided into

The development and variety of attachments

The formation of attachments

Individual differences: Secure and insecure attachments

Individual differences: Cross-cultural variations

Explanations of attachment

End of section review

Deprivation and privation

Maternal deprivation hypothesis

Effects of privation

End of section review

Critical issue: Day care

Effects of day care on cognitive development

Effects of day care on social development

End of section review

The formation of attachments

DEVELOPMENTAL PSYCHOLOGY: ATTACHMENTS IN DEVELOPMENT

Specification extract
Stages in the formation of attachments (e.g. Schaffer).

research methods Q

a) What is a naturalistic observational study?

b) What is observer bias?

Schaffer and Emerson conducted a naturalistic observation of infants in Glasgow. The researchers visited the children and their mothers at home and made notes about the infants' behaviour.

c) Give **one** advantage and **one** weakness of conducting a naturalistic observation in the context of this study.

d) Suggest **one** ethical problem that may arise when conducting an observation in the context of this study.

Candidates often provide *too* many details when explaining what is meant by attachment. Keep your explanation brief but with sufficient detail for 3 marks.

In this part of the specification there are no APFCC studies but you do need to know about relevant research, which can be theories (such as what Bowlby *found* about the development of attachment) or could be studies (or even the findings from just one study).

This answer should be different to your answer to question 2, though it may be drawn from the same research.

You can think of short-term consequences (such as maintaining proximity) or long-term consequences (such as the development of adult relationships).

For example, you might think about why some children become securely attached and others don't. Or you might think about who an infant becomes attached to and why.

The obvious way to answer this is to describe the stages or phases through which an infant passes as attachment develops. When answering this question make sure you provide a comprehensive account but one that doesn't take too much time; in other words, write a good précis.

Remember that criticisms can be positive as well as negative, and can relate to supporting evidence from research studies.

Ensure that the contents of your answer reflect the way the marks are distributed: 1/3 marks are for AO1 (description of research) and 2/3 marks for AO2 (commentary, analysis and effective use of material). You are permitted to describe either theory (a stage account) or studies (such as Schaffer and Emerson) but it might be better to use the latter study as part of your commentary, for example saying that the stage account is supported by the study's findings.

AO1 questions

1. Explain what is meant by attachment in the context of child development.
(3 marks)

2. Outline findings of research into the formation of attachments. *(6 marks)*

3. Outline conclusions of research into the formation of attachments.
(6 marks)

4. Give **two** effects of the formation of attachments.
(3 marks + 3 marks)

5. Describe **two** factors that influence the formation of attachments.
(3 marks + 3 marks)

6. Outline the formation of attachments. *(6 marks)*

7. Give **two** criticisms of this account of the formation of attachments.
(3 marks + 3 marks)

AO1/AO2 question

Outline and evaluate research (theories **and/or** studies) into the formation of attachments.
(18 marks)

Possible plan

AO1 1/3 of your time	AO2 2/3 of your time	
Outline of research on the development of attachments	Commentary	Make comments about particular features of the stage account and point to research support for the features
	Analysis	Question certain features of the account in terms of whether these features are supported or whether the research support is flawed
	Effective use of material	Avoid *describing* any evidence presented. Use phrases like 'This shows that …'

1 Attachment is an emotional bond between two people. It is a two-way process that endures over time. It leads to certain behaviours such as clinging and proximity-seeking, and serves the function of protecting an infant.

In order to get all 3 marks you must elaborate your answer sufficiently. Three distinct points are made here.

2 Schaffer and Emerson (1964) found that most infants first showed signs of separation protest and stranger anxiety at around the age of seven months, indicating the onset of specific attachments. Soon after an infant formed one specific attachment, other attachments were formed; the infants also displayed separation anxiety when separated from other people. Within one month of first becoming attached 29% of the infants had multiple attachments; within six months this had risen to 78%. Schaffer and Emerson reported that there was little relationship between time spent together and attachment. In 39% of the cases, infants were attached to someone other than the person who bathed or fed them.

You can be given 6 marks even if you have only described the findings from one study as long as there is enough detail for 6 marks.

3 Schaffer and Emerson (1964) concluded that responsiveness appeared to be the key to attachment. Intensely attached infants tend to have mothers who respond quickly to their demands. Infants who are weakly attached tend to have mothers who fail to interact. Ainsworth's observations of children in Uganda and the US led her to conclude that there are two distinctive features of attachment, both of which have adaptive value. First, infants seek to be close to their mothers especially at times when they are threatened by something in the environment. Second, infants who are close to their attachment figure will be more willing to explore in the knowledge that they are safe. They use their caregiver as a secure base.

There is a subtle difference between conclusions and findings. If you wrote 'Intensely attached infants had mothers who failed to interact', this would be a finding. It has been rephrased slightly to make the same thing into a conclusion.

4 **Effect 1:** Young children who have developed an attachment seek the company of their mother (or caregiver) and are disturbed when they are separated from her/him, even for short periods of time. As a result, the infant tries to get close to and then maintain proximity with the caregiver.
Effect 2: Adults who have developed a secure attachment bond in childhood find it relatively easy to get close to others and are comfortable depending on others and having others depend on them. Insecurely attached adults may find it difficult to trust or depend on others completely, or their desire to merge completely with another person scares others away.

5 **Factor 1:** Certain patterns of maternal behaviour seem to represent 'good mothering' and enable the child to become securely attached. These behaviours appear to be maternal sensitivity and maternal responsiveness. The mother of a securely attached child is a mother who notices what her child is doing, and responds appropriately.
Factor 2: Maccoby (1980) suggests that certain temperamental characteristics of the infant can shape the mother's responsiveness. Normal infants tend to take the initiative in inviting a maternal response whereas other children do not take this initiative.

There is an important difference between 'factors' and 'effects', which should be evident from this and the previous answer.

research methods A

a) In an observational study, everything is left as normal, with all variables free to vary. The observer does not manipulate any variables, but merely observes behaviour.

b) An observer might see what they expect to see, rather than what actually happens, and this leads to inaccurate observations.

c) Advantage: Because mothers and their children were studied in their own homes, they would be more likely to be behaving in a natural manner (rather than behaving in response to the artificial set-up of a laboratory).

Weakness: Mothers may have acted differently as they knew they were being observed. They may have been apprehensive about being evaluated, thus making any observations less valid.

d) One ethical problem with this study is the invasion of privacy. The researchers must take care that their presence is not intrusive in any way, and that mothers do not feel pressurised into letting them into their personal space.

6 In phase 1, newborn infants show indiscriminate social responsiveness; they are equally happy being picked up or comforted by familiar and unfamiliar people. Phase 2 is characterised by the increasing ability to recognise familiar people. An infant is more easily comforted by someone familiar but still does not show anxiety with strangers or less familiar people. Phase 3 is signalled by the appearance of separation protest – the distress when an infant is separated from his/her caregiver, and stranger anxiety – distress when approached by someone who is unfamiliar. In phase 4, initially infants show attachments to one primary caregiver but soon after most infants also show attachments to other people. In phase 5 the infant learns to predict the responses of others and this means that it is possible to consciously influence their behaviour.

7 **Criticism 1:** One weakness in any stage account of development is that it suggests a fixed pattern of development. However, it is the *sequence* of the development of attachment that is important; the actual ages at which children attain the different stages are only approximate.

Criticisms can be negative and positive, but remember to use research evidence as part of a critical evaluation.

Criticism 2: This account is supported by research evidence. Schaffer and Emerson (1964) found that within one month of first becoming attached 29% of the infants studied had multiple attachments; within six months this had risen to 78%.

AO1 (1/3 of the answer)	AO2 (2/3 of the answer)
In phase 1, newborns show indiscriminate social responsiveness; they are equally happy being picked up or comforted by familiar and unfamiliar people. Phase 2 is characterised by the increasing ability to recognise familiar people. An infant is more easily comforted by someone familiar but still does not show anxiety with strangers or less familiar people. Phase 3 is signalled by the appearance of separation protest – the distress when an infant is separated from his/her caregiver, and stranger anxiety – distress when approached by someone who is unfamiliar. In phase 4, initially infants show attachments to one primary caregiver but soon after most infants also show attachments to other people. In phase 5 the infant learns to predict the responses of others and this means that it is possible to consciously influence their behaviour.	• As predicted by the stage model, Schaffer and Emerson (1964) found that most infants first showed signs of separation protest and stranger anxiety at around the age of seven months, indicating the onset of specific attachments. • One problem with this evidence is that it only considered infants from a Western cultural background and thus may not apply universally. A further problem is that the observations were recorded by the mothers, who may not have been able to keep a very reliable record. • One weakness in any stage account of development is that it suggests a fixed pattern of development. However, it is the *sequence* of the development of attachment that is important; the actual ages at which children attain the different stages are only approximate. • The development of secure attachments in infancy has consequences for development in adult life. Adults who have developed a secure attachment bond in childhood find it relatively easy to get close to others and are comfortable depending on others and having others depend on them. Insecurely attached adults may find it difficult to trust or depend on others completely, or their desire to merge completely with another person scares others away. This demonstrates the long-term impact of early attachment experiences.

Individual differences: Secure and insecure attachments

Specification extract
Research into individual differences in attachment, including secure and insecure attachments (e.g. Ainsworth).

research methods
Q.

Comment You may be asked in an exam about methods or techniques. Don't make the mistake of getting confused between them. There are experimental methods and experimental techniques, observational methods and observational techniques.

a) *What is an observational technique?*

b) *What is the difference between an observational study and observational techniques?*

c) *Explain the difference between time sampling and event sampling.*

d) *Why are sampling methods needed when conducting some observational studies?*

e) *Describe* **one** *method to record observations.*

Some candidates give a tautological answer such as 'insecure attachment is one that was not secure'. This would receive no marks as it displays no psychological understanding.

Successful answers refer to the Strange Situation as a way of distinguishing between the two behavioural types. Weak candidates write about attachment in basic terms saying, for example, that insecure attachment is when you have a weak bond with your mother.

The greatest problem here is that candidates know too much about the procedures of the Strange Situation (if they use this study – which most do). You should practise producing a very short but comprehensive account of the Strange Situation. If you only describe the seven episodes, this is not a full account of the procedure.

No problem here distinguishing between findings and conclusions, because they both count! But you do have to make sure you don't just write about findings or conclusions. Aim to get a *reasonable* balance.

Don't forget the **three-point rule**: identify, describe, contextualise.

Some candidates choose inappropriate studies on attachment that do not focus on individual differences such as Harlow's study of attachment in monkeys. You do not need to refer to more than one study as long as you know a number of findings from one study.

Some candidates produce two short criticisms despite the requirement to give *one* criticism. You will only get credit for the better criticism (examiners do try to be kind).

What happens to a securely (or insecurely) attached infant when they grow older? You need to identify two different effects and apply the three-point rule: name the effect, explain it and elaborate using, for example, research evidence.

Possible plan

	A01 Description of the study (1/3 of answer) About 100 words	**A02** Criticism of the study (2/3 of answer) About 200 words
Study 1		
Study 2		
Study 3		

AO1 questions

1. Explain what is meant by secure attachment and insecure attachment.
   (3 marks + 3 marks)

2. Describe **two** differences between secure and insecure attachment.
   (3 marks + 3 marks)

3. Describe the aims and procedures of **one** study of secure and insecure attachment. *(6 marks)*

4. Describe the findings and conclusions of **one** study of secure and insecure attachment. *(6 marks)*

5. Give **two** criticisms of the study that you have described in question 4.
   (3 marks + 3 marks)

6. Outline findings of research into secure and insecure attachments. *(6 marks)*

7. Outline the procedures used in **one** study that has investigated individual differences in attachments and give **one** criticism of this study. *(3 marks + 3 marks)*

8. Give **two** effects of secure and insecure attachments.
   (3 marks + 3 marks)

9. Give **two** explanations for secure and insecure attachment.
   (3 marks + 3 marks)

There is no requirement in this question to consider more than one research study if you can describe one study in sufficient detail. Leave yourself enough time to provide sufficient AO2 material for the larger share of the marks that are given for evaluation. Any evaluation of the validity of the studies will also be relevant to AO2. This can be done by considering other research evidence and/or the methodology of the study.

AO1/AO2 question

Outline and evaluate research (studies **and/or** theories) into secure and insecure attachment.
   (18 marks)

1 Secure attachment is a strong and contented attachment of an infant to its caregiver, which develops as a result of sensitive responding by the caregiver to the infant's needs. Secure attachment is related to healthy subsequent cognitive and emotional development.

Insecure attachment is a form of attachment between infant and caregiver that develops as a result of the caregiver's lack of sensitive responding to the infant's needs. It may be associated with poor subsequent cognitive and emotional development.

2 **Difference 1:** Secure attachment develops as a result of consistently sensitive responding by the parent to the infant's needs. Insecure attachment may develop if there is a lack of such sensitive responding.

Difference 2: Securely attached children seek and are comfortable with social interaction and intimacy. Insecurely attached children tend to avoid social interaction (avoidant type) or both seek and reject contact with others.

3 A study of secure and insecure attachment (Ainsworth *et al.*, 1978).
Aims: The aim was to see how an infant behaves under conditions of mild stress and also novelty. The Strange Situation is novel and this aims to encourage exploration and test the secure base concept.
Procedures: In this study data was combined from several other studies, to make a total of 106 middle-class infants observed in the Strange Situation. The Strange Situation consists of eight episodes, each one lasting about three minutes. Three people are involved: a caregiver, her infant and a stranger. Observers recorded infant behaviour in terms of five categories such as proximity and contact-seeking behaviours.

4 A study of secure and insecure attachment (Ainsworth *et al.*, 1978).
Findings: Ainsworth *et al.* found that exploratory behaviours declined in all infants from episode two onwards. Proximity-seeking and contact-maintaining behaviours intensified during separation and when the stranger appeared. They found three main types of children (secure, insecure-avoidant and insecure-resistant).
Conclusions: The Strange Situation highlights important behaviours related to attachment: willingness to explore, stranger and separation anxiety, and behaviour at reunion. Infants vary in the way they behave, showing individual differences that may be related to the behaviour of their caregiver. This suggests that an innate tendency (attachment) is affected by life experiences (caregiver's behaviours).

5 **Criticism 1:** The Strange Situation procedure has been used widely in attachment research with infants, and has been adapted for studies of children and even adults. This is a positive criticism of both the technique and the classification system pioneered in this study.
Criticism 2: The intention of the Strange Situation is to cause mild distress. Ainsworth *et al.* claimed that the situation as a whole was not intended to be any more disturbing than ordinary life experiences. However, in episode six 20% of the infants reportedly cried 'desperately'. Ethical guidelines state that psychologists should avoid causing any distress to participants.

6 In the Strange Situation study, Ainsworth *et al.* found evidence of three main types of attachment (secure, insecure-avoidant and insecure-resistant). Securely attached children were willing to explore in the absence of the mother, showed high levels of stranger anxiety and were enthusiastic at the mother's return. Insecure-avoidant children were also willing to explore in the mother's absence, but showed low levels of stranger anxiety and avoided contact with the mother on her return. Insecure-resistant children were reluctant to explore, showed high levels of stranger anxiety and both sought and rejected the mother upon her return. They found the majority of children fitted the first type, with one-third being classified as insecurely attached.

> *Notice how the findings have been reported differently here from question 4. Both answers are creditworthy.*

AO1 Description of study	AO2 Criticism of the study
Can use parts from answers 3 and 4	Can use answer 5
Can use part of answer 8	Can use part of answer 8
Repeat for study 3 if time (and space) allow.	

7 A study of individual differences in attachment (Van IJzendoorn and Kroonenberg, 1988).

> *You can use a study related to secure and insecure attachment or on cross-cultural variations as an example of individual differences.*

Procedures: Van IJzendoorn and Kroonenberg looked through various databases to find studies on attachment, selecting only those studies of mother–infant interaction that used the Strange Situation procedure. Altogether they examined over 2,000 Strange Situation classifications from 32 studies conducted in eight different countries.
Criticism: Some US studies looked at urban populations whereas others were more rural. Rural societies in the US may be more similar to rural societies in Israel than they are to urban societies in the US. What this means is that data was collected on different *subcultures* within each country and that it is a mistake to think of behaviour within one country as representing a homogeneous culture.

8 **Effect 1:** The quality of attachment is related to different patterns of behaviour. Children who are securely attached explore their environments more thoroughly, are better able to deal with challenging situations, and are better at problem solving, whereas insecure (avoidant) children often develop behaviour problems and lack persistence in learning.
Effect 2: The quality of attachment is also related to different patterns of adult behaviour. For example, adults who were securely attached as infants find it relatively easy to get close to others and are comfortable depending on others and having others depend on them, whereas insecure-avoidant adults are somewhat uncomfortable being close to others.

9 **Explanation 1:** Children are born with innate temperamental differences. It is quite possible that children form more secure relationships simply because they have an 'easy' temperament whereas 'difficult' children are likely to form insecure relationships.
Explanation 2: Numerous studies have demonstrated that the quality of infant attachment to the mother is influenced by maternal sensitivity to the infant during interactions. For example, recent research has shown a significant association between maternal depression and infant attachment insecurity.

research methods **A**

a) An observational technique is simply one way of collecting data, by observing behaviour rather than manipulating it.

b) An observational study is the method used to investigate a particular behaviour; the observational technique is a component part of that study, a way of collecting data.

c) Time sampling involves making a note of a target behaviour at fixed time intervals. In event sampling, a list of behaviours is drawn up (e.g. crying, smiling, cuddling), and a count is kept of every time each behaviour occurs.

d) An observer needs some way to decide how often and for how long to make observations. It would be impossible and inappropriate to watch participants 24 hours a day or to record every single behaviour.

e) One method to record observations would be to have some sort of observation checklist of behaviours to be observed. This involves dividing the behaviours to be observed into categories and noting every time a behaviour occurs that fits one of the categories.

Individual differences: Cross-cultural variations

Specification extract

Research into individual differences in attachment, including cross-cultural variations.

research methods Q!

You would not be asked a research methods question on cross-cultural research because it is not a term listed in the specification. However, it is useful to be aware of some of the problems with such research so you can use this when evaluating cross-cultural research.

a) *In what way is cross-cultural research a kind of natural experiment? [Hint: Think of a cross-cultural study and identify the IV and DV.]*

b) *Describe one other limitation that is likely with cross-cultural studies.*

What's wrong with this explanation? 'Cross-cultural variation is when there are differences between cultural groups.'

A cross-cultural study does not need to make specific comparisons between two or more cultures. This comparison is implicit in any study of attachment in a cultural setting. Some candidates think that Harlow's research is cross-cultural. It isn't.

Candidates frequently include percentages when describing the findings of a study but these are often wrong. It is better to give approximate numbers rather than inaccurate ones.

Remember that criticisms can be positive. Positive criticisms can refer to applications of the research or describe support from another study.

Many candidates feel they need to outline in detail the procedures of the Strange Situation before they answer a question like this. Don't do it!

If you start a sentence 'This suggests that …' or 'Therefore …' you are more or less forced to record a conclusion.

You are asked to describe general criticisms of research in this area but can adapt your knowledge of criticisms of specific studies.

Always read the question first. Don't answer the quotation, you must answer the question. Use the quotation to clarify what points you might include in your answer.

AO1 questions

1. Explain what is meant by cross-cultural variations.
   (3 marks + 3 marks)

2. Describe the aims and conclusions of **one** study of cross-cultural variations.
   (6 marks)

3. Describe the procedures and findings of **one** study of cross-cultural variations.
   (6 marks)

4. Give **two** criticisms of the study that you have described in question 3.
   (3 marks + 3 marks)

5. Outline findings of research into cross-cultural variations.
   (6 marks)

6. Outline conclusions of research into cross-cultural variations. *(6 marks)*

7. Give **two** criticisms of research into cross-cultural variations.
   (3 marks + 3 marks)

8. Give **two** effects of cross-cultural variations.
   (3 marks + 3 marks)

Possible plan

	Brief description of the study **(AO1)**	What does this study tell us about cross-cultural variations in attachment? **(AO2)**	Further commentary on the study **(AO2)**
Study 1			Limitations of using the Strange Situation in a different cultural setting, etc.
Study 2			General commentary on cross-cultural research, etc.
Study 3			Ways of explaining cross-cultural differences/similarities, etc.

AO1/AO2 question

'Psychological research has found important differences in child-rearing styles in different cultures. Such differences are likely to affect styles of attachment.' To what extent are there cross-cultural variations in attachments? *(18 marks)*

1 Cross-cultural variations are the ways that different groups of people (e.g. members of a society or subcultures within a society) vary in terms of their social practices and the effects these practices have on development and behaviour.

2 A study on cross-cultural variations (Van IJzendoorn and Kroonenberg, 1988).
Aims: Van IJzendoorn and Kroonenberg aimed to establish whether there really are differences in attachment patterns in different cultures or whether the apparent differences are due to research error. They were also interested to find out whether there were *intra*cultural differences – differences in the findings from studies conducted within the same culture.
Conclusions: Van IJzendoorn and Kroonenberg concluded that *inter*cultural differences were not likely to be due to methodological problems because most of the studies within the *same* culture were conducted by the same investigator and yet showed even greater variation in Strange Situation classifications.

> When you answer a question on aims and conclusions (or procedures and findings) you can gain full marks even if you have not provided the same amount of information for both.

3 A study on cross-cultural variations (Van IJzendoorn and Kroonenberg, 1988).
Procedures: Van IJzendoorn and Kroonenberg carried out a meta-analysis of studies on attachment, selecting only those studies of mother–infant interaction that used the Strange Situation procedure. Studies were excluded if they looked at special groups such as Down syndrome or twins, or those that involved fewer than 35 infants. Altogether they examined over 2,000 Strange Situation classifications from 32 studies conducted in 8 different countries.
Findings: With reference to variation *between* cultures/countries, Van IJzendoorn and Kroonenberg found that the differences were small. Secure attachment was the most common classification in every country. Insecure-avoidant attachment was the next most common in every country except Israel and Japan. With reference to variation *within* cultures, they found that this was *1.5 times* greater than the variation between cultures.

4 **Criticism 1:** The Strange Situation is based on the notion that independence (valued in individualist societies) is the outcome of secure attachment. Rothbaum *et al.* (2000) suggest that secure attachment in collectivist societies leads to dependence rather than independence. This means that the Strange Situation assessment is not a valid measure of attachment collectivist cultures.
Criticism 2: One explanation for the large within-culture variation is that some studies involved middle-class infants whereas other studies involved working-class infants. What this means is that data was collected on different *subcultures* within each country and that it is a mistake to think of behaviour within one country as representing a homogeneous culture.

5 Grossmann and Grossmann (1991) found that German infants tended to be classified as insecurely attached rather than securely attached. Takahashi (1990) found that Japanese infants were more distressed in the Strange Situation than their American counterparts. Tronick *et al.* (1992) studied an African tribe, the Efe, who live in extended family groups. The infants are looked after by different women but usually they sleep with their own mother at night. Despite such differences in child-rearing practices the infants, at six months, still showed one primary attachment.

research methods **A**

a) Cross-cultural research may be thought of as a natural experiment because naturally occurring variations in some aspect of development (e.g. child-rearing styles – the independent variable) can be investigated for their effects on some defined behaviour (e.g. attachment style – the dependent variable).

b) A second limitation is that the group of participants may not be representative of that culture and yet we make generalisations about the whole culture.

6 Van IJzendoorn and Kroonenberg (1988) concluded that *inter*cultural differences were not likely to be due to methodological problems because most of the studies within the *same* culture were conducted by the same investigator and yet showed even greater variation in Strange Situation classifications. Grossmann and Grossmann (1991) concluded that because of different child-rearing practices in Germany, which require some interpersonal distance between parents and children, infants *appear* to be insecurely attached. In the Takahashi (1990) study, it is likely that Japanese infants appeared to be insecurely attached because they rarely experience separation from their mothers.

7 See answer to question 4.

8 **Effect 1:** In some cultures it is the norm for women to bear many children and to breastfeed them all. In such cultures it is more efficient for the child-care duties to be assigned almost entirely to the mother. As a result, the mother's role as primary caregiver leads to a strong attachment between mother and infant, such that she becomes the main agent of socialisation in the child's early years.
Effect 2: Cultural differences in attachment behaviours may lead children to behave in predictable ways as adults. Closeness between mother and child in infancy (as in Japanese infants) leads to closer-knit family groups, consistent with the Japanese ideal of the importance of the group. In the West there is greater emphasis on the need to cope with separation, which leads to greater individuality as adults.

Brief description of the study (AO1)	What does this study tell us about cross-cultural variations in attachment? (AO2)	Further commentary on the study (AO2)
Van IJzendoorn and Kroonenberg (1988) found that differences between cultures were small. Secure attachment was the most common classification in every country. Insecure-avoidant attachment was the next most common in every country except Israel and Japan. With reference to variation *within* cultures, they found that this was *1.5 times* greater than the variation between cultures.	Van IJzendoorn and Kroonenberg concluded that *inter*cultural differences were not likely to be due to methodological problems because most of the studies within the *same* culture were conducted by the same investigator and yet showed even greater variation in Strange Situation classifications.	The Strange Situation is based on the notion that independence is the outcome of secure attachment. Rothbaum *et al.* (2000) suggest that secure attachment in collectivist societies leads to dependence rather than independence. This means that the Strange Situation assessment doesn't make sense in collectivist cultures and is not a valid measure of attachment.
Grossmann and Grossmann (1991) found that German infants tended to be classified as insecurely attached rather than securely attached. German infants did not engage in proximity-seeking behaviours in the Strange Situation.	Grossmann and Grossmann (1991) concluded that because of different child-rearing practices in Germany, which require some interpersonal distance between parents and children, infants *appear* to be insecurely attached.	This is supported by the research by Takahashi (1990) which found that Japanese infants also appear to be insecurely attached because of their mother–infant experiences. They are rarely separated from their mothers and therefore separation is more stressful for them than for their US counterparts.
Repeat for study 3 if time (and space) allow.		

Explanations of attachment

Specification extract

Explanations of attachment (e.g. learning theory, Bowlby's theory).

Keep it brief – there are only 3 marks for each explanation. Don't write about more than two explanations even though you may know three; it won't impress the examiner.

You can reuse one of the explanations you gave in question 1 but this time you should provide twice as much detail. If your first answer now seems a bit too long, make it shorter. Practise the art of précis; it will increase your understanding of the topic you are précising.

Knowing criticisms of the explanation will be useful if you have to answer an AO1/AO2 question.

Remember that criticisms can be positive or negative (strengths or limitations).
When you are asked to give two criticisms, don't write more than two, but here you might practise describing more than two criticisms in case you need to use them for an AO1/AO2 question. It also might enable you to see which two criticisms you can do best, in case you are asked this as an AO1 question.

Consider research that has used non-human animals in order to increase our understanding of human behaviour, such as the research by Lorenz and by Harlow.

a) Is it reasonable to make generalisations about human behaviour from this research?

b) What is the value of conducting research with non-human animals?

c) Describe **one** negative criticism of this research.

d) Describe **one** positive criticism of this research.

This question invites you to put together all the material provided in the AO1 questions above. The difference is that you should now weave it into a 'story'. Briefly describe explanations of attachment and for each one consider its strengths and weaknesses (there is no requirement for strengths and weaknesses but it gives a balanced answer). If you prefer, you can focus on one explanation only and evaluate this. You can even use a second explanation as a means of evaluating the first explanation but you must *use it effectively* as evaluation, not merely describe the alternative explanation (in which case it would get AO1 credit). Whatever you do, don't simply write everything you know about Bowlby.

Possible plan

	Description	Strengths (with reference to research studies, for example)	Weaknesses
Explanation 1			
Explanation 2			

AO1 questions

1. Outline **two** explanations of attachment.
(3 marks + 3 marks)

2. Describe **one** explanation of attachment. *(6 marks)*

3. Give **two** criticisms of explanation 1.
(3 marks + 3 marks)

4. Give **two** criticisms of explanation 2.
(3 marks + 3 marks)

AO1/AO2 question

Outline and evaluate **one or more** psychological explanations of attachment.
(18 marks)

1 **Explanation 1:** Behaviourists suggest that attachment is learned either through classical or operant conditioning. This approach has been called the *cupboard love* theory of attachment because it suggests that the infant becomes attached because they are fed and through association they become attached to the person who feeds them.

Both explanations have been well précised as appropriate for 3 marks, but they still contain a good amount of detail.

Explanation 2: Bowlby proposed that infants become attached to a caregiver because attachment is adaptive. Infants who do not become attached are less likely to survive and reproduce. Thus the attachment 'gene' is perpetuated and infants are born with an innate drive to become attached to a caregiver.

2 Behaviourists suggest that attachment is learned either through classical or operant conditioning. Food (an unconditioned stimulus) produces a sense of pleasure (an unconditioned response). The person who feeds (a conditioned stimulus) the infant becomes *associated* with the food, and eventually produces the conditioned response – pleasure. This association between an individual and a sense of pleasure is the attachment bond. Dollard and Miller (1950) suggested that a hungry infant feels uncomfortable and this creates a drive to reduce the discomfort. When they are fed, the drive is reduced, producing a sense of pleasure. Food becomes a primary reinforcer because it reinforces the behaviour in order to avoid discomfort. The person who supplies the food is associated with avoiding discomfort and becomes a secondary reinforcer, and a source of reward in his/her own right. This rewardingness is attachment.

3 **Criticism 1:** Schaffer and Emerson found that infants were *not* most attached to the person who fed them, nor to the person who spent most time with them. They were most attached to the person who was most responsive and interacted with them. This shows that reinforcement through feeding does not explain attachment.
Criticism 2: Harlow (1959) demonstrated that food isn't everything. This study concerned motherless rhesus monkeys who were raised on their own by two 'wire mothers'. According to learning theory, the young monkeys should have become attached to a 'mother surrogate' associated with food and offering drive reduction. In fact, the monkeys spent most time with a cloth-covered mother (offering contact comfort).

 research methods **A**

a) Animals (particularly other primates) and humans have sufficient of their physiology and evolutionary history in common to justify conclusions drawn from one to be applied to the other. However, animals and humans differ in terms of the importance of learning and cognition, which may challenge the validity of generalisations from one species to another.

b) The value of research using non-human animals lies in the fact that they offer the opportunity for greater experimental control and objectivity, and have been used in situations where it would have been impossible to use humans.

c) Harlow and Lorenz's research used non-human species and it may not be wholly appropriate to generalise the findings to human behaviour.

d) Harlow and Lorenz's research allowed for a degree of control that would have been impossible in studies using human children, and so allowed conclusions about cause and effect to be drawn.

4 **Criticism 1:** It follows, from Bowlby's theory, that we would expect securely attached infants to develop different social and emotional relationships in comparison to those who were insecurely attached, with emotionally secure infants going on to become emotionally secure, trusting and socially confident adults. A number of studies (e.g. Hazan and Shaver, 1987) support this.
Criticism 2: However, this continuity in development can be explained without using Bowlby's theory. An alternative explanation is that some infants are born trusting and friendly. This would explain why they become securely attached and also why they later form similar kinds of relationship. This is called the temperament hypothesis.

Explanation (AO1)	AO2 Strengths	AO2 Weaknesses
Behaviourists suggest that attachment is learned either through classical or operant conditioning. This approach has been called the *cupboard love* theory of attachment because it suggests that the infant becomes attached because they are fed and through association they become attached to the person who feeds them.	Learning theory can explain attachment. We do learn through association and reinforcement. Reinforcement may be provided in ways other than food. Attention and responsiveness from a caregiver are also rewarding.	The importance of food is not supported by research. For example, Harlow (1959) demonstrated that food isn't everything. According to learning theory, young monkeys should have become attached to a 'mother surrogate' associated with food and offering drive reduction. In fact, these monkeys spent most time with a cloth-covered mother (offering contact comfort).
Bowlby proposed that infants become attached to a caregiver because attachment is adaptive. Infants who do not become attached are less likely to survive and reproduce. Thus the attachment 'gene' is perpetuated and infants are born with an innate drive to become attached to a caregiver.	It follows, from Bowlby's theory, that we would expect securely attached infants to develop different social and emotional relationships in comparison to those who were insecurely attached, with emotionally secure infants going on to become emotionally secure, trusting and socially confident adults. A number of studies (e.g. Hazan and Shaver, 1987) support this.	However, this continuity in development can be explained without using Bowlby's theory. An alternative explanation is that some infants are born trusting and friendly. This is called the temperament hypothesis. This would explain why they become securely attached and also why they later form similar kinds of relationship.

End of section review

Note that this entire question has been drawn from the one section (the development and variety of attachments). This is acceptable. It is also acceptable to set an entire question on two or three sections.

Sample exam question

a. Outline the stages in the formation of attachments. *(6 marks)*

b. Outline findings of research on secure and insecure attachment. *(6 marks)*

c. Outline and evaluate **one** explanation of attachment. *(18 marks)*

See page viii for an explanation of how questions are marked.

Student answer

(a) When they are born infants are not attached at all. At this stage they respond in a similar way to most people. In the second stage, infants become better at recognising special people. However, they still do not seem very upset when they are left on their own with a stranger. This means they do not show stranger anxiety yet at this stage. Finally, at around 7 months they enter the stage of attachment proper when they get very upset (separation distress) when they are left by one special caregiver and they also show stranger anxiety for the first time.

(b) Ainsworth conducted the Strange Situation which involved a stranger, a caregiver and an infant. The aim was to test separation anxiety and stranger anxiety and attachment. It was found that some children were securely attached whereas others (about 30%) were insecurely attached. The insecurely attached were divided into two groups: resistant insecure and avoidant insecure. Another study looked at children all over the world and found that rates of classification into secure and insecure types were very similar to the Ainsworth study, though a Japanese study found that no children were classified as avoidant. This may be because the Strange Situation doesn't make sense to them.

(c) Learning theory has been used to explain attachment. It is said that infants become attached to their mother because their mother gives them food. This leads to conditioning and the infant thinks positively of his mother. The main problem with this explanation is that when Harlow studied monkeys he found this wasn't true. The monkeys were raised in a cage with two wire mothers. One 'mother' had a feeding bottle and the other had no bottle but was wrapped in a cloth so it was nice to cuddle. The monkeys spent most of their time with the cuddly mother and ran to her when they were frightened. This shows that they were not attached to the mother that fed them. However we should not generalise from animals to humans.

Another explanation of attachment was Freud's cupboard love theory. He again suggested that food was the key factor. Babies have their oral needs satisfied by their mothers and this leads to love.

The third theory was proposed by Bowlby. He said that babies become attached because it keeps them safe and therefore they survive and have babies themselves. And therefore the behaviour continues. It is impossible to prove that this theory is correct but it is a good explanation of the facts. [212 words]

Examiner's comments

A reasonably short description but an outline is all that is required and there is sufficient detail for the full **6 marks**.

A mixed bag of aims, findings and conclusions. Findings from three studies are given but not all are detailed. The *breadth* of this answer compensates to some extent for the lack of depth (detail) but not sufficiently to give full marks, thus *5 marks*.

The candidate has overlooked the fact that the question requires only one explanation and therefore AO1 credit can only be given to the best explanation (and only the evaluation of this one explanation would be creditworthy). The description of learning theory is the best but it is basic and lacking detail, thus **2 marks for AO1**.

The second half of the first paragraph offers commentary on this theory; however, much of this is a *description* of the Harlow study. Credit is awarded to the extent that such material has been used as commentary (e.g. 'This shows that …'). The remaining paragraphs provide descriptions of other theories, material that could have been used as commentary if contrasts were made with learning theory (e.g. saying that Freud's theory was similar because it identified feeding as the course of attachment). Overall the AO2 material is rudimentary, thus **4 marks for AO2**, a **total of 6 marks**.

Total for whole question is **17 marks**, equivalent to a Grade B.

This module is divided into

The development and variety of attachments

The formation of attachments

Individual differences: Secure and insecure attachments

Individual differences: Cross-cultural variations

Explanations of attachment

End of section review

Deprivation and privation

Maternal deprivation hypothesis

Effects of privation

End of section review

Critical issue: Day care

Effects of day care on cognitive development

Effects of day care on social development

End of section review

COGNITIVE PSYCHOLOGY:
HUMAN MEMORY

DEVELOPMENTAL PSYCHOLOGY:
ATTACHMENTS IN DEVELOPMENT

PHYSIOLOGICAL PSYCHOLOGY:
STRESS

INDIVIDUAL DIFFERENCES:
ABNORMALITY

SOCIAL PSYCHOLOGY:
SOCIAL INFLUENCE

RESEARCH
METHODS

Maternal deprivation hypothesis

The phrase 'in relation to attachments in development' is added to restrict your definitions to this area of study rather than deprivation of anything. So, keep your answer specific.
It may be helpful to think of how these concepts are different when trying to explain them.

Specification extract
Bowlby's maternal deprivation hypothesis, including evidence on which it is based.

Some candidates provide lengthy accounts of Bowlby's study of juvenile thieves when trying to outline the maternal deprivation hypothesis. This approach will gain some marks but you really should be able to state the hypothesis that led to this study. Three key points on the hypothesis (e.g. consequences of deprivation, critical period, monotropy) are better than six sentences about the study.

State the criticism, explain it (possibly with reference to a research study) and explain why it is a criticism.

Some candidates answer this question by identifying all the findings from Ainsworth's Strange Situation, but they restrict their marks because they waste time including procedures as well.

Criticising a study is slightly different to criticising an explanation – contextualisation is often an issue. 'Contextualisation' means placing your answer in the context of the study not just making a general comment that could fit after every study.

research methods Q

a) Why is it important for the findings of a study to be generalisable?

b) Explain what is meant by a 'representative sample'.

c) What is a 'population' (in the context of research)?

Many exam questions are very straightforward, such as this one. The greatest danger in a question like this is that you may feel tempted to describe (AO1) a number of research studies and overlook the requirement to provide twice as much AO2. You must restrict the number of studies described (two will be plenty) to leave yourself time to offer thoughtful commentary on the studies.

AO1 questions

1. What is meant by deprivation in relation to attachments in development?
(3 marks)

2. Outline Bowlby's maternal deprivation hypothesis.
(6 marks)

3. Give **two** criticisms of this hypothesis.
(3 marks + 3 marks)

4. Outline findings of research into the maternal deprivation hypothesis.
(6 marks)

5. Give **two** criticisms of the study that you described in question 4.
(3 marks + 3 marks)

6. Outline conclusions of research related to the maternal deprivation hypothesis.
(6 marks)

AO1/AO2 question

Outline and evaluate the evidence on which the maternal deprivation hypothesis is based.
(18 marks)

Possible plan

	Outline key details **(AO1)**	What does this tell us about 'lasting effects'? **(AO2)**	General commentary on the theory/study e.g. good research support, methodological problems **(AO2)**
Study 1			
Study 2			

1 To be deprived means to lose something, so in this case the child has lost the emotional care usually provided by their caregiver, and this loss is not compensated by suitable levels of care from another person.

2 Bowlby believed that, during development, emotional care was as important as physical care. He believed that infants and children needed a mother's emotional care to ensure continuing normal *mental* health. A child who is denied such care because of frequent and/or prolonged separations will become emotionally disturbed if this happens before the age of about two

> To get 6 marks your answer must be detailed and accurate but need not be more than about 100 words (that's about what you can write in 6 minutes if you include thinking time as well). This answer is 108 words.

and a half years, and if there is no substitute mother-person available. Bowlby also felt there was a continuing risk up until the age of five. Separation alone may not be harmful but Bowlby claimed that a child who is deprived of emotional care will suffer permanent consequences in terms of their mental health.

3 **Criticism 1:** This hypothesis had an enormous impact on how children are looked after in hospitals. Before the research by Bowlby, children were separated from parents when they spent time in hospital or if their mother spent time in hospital. Visiting was discouraged or even forbidden. Bowlby's maternal deprivation hypothesis changed all that.
Criticism 2: Some research shows that Bowlby was wrong about the effects of early separation. For example, some studies of isolated children (e.g. Koluchová, 1976) demonstrate good recovery despite many years of deprivation.

4 In Bowlby's study (Bowlby, 1944), it was found that the affectionless thieves had experienced frequent early separations from their mothers, with 86% of the affectionless thieves having experienced frequent separations compared with 17% (5 out of 30) of the other thieves. Furthermore almost none of the control participants experienced early separations whereas 39% of all the thieves had experienced early separations, such as repeated stays in foster homes or hospitals. Bowlby *et al.* (1956) studied a group of children staying in a TB hospital. When these children were assessed in adolescence there were no significant differences between them and their 'normal' peers in terms of intellectual development. Some members of the TB group were more maladjusted but there was no serious maladjustment.

5 **Criticism 1:** The information about early separation in Bowlby's (1944) study was collected *retrospectively*. Parents were asked to recall events from up to 14 years previously about when they had been separated from their children. It is likely that such recall was not completely accurate.
Criticism 2: It is wrong to think that early separations *caused* later maladjustment in the children just because the two are linked together. Rutter (1981) suggested that there may be a factor which causes both and this is why separations and maladjustment are linked. It could be that some family environments are full of stress because parents are arguing and also lack resources to care for the children.

research methods **A**

a) If the findings of a study are generalisable, it means that they can be applied beyond the sample of people studied towards the rest of the population.

b) A representative sample allows the researcher to draw conclusions based on the population under study, in that he/she is confident that the sample studied adequately represents the underlying characteristics of the population.

c) A population is the group of people from whom a sample is drawn.

6 Bowlby's study of 44 thieves (Bowlby, 1944) suggests a link between early separation and becoming a thief (i.e. lacking a social conscience). The findings also suggest that early separations are linked to affectionless psychopathy. In other words, lack of continuous care may well cause emotional maladjustment, especially in the extreme form of affectionless psychopathy. Another study by Bowlby (Bowlby *et al.*, 1956) looked at children hospitalised for TB who, despite a lack of maternal care, appeared to show no long-term effects from their prolonged maternal deprivation. This suggests that the dangers of maternal deprivation may have been overstated. Early deprivation does not invariably cause emotional maladjustment.

Key details (AO1)	What does this tell us? (AO2)	General commentary (AO2)
Bowlby (1944) found that 86% of his affectionless thieves had experienced frequent early separations from their mothers, compared with 17% of the other thieves. Furthermore, almost none of the control participants experienced early separations.	Bowlby's data suggest a link between early separation and becoming a thief (i.e. someone lacking a social conscience). They also suggest that lack of continuous care may well cause emotional maladjustment, especially in the extreme form of affectionless psychopathy.	The information about early separation was collected *retrospectively*. Parents were asked to recall events from up to 14 years previously about when they had been separated from their children. It is likely that such recall was not completely accurate.
Bowlby *et al.* (1956) studied children under the age of four who were hospitalised for the prolonged treatment of TB. When assessed in adolescence there were no significant differences between them and their 'normal' peers in terms of intellectual development or in terms of maladjustment.	Bowlby *et al.* concluded that the dangers of maternal deprivation may have been overstated. In this case early deprivation did not invariably cause emotional maladjustment. One explanation for the individual differences may be that some children were more securely attached and therefore able to cope better.	There are many other studies that support the view that deprivation effects can be reversed. Bohman and Sigvardsson (1980) studied adopted children in Sweden, discovering that despite some problems at age 11, none of the children were any worse off than the rest of the population at age 21. This would suggest that early, negative effects were reversed.

Effects of privation

🪱🪱🪱🪱🪱🪱🪱🪱🪱🪱🪱🪱🪱

Specification extract
Research into the effects of privation
(e.g. studies of extreme privation
and institutionalisation), including
the extent to which the effects of
privation can be
reversed.

research methods

Q

a) What is a longitudinal design?

b) What is a cross-sectional
design?

c) Give **two** reasons why the study
by Hodges and Tizard can be
considered to be a natural
experiment.

Candidates frequently confuse these two terms,
somehow getting the idea that they are
opposites, i.e. that privation = enrichment.

Those candidates who select the study of Genie
when answering this question often spend time
describing her early life, thinking this is a
description of the procedures of the study. It isn't.
Make sure you are writing about a study of
privation and not a study of deprivation. If you're
not sure, try to explain in what way this is a study
of privation so the examiner is informed about why
you felt this was an appropriate study.

Candidates tend to find it more difficult to report the
conclusions of research. Have you got any ideas why this is?
Perhaps they are less clear-cut than findings. If you aren't
sure what to write, think of the findings and then ask
yourself what these findings show – and that's a conclusion.

Candidates who use the study of Genie are often limited
here because they know little else other than the ethical
problems and these are often not criticisms of the study
anyway – her father's behaviour is not an ethical problem
for the study. Some candidates get even more muddled
and accuse the researchers of causing the privation.

It is permissible to refer to the findings from just one
study but this may limit your answer.
Don't include the peripheral details of any research
study (such as how Genie was treated) as they will gain
no credit in answer to this question.

It is also permissible to discuss the conclusions from just
one study – if you can write 6 marks-worth. It may be
easier to write about the conclusions of several studies.

Which of the following is *not* an effect of privation: poor
cognitive development, poor emotional development,
difficulty as a parent later in life, difficulty in relationships,
difficulty getting a job, or physical underdevelopment?

AO1 credit will be achieved through your description of research. AO2 credit can be through
your use of such research to (a) consider what effects deprivation or privation has on
development, and (b) draw conclusions about whether the effects of deprivation differ from
those of privation. This means that you must examine research on deprivation and privation. An
answer that only looks at one kind of study (deprivation or privation only) would be
described as a *partial performance*, and a maximum of 2/3 of the marks would be available.

Possible plan

	Brief outline of the study **(AO1)**	Conclusions regarding the effects of deprivation/ privation **(AO2)**	Conclusion(s) about whether this shows that deprivation/ privation is different **(AO2)**
Study on deprivation			
Study on deprivation			
Study on privation			

AO1 questions

1. Explain what is meant by
   deprivation and privation, and
   explain the difference
   between them. (*2 marks +
   2 marks + 2 marks*)

2. Describe the aims and
   findings of **one** study of the
   effects of privation.
   (*6 marks*)

3. Describe the procedures and
   conclusions of **one** study of
   the effects of privation.
   (*6 marks*)

4. Give **two** criticisms of the
   study that you have described
   in question 3.
   (*3 marks + 3 marks*)

5. Outline findings of research
   into the effects of privation.
   (*6 marks*)

6. Outline conclusions of
   research into the effects of
   privation.   (*6 marks*)

7. Describe **two** effects of
   privation.
   (*3 marks + 3 marks*)

AO1/AO2 question

'It has been suggested that only
the effects of privation are lasting;
children recover from early
maternal deprivation.' To what
extent does psychological research
(theory **and/or** studies) suggest
that the effects of deprivation and
privation on development are
different?   (*18 marks*)

1 To be deprived means to lose something, so in this case the child has lost the emotional care usually provided by their caregiver, and this loss is not compensated for by suitable levels of care from another person. Privation describes those children who have never managed to develop an attachment bond.

The difference between them is that deprivation may not lead to permanent emotional damage but this is more likely if privation occurs.

These answers may seem brief but would get 2 marks (1 mark would be 'muddled or flawed').

2 A study of the effects of privation (Hodges and Tizard, 1989).

Aims: Bowlby's maternal deprivation hypothesis suggested that a discontinuous relationship between a mother figure and infant would result in emotional maladjustment. To test this, Hodges and Tizard undertook a longitudinal study following a group of institutionalised children from early life to adolescence to see if there were any differences between those children who were returned home and those children who were adopted.

Findings: At age 4, the institutionalised children did not have any deep relationships. They were more attention-seeking than non-institutional children. At age 8, most of the ex-institutional children had formed close attachments with their parents or adopted parents. At age 16, the adopted children were about as closely attached to their parents as the control group, whereas the 'restored' group where much less likely to be closely attached. All the ex-institutional adolescents were less likely to have a special friend or to be liked by other children.

3 A study of the effects of privation (Hodges and Tizard, 1989).

Findings can be used to inform conclusions.

Procedures: The study focused on a group of 65 children who had been placed in one institution when they were less than 4 months old. By the age of 4, 24 of the children had been adopted, 15 returned to their natural homes and the rest remained in the institution. The children were assessed at age 4 and again at ages 8 and 16, and compared to a control group of children raised in a 'normal' home environment.

Conclusions: The findings at age 4 and 8 suggest that the children did show signs of permanent damage as a result of their early institutional life. The findings at age 16 suggest that early privation had a negative effect on the ability to form relationships when the relationship involved someone who wasn't going to work hard at it, i.e. in peer relationships.

4 **Criticism 1:** The original sample was reduced in subsequent follow-ups, a problem known as *attrition*. It is possible that more troubled children dropped out, although this should have affected both the adopted and restored children equally and therefore not have biased the findings.

Criticism 2: Hodges and Tizard suggest that, at age 16, might be explained in other ways. For example, it could be that the adopted children suffered from poor self-esteem stemming from being adopted, which would explain their problems outside the home.

5 Hodges and Tizard (1989) found that at age 4, institutionalised children did not have any deep relationships. They were more attention-seeking than non-institutional children. At age 8, most of the ex-institutional children had formed close attachments with their parents or adopted parents. At age 16, the adopted children were about as closely attached to their parents as the control group, whereas the 'restored' group were much less likely to be closely attached. All the ex-institutional adolescents were less likely to have a

research methods **A**

a) A longitudinal design is when a study is conducted over a long period of time, to compare the same individual at different points in time (i.e. the IV = age).

b) A cross-sectional design is an alternative to a longitudinal design, with individuals of different ages compared at the same point in time (i.e. the IV = age).

c) Reason 1: The IV (level of early emotional privation) was not controlled by the experimenter but already existed.

Reason 2: It would have been impractical (and unethical) for the experimenter to allocate participants to conditions, but they could make use of divisions that already existed.

special friend or to be liked by other children. The Czech twins (Koluchová, 1976) after seven years of privation, were cared for by two loving sisters and by age 14 had near normal intellectual and social functioning. By the age of 20, they were of above average intelligence and had excellent relationships with the members of their foster family.

6 In the Hodges and Tizard study, the findings at age 4 and 8 suggest that the children did show signs of permanent damage as a result of their early institutional life. The findings at age 16 suggest that early privation had a negative effect on the ability to form relationships when the relationship involved someone who wasn't going to work hard at it, i.e. in peer relationships. The study of the Czech twins who suffered seven years of privation (Koluchová, 1976) shows that recovery is possible. This may be because they were 'discovered' at a young enough age, or it may be that they provided emotional care for each other, and thus did experience early attachment rather than privation.

7 **Effect 1:** Poor parenting. It may be that children who experience early privation are in some way 'driven' to recreate the conditions of their own childhood when they themselves become parents. There is some evidence for this 'cycle of privation' in that ex-institutional women experienced extreme difficulties as parents, and a high proportion of their children spent time in care themselves (Quinton *et al.*, 1984).

Effect 2: Poor adult relationships. Children with reactive attachment disorder have learned that the world is unsafe, and have learned not to depend on adult caregivers. Individuals with this disorder, if left untreated, may grow up to become sociopaths who fail to develop a conscience and do not learn to trust others or form lasting intimate relationships.

Brief outline (AO1)	Conclusions regarding the effects of deprivation/ privation (AO2)	Conclusion(s) about whether this shows that deprivation/privation is different (AO2)
Bowlby (1944) found that 86% of his affectionless thieves had experienced frequent early separations, compared with 17% of the other thieves and none of the control participants.	Bowlby's data showed that lack of continuous care may well cause emotional maladjustment, especially in the extreme form of affectionless psychopathy.	Rutter (1972) criticised this view of deprivation because it did not make clear whether the child's attachment bond had formed but been broken, or in fact had never formed in the first place.
Bowlby *et al.* (1956) found that children who had been hospitalised when under 4, were no more intellectually or emotionally maladjusted in adolescence than their peers.	Bowlby *et al.* concluded that the dangers of maternal deprivation may have been overstated. In this case early deprivation did not invariably cause emotional maladjustment.	Rutter believed that deprivation may not have irreversible consequences whereas privation might have. This distinction is supported by the findings of these two studies.
Hodges and Tizard (1989) found at age 4, institutionalised children did not have any deep relationships, and showed other behavioural and emotional difficulties compared to non-institutionalised children.	In the Hodges and Tizard study, the findings supported the claim that children did show signs of permanent damage as a result of their early privation.	Hodges and Tizard suggest that their findings might be explained in other ways. Adopted children may have suffered from poor self-esteem stemming from being adopted. This makes it more difficult to disentangle the specific effects of early privation from other factors.

End of section review

Sample exam question

a. Explain what is meant by attachment, deprivation and privation.
(2 marks + 2 marks + 2 marks)

b. Outline the findings of **one** study in which the effects of privation have been investigated and give **one** criticism of this study.
(3 marks + 3 marks)

c. To what extent do research studies support the view that maternal deprivation can have long-term effects on individuals? *(18 marks)*

> Note that this entire question has been almost completely drawn from the one section (deprivation and privation). This is acceptable. It is also acceptable to set an entire question on two or three sections.

> See page viii for an explanation of how questions are marked.

Student answer	Examiner's comments
(a) Attachment is a bond between two people. It is a mutual bond between two people such as a caregiver and infant. Privation is the lack of having attachment, when someone has had no attachment to a special caregiver. Deprivation is when you are deprived of something.	The first two terms are described in sufficient detail for 2 marks. The final one includes nothing of relevance. For 1 mark you need to say what you are deprived of. Thus **2+2+1 marks**.
(b) Bowlby conducted a study on 44 thieves compared to 44 non-thieves. Of the 44 thieves, 17 were cold and uncaring and 14 of these had been maternally deprived. Bowlby called these 17 children 'affectionless psychopaths'. Of the 44 non-thieves, only 2 had been maternally deprived. One criticism of this study was that only 17 of the 44 thieves had been maternally deprived, so then why have the other 27 committed crimes?	The 44 thieves study is not a study of privation. There was nothing to suggest that the children had no attachments, just that they experienced frequent deprivation of emotional care. Even if the study had been creditworthy there would be few marks for the criticism, which is at best muddled, but as the study is not creditworthy there are no marks for the criticism. In total **0 marks**.
(c) Bowlby proposed the theory of maternal deprivation stating that if children were separated from their mothers for a long period that would have an irreversible effect on their emotional development. Bowlby conducted a study called '44 thieves' to support this theory. The study looked at children in a child guidance clinic. A lot of them had been separated from their mothers before the age of two. Bowlby diagnosed many of them as having affectionless psychopathy and blamed maternal deprivation for this condition. Support for Bowlby's view came from the Robertsons, who described the protest, despair, detachment model. This was shown by John, who was in a nursery while his mother went to hospital. However, not all psychologists have supported Bowlby. Rutter suggested that it was wrong to say that maternal deprivation was the sole cause of damaged emotional development. He stated that it was a chain of adversity, a combination of outside factors such as social status and individual differences that affected people. [163 words]	AO1 credit is given to the description of any studies, as has been done in the first paragraph. In the next two paragraphs the studies have been mentioned but not described. They have been *used* (appropriately) as commentary and will be credited as AO2. Thus the **AO1 mark is 4** (limited but closer to detailed than to muddled or flawed). The first paragraph could have been used effectively to argue that such evidence supports the maternal deprivation hypothesis. The remainder of the essay is reasonably well directed at evaluation but basic in its scope. As the mark for AO1 was a bit generous, the **AO2 mark is 5** rather than 6, a **total of 9 marks**.
	Total for whole question is **14 marks**, equivalent to a Grade C.

COGNITIVE PSYCHOLOGY: HUMAN MEMORY

DEVELOPMENTAL PSYCHOLOGY: ATTACHMENTS IN DEVELOPMENT

PHYSIOLOGICAL PSYCHOLOGY: STRESS

INDIVIDUAL DIFFERENCES: ABNORMALITY

SOCIAL PSYCHOLOGY: SOCIAL INFLUENCE

RESEARCH METHODS

Section 3:

DEVELOPMENTAL PSYCHOLOGY: ATTACHMENTS IN DEVELOPMENT

This module is divided into

The development and variety of attachments

The formation of attachments

Individual differences: Secure and insecure attachments

Individual differences: Cross-cultural variations

Explanations of attachment

End of section review

Deprivation and privation

Maternal deprivation hypothesis

Effects of privation

End of section review

Critical issue: Day care

Effects of day care on cognitive development

Effects of day care on social development

End of section review

Effects of day care on cognitive development

DEVELOPMENTAL PSYCHOLOGY: ATTACHMENTS IN DEVELOPMENT

Specification extract
The effects of day care on children's cognitive and social development.

research methods Q

a) What is meant by a correlation?

b) Describe a positive correlation, a negative correlation and a zero correlation.

c) What kind of graph is used to display correlational data?

Look at the graph below.

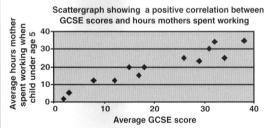

Scattergraph showing a positive correlation between GCSE scores and hours mothers spent working

Average hours mother spent working when child under age 5

Average GCSE score

d) What kind of correlation is shown in this graph?

e) What can you conclude from this graph?

In this case there are only 2 marks per definition so you should adjust your definition/explanation accordingly and not provide your three marks' worth explanation because this will waste valuable examination time.

Don't get sidetracked and start providing other details such as conclusions or criticisms. Some candidates forget themselves and start writing an **AO2**-type answer since this is what they have practised.

Day care is not the same as institutional care. The study by Hodges and Tizard is a study of institutional care.

Some candidates fail to distinguish between social and cognitive development, and therefore lose marks on a question such as this. You need to know the difference in order to be able to define the terms and in order to answer a question such as this.

On this occasion there are no numbers. You are not asked for one explanation or two explanations of how day care may affect cognitive development; you decide yourself whether to write about one explanation (and give lots of detail) or more than one (and get marks from variety rather than detail).

You can base your answer on criticisms you know in relation to a particular study.

Some questions do not clearly identify the AO1 and AO2 content, as is the case here, but it should always be fairly obvious how to do this. In order to consider what research has shown you must offer some (brief) description of this research. It would then be appropriate for AO2 to consider the validity of this research and finally offer a conclusion.
You might note that this answer plan is the same as the one on the next double-paged spread even though the questions are phrased differently.

AO1 questions

1. What is meant by day care and cognitive development?
   (2 marks + 2 marks)

2. Outline findings of research into the effects of day care on cognitive development.
   (6 marks)

3. Outline conclusions of research into the effects of day care on cognitive development. *(6 marks)*

4. Give **two** effects of day care on cognitive development.
   (3 marks + 3 marks)

5. Explain how day care may affect cognitive development.
   (6 marks)

6. Give **two** criticisms of research on the effects of day care on cognitive **and/or** social development.
   (3 marks + 3 marks)

AO1/AO2 question

To what extent has research (theories **and/or** studies) supported the view that day care has a negative effect on cognitive development?
(18 marks)

Possible plan

	Describe the study **(AO1)**	Refer to any flaws **(AO2)**	Discuss the conclusions **(AO2)**	Contrast with other research that reached alternative conclusions (do not describe this research but *use* it as part of your argument). **(AO2)**
Study 1				
Study 2				

1 Day care is a form of temporary care (i.e. not all day and night long), not given by family members or someone well known to the child, and usually outside the home.

Cognitive development refers to the changes in a person's mental structures, abilities and processes that occur over their lifespan.

2 Ruhm (2000) found that three- and four-year-olds tend to have lower verbal ability if their mothers worked during the child's first year. Five- and six-year-olds tend to have worse reading and maths skills if their mothers worked during any of the child's first three years. Andersson (1992) found that school performance was highest in those children who entered day care before one year, and lowest for those who did not have any day care. Burchinal *et al.* (2000) studied 89 African–American children from the age of three months to three years. Those placed in high-quality childcare had improved cognitive development, language development and communication skills.

> There are so many studies to choose from but selecting just three will give you the right balance of depth and breadth.

3 Harvey (1999) evaluated the development of more than 6,000 youngsters and concluded that being at home during the early years, or being employed during those years, can both result in healthy, well-developed children. Burchinal *et al.* (2000) concluded that policymakers should strive to improve the quality of childcare to enhance early development of vulnerable children because they found significant improvement in the cognitive development of Afro-American children given high-quality day care.

4 **Effect 1:** Day care has a negative effect. For example, Rhum (2000) found that three- and four-year olds tend to have lower verbal ability if their mothers work during the child's first year. Rhum also found that five- and six-year olds tend to have worse reading and maths skills if their mothers work during any of the child's first three years.

> Research studies can be used to provide information on effects.

Effect 2: Day care has a positive effect. For example, Andersson (1992) found school performance was highest in children who entered day care before the age of one and lowest in those who had no day care.

5 Holding and interacting with babies leads to more connections being made in the brain – connections between neurons. The more an infant is stimulated, the more neural connections are made. The nervous system relies on experience for development. Willingness to explore the environment is important for cognitive development. The more you explore, the more you learn. Separation through day care may harm the continuous relationship between mother and child, and this may lead to insecure attachment. Children who are insecurely attached will be less willing to explore, and their cognitive development may suffer as a result.

research methods

A

a) A relationship between two variables, such that systematic increases (or decreases) in the magnitude of one variable are accompanied by systematic increases (or decreases) in the magnitude of the other.

b) In a positive correlation the covariables increase together. In a negative correlation one variable increases while the other decreases. In a zero correlation there is no relationship between the variables.

c) A scattergraph.

d) A high positive correlation.

e) We can conclude that there is a strong relationship between the average number of hours worked by the mother when the child was under age five and the GCSE score subsequently achieved by that child. Children whose mothers worked the most hours tended to achieve the highest GCSE scores, and children whose mothers worked the least hours tended to achieve the lowest GCSE scores.

6 **Criticism 1:** Many of the studies involve a correlation. Therefore day care may be related to certain outcomes *but may not be the cause of them.* There may be other variables. For example working mothers may be more stressed, on average, than those who stay at home and this might cause increased aggressiveness in their children.

Criticism 2: An important variable, when considering whether day care has good or bad effects, is how long a child spends each day or week in day care. It may be that there is a limit to how much a small child can take. An NICHD report (2001) found that babies in day care for more than ten hours a week were more aggressive once they reached school.

Describe the study (AO1)	Refer to any flaws (AO2)	Discuss the conclusions (AO2)	Contrast with other research that reached alternative conclusions (AO2)
Ruhm (2000) surveyed 4000 three- and four-year-olds and found lower verbal ability in those whose mothers worked during the child's first year. Five- and six-year-olds tend to have worse reading and maths skills if their mothers worked during any of the child's first three years.	In such a large-scale study (which is a strength of this study) there are bound to be significant differences in the quality of care experienced by individual children.	This suggests that it might be hasty to conclude that day care would have the same negative effects on cognitive development in all day care situations.	Many studies have found negative effects but there are also many studies that have found no effects or positive effects. For example, Harvey (1999) found that children of working mothers displayed some cognitive delays at age three and four but these had disappeared by the age of 12.
Ermisch and Francesconi (2000) found a negative correlation between a child's educational attainment and how much the child's mother had been working when the child was under five.	It may be that some of the children studied were especially sensitive to being apart from their mothers and this affected the findings.	There are so many uncontrolled variables in any study of day care that it is difficult to draw clear conclusions.	Andersson (1992) found that school performance was highest in those children who entered day care before one year, and lowest for those who did not have any day care. This was a Swedish study where day care is high in quality.
			Research related to the Headstart projects has shown that for disadvantaged children day care has positive effects on academic achievement even 20 years later (Campbell *et al.*, 2001), but again this may apply only to high-quality day care.

Effects of day care on social development

Specification extract
The effects of day care on children's social development.

In this case there are only 2 marks so you should adjust your definition/explanation accordingly and not provide your three marks' worth explanation because this will waste valuable examination time.

Weak candidates write about day care generally without focusing on specific research findings.

The same problem may arise here as for question 2.

The most likely way to provide detail in your answer is to support the named effect by identifying a relevant research study and saying what this demonstrates about the named effect.

You can base your answer on criticisms you know in relation to a particular study.

research methods Q

a) Describe **two** factors you would take into consideration when designing a good questionnaire.

b) What is the difference between an open question and a closed question?

You plan to conduct a survey of children's experiences in day care.

c) Write two suitable questions for the survey.

d) What would be **one** advantage of interviewing respondents face-to-face?

e) What would be **one** disadvantage of doing this?

f) You wish to find out what (if any) feelings of distress were experienced at the time the respondents were in day care. How would you operationalise the variable 'distress'?

AO1 questions

1. What is meant by social development?

    (2 marks)

2. Outline findings of research into the effects of day care on social development.

    (6 marks)

3. Outline conclusions of research into the effects of day care on social development. *(6 marks)*

4. Give **two** effects of day care on social development.

    (3 marks + 3 marks)

5. Give **two** criticisms of research on the effects of day care on cognitive **and/or** social development.

    (3 marks + 3 marks)

The question asks about positive effects but that does not mean that evidence about negative effects would be uncreditworthy – such evidence is highly relevant to a consideration of whether day care has positive effects or not. You might also consider evidence that day care appears to have no effects. You should take care to limit any discussion to research on social development, though you could mention research on cognitive development if this is used as part of an evaluation (e.g. 'day care may harm social development but this is less true of its effects on cognitive development'). Don't forget to evaluate any studies that you describe – we can only make generalisations from sound research.
Note: You could try answering this question a second time, this time changing to cognitive development.

You will get credit for descriptions of studies that have found negative effects *but* the maximum mark for the description of studies is 6, therefore you must not spend too long describing studies.

AO1/AO2 question

Consider the extent to which psychological research (theories **and/or** studies) supports the view that day care has a positive effect on social development.

(18 marks)

Possible plan

Research that demonstrates positive effects	Describe the study **(AO1)** **(AO2)**	Refer to any flaws **(AO2)**	Discuss the conclusions	Contrast with other research that reached alternative conclusions (do not describe this research but *use* it as part of your argument) **(AO2)**
Study 1				
Study 2				
Study 3				

1 Social development is that aspect of a child's growth that is concerned with the development of sociability and with the process of socialisation.

2 Belsky and Rovine (1988) found that infants who had been receiving 20 hours or more of day care per week before they were one year old were more likely to be insecurely attached compared with children at home. Clarke-Stewart et al. (1994) found no difference in attachment security when comparing children spending a lot of time in day care (30 hours or more a week from age three months) with children who spent less time (less than 10 hours a week). Schweinhart et al. (1993) found decreased rates of self-reported delinquency at age 14 for children who had been involved in the High/Scope Perry Preschool Project, decreased official chronic delinquency at age 19, and, at age 27, lower adult criminality.

3 Violata and Russell (1994) carried out a meta-analysis of the findings from 88 studies, concluding that regular day care for more than 20 hours per week had an unmistakably negative effect on socio-emotional development, behaviour and attachment of young children. An NICHD report (2001) concluded that children who are separated from their mothers for more than 10 hours a week early in life are more aggressive once they reach kindergarten, as rated by their mothers and by their teachers. Creps and Vernon-Feagans (1999) concluded that day care may be better for social development because they found that infants who started day care before the age of six months were more sociable later than those who started later.

> Writing effective conclusions without including too much on findings requires practice. This answer has that suitable balance.

4 **Effect 1:** Belsky and Rovine (1988) assessed attachment in infants who had been receiving 20 hours or more of day care per week before they were one year old. These children were found to be more likely to be insecurely attached compared with children at home.
Effect 2: Creps and Vernon-Feagans (1999) found that infants who started day care before the age of six months were more sociable later than those who started later. This suggests that early day care may be better for social development.

5 **Criticism 1:** It may be that some children find day care harder to cope with than others. Children who are insecurely attached at home may also find that separation is hard to cope with. An NICHD study (1997) found that children whose mothers lacked responsiveness (and thus might be insecurely attached) did less well in day care.
Criticism 2: There are so many possible variables that contribute to the effects of day care that it is difficult to state with certainty which are the most important factors. It could be related to home background, attachment to caregiver, quality of day care, hours spent in day care, age when first started and so on.

research methods **A**

a) *Factor 1: Writing good questions (issues include clarity, bias, analysis).*

   Factor 2: Using different kinds of questions (e.g. open/closed, fixed choice, Likert scale, semantic differential).

b) *Closed questions provide only a limited range of possible answers whereas open questions allow respondents to give a more exact answer to suit their circumstances.*

c) *Question 1: How many hours a week did you work when your son/daughter was under one year old?*

   ☐ *0 hours*   ☐ *Between 20 and 30 hours*
   ☐ *Less than 10 hours* ☐ *More than 30 hours*
   ☐ *Between 10 and 20 hours*

   Question 2: If you worked when you had pre-school children, how do you think that this may have affected your children?

d) *Questions can be created in response to answers.*

e) *Participants feel that they are being evaluated by the investigator, and alter their behaviour accordingly.*

f) *Distress could be operationalised as the time spent in proximity-seeking behaviour with the substitute caregiver.*

Describe the study (AO1)	Refer to any flaws (AO2)	Discuss the conclusions (AO2)	Contrast with other research that reached alternative conclusions (AO2)
Vandell et al. (1988) reported that children in higher-quality care have more friendly and fewer unfriendly interactions than those in lower-quality care.	Most research involves American children and therefore cannot be applied universally.	These findings suggest that, at least for American children, high-quality day care may have a positive effect on some social interactions.	In contrast, many studies have found negative effects of day care on social development. For example, Belsky and Rovine (1988) assessed attachment in infants who had been receiving 20 hours or more of day care per week before they were one year old. These children were found to be more likely to be insecurely attached compared with children at home.
Clarke-Stewart et al. (1994) found that those children who attended day care could cope better in social situations and negotiate better with peers.	It may be that children who didn't cope well with day care were withdrawn by their parents, leaving a biased sample.	There are so many uncontrolled variables in any study of day care that it is difficult to draw clear conclusions.	Equally, there is evidence of no effects. For example, Clarke-Stewart et al. (1994) found no difference in attachment security in children who spent a lot of time in day care and those spending less time. Attachment should promote better relationships.
Creps and Vernon-Feagans (1999) found that infants who started day care before the age of six months were more sociable later than those who started later.	Parents who seek day care for very young children may be more ambitious or may be less well-off than parents who don't.	Such parent differences may be used to explain differences in sociability.	

End of section review

Sample exam question

a. Outline Bowlby's maternal deprivation hypothesis. *(6 marks)*

b. Give **two** criticisms of this hypothesis. *(3 marks + 3 marks)*

c. 'Many parents want to know whether they are harming their children by placing them in day care'.

Outline and evaluate research (theories **and/or** studies) into the effects of day care on children's cognitive and/or social development. *(18 marks)*

See page viii for an explanation of how questions are marked.

Student answer	Examiner's comments
(a) Bowlby proposed that children who experienced deprivation for the first few years of their lives will suffer severe and permanent consequences in terms of their emotional development. The consequences include mental subnormality, delinquency, depression, affectionless psychopathy and even dwarfism. He supported this hypothesis with research on adolescent delinquents.	Everything in the answer is relevant except the last sentence, which is more like an evaluative statement. Accurate and detailed but limited, thus **4 marks.**
(b) One criticism is that there is not much evidence to support the age of two and a half. Many children who experience deprivation before this age turn out OK. A second criticism is that the effects may be due to privation rather than deprivation. Bowlby's idea that deprivation led to harm may not have been accurate enough.	More detail could have been given for the first criticism by mentioning an appropriate study. As it stands, it is less detailed than required for 3 marks. The second criticism contains detail but it is not entirely clear why this is a criticism. Both criticisms are not worth the full 3 marks, **2+2 marks**.
(c) Andersson carried out a study involving children in his native Sweden. He had a control group of about 30 children who attended day care, another group stayed at home with their mothers and a third group were looked after by childminders. He started the study when they were three to five years of age. They were tested using an IQ test. At age 13 the day care children were the most intelligent, with the children who were with childminders being the least intelligent. Some research has shown that children from lower-class families benefit from good-quality day care but poor-quality day care benefits no one. One study found that children benefited if the day care provider gave physical, intellectual and emotional stability. Day care does not appear to have any harmful effect on children's cognitive or social development as all the research shows only positive effects. Of course a shy, backward child is going to find day care a daunting experience but that's down to personality. [169 words]	The first paragraph contains a detailed description of one study. The second paragraph mentions a further two studies at a rather basic level. Thus we have some breadth and some depth for an overall **6 marks for AO1.** The only commentary is offered in the last paragraph. The first sentence is not clearly linked to the evidence but could have been. The last sentence is a valuable piece of commentary, which lifts this to better than 'mainly irrelevant', so **3 marks for AO2, a total of 9 marks**.
	Total for whole question is **17 marks**, equivalent to a Grade B.

Physiological psychology seeks to explain behaviour in terms of the systems that operate in our bodies, such as the action of blood, hormones, nerves and the brain. The way you think and feel has important influences on these physiological systems, as is illustrated by the study of stress.

This module is divided into

Stress as a bodily response

The body's response to stressors

Stress and physical illness: Cardiovascular disorders and the immune system

End of section review

Sources of stress

Life changes

Workplace stressors

Individual differences: Personality and gender

End of section review

Critical issue: Stress management

Physiological methods of stress management

Psychological methods of stress management

End of section review

COGNITIVE PSYCHOLOGY: HUMAN MEMORY

DEVELOPMENTAL PSYCHOLOGY: ATTACHMENTS IN DEVELOPMENT

PHYSIOLOGICAL PSYCHOLOGY: STRESS

INDIVIDUAL DIFFERENCES: ABNORMALITY

SOCIAL PSYCHOLOGY: SOCIAL INFLUENCE

RESEARCH METHODS

The body's response to stressors

Specification extract

The body's response to stressors (e.g. pituitary–adrenal system) including the General Adaptation Syndrome (Selye).

research methods

Q

A study set out to investigate whether people who were stressed were more likely to become ill. The intention was to collect information using a questionnaire.

a) Write a suitable non-directional hypothesis for this study.

b) Describe **one** advantage of using a written questionnaire rather than a face-to-face interview.

c) Describe **one** disadvantage.

d) Suggest **two** ways that you could operationalise the concept of being ill.

e) What are the covariables in this study?

Keep your answers brief (for 2 marks) and make three separate points (two definitions and one difference).

Some candidates are very good on physiological detail. You don't have to use technical language such as 'sympathetic branch' and 'cortisol' but it does provide your answer with the detail necessary for full marks. On the other hand, take care not to write too much as each part of your answer is only worth 3 marks.

A good answer goes beyond just giving a list of the stages and provides physiological detail for each of the stages. Don't include any evaluation.

If you say one limitation is that the research was all done on animals, this is wrong as Selye did some research on humans. It is usually wise to avoid definite statements. For example, you would be right in saying that Selye *based* his account *mainly* on research with animals. Remember the **three-point rule**: state it, explain it, explain how it is an issue in this model.

This is just a different way of asking question 2, though you could discuss the effects on the cardiovascular system and/or the immune system.

Do you think that physiological explanations can explain the way we respond to stress? How can you decide? By considering what research (theory and/or studies) has told us and whether this research is valid. Later on in your studies you will find out about psychological methods of stress management which may extend what you can write about the psychology of stress (as distinct from the physiology of stress). If you do introduce material on the psychology of stress, ensure that you use this material *effectively*, rather than just describing it, in order to attract AO2 marks.

AO1 questions

1. Explain what is meant by stress and a stressor and identify **one** difference between them. *(2 marks + 2 marks + 2 marks)*

2. Outline **two** ways the body responds to stressors. *(3 marks + 3 marks)*

3. Outline the main features of Selye's general adaptation syndrome. *(6 marks)*

4. Give **two** criticisms of Selye's general adaptation syndrome. *(3 marks + 3 marks)*

5. Describe **two** effects of stress on the body. *(3 marks + 3 marks)*

AO1/AO2 question

'Physiological psychologists claim that the stress response can be explained entirely in terms of bodily responses.' Describe and evaluate research (theories **and/or** studies) into stress as a bodily response. *(18 marks)*

Possible plan

	Description **(AO1)**	What conclusions can you draw from this research? **(AO2)**	Are there any strengths/weaknesses in the research? **(AO2)**
Explanation (e.g. GAS model)			
Study 1			
Study 2			

1 Stress is the subjective experience of a lack of fit between a person and their environment (i.e. where the perceived demands of a situation are greater than a person's perceived ability to cope).

The term 'stressor' refers to any event that causes a stress reaction in the body, for example environmental stressors such as the workplace.

Stress is used to refer to the way the body reacts to a stressful situation whereas a stressor is whatever event led to this physiological reaction.

> *These are similar terms, so you should be clear in your own mind what is different about their use, and be able to communicate this effectively.*
> *Do not repeat your explanations when you identify a difference.*

2 **Way 1:** The hypothalamus controls the pituitary gland, which in turn controls the adrenal cortex (part of the adrenal gland). The pituitary releases ACTH into the bloodstream. This travels to the adrenal cortex and stimulates the release of corticosteroids, which produces a stress response.

Way 2: The ANS controls the adrenal medulla. Stimulation by the sympathetic division of the ANS causes the adrenal medulla to release adrenaline and noradrenaline into the bloodstream. These increase heart rate and blood pressure and the 'fight or flight' response.

3 There are three stages in GAS:

The *alarm* stage, where the threat or stressor is recognised and a response made to the alarm. The ANS is activated, which increases heart rate and blood pressure, and hormones are released that maintain and increase sympathetic activity.

> *Students often forget the names of these stages, and what each involves. Try to create a mnemonic to help you remember them (ARE).*

The *resistance* stage, where the body adapts to the demands of the stressor, but at the same time resources are gradually being depleted.

The *exhaustion* stage, where the body's systems can no longer maintain normal functioning. At this stage, stress-related conditions such as ulcers may develop.

4 **Criticism 1:** The GAS model is derived from research with non-human animals and so emphasises *physiological* factors. Humans are capable of thinking about their situation, which is less true of non-human animals. This ability to think

> *Criticisms come in all shapes and sizes, but it is important that you make any comments critical, in that you show you have something to say about this material.*

research methods A

a) Respondents' likelihood of becoming ill is related to their current levels of stress as measured by a stress questionnaire.

b) A questionnaire guarantees the respondent a certain degree of anonymity that might not be possible in a face-to-face interview.

c) A disadvantage is the relatively high attrition rate among questionnaire respondents, who feel less pressured to complete than those who take part in a face-to-face interview.

d) Respondents may be asked to indicate the number of days they had taken off work/college due to ill health in the last 12 months.

   Or their blood pressure and cholesterol levels might be measured to assess their cardiovascular system.

e) The covariables would be the measure of ill heath (e.g. number of days off work), and current levels of stress as measured by the stress questionnaire.

may mean that humans have the potential to control the extent to which an experience is stressful.

Criticism 2: The GAS model proposes that resources become depleted, so the body can no longer fight infections. However, more recent research has shown that many 'resources' do not become depleted even under extreme stress. The current view is that the exhaustion phase is associated with increased hormone activity and it is this rather than depletion of resources that leads to stress-related illness.

5 See answer to question 2.

> *An alternative way of answering this question would make use of material on the next spread.*

Description (AO1)	Conclusions (AO2)	Strengths/weaknesses (AO2)
Description of Selye's GAS model (see question 3)	The GAS model proposes that resources become depleted so that the body can no longer fight infections. However, more recent research has shown that many 'resources' do not become depleted even under extreme stress. The current view is that the exhaustion phase is associated with increased hormone activity, such as cortisol and it is this rather than depletion of resources that leads to stress-related illness (Sheridan and Radmacher, 1992).	The GAS model has had an important influence on our understanding of the relationship between stress and illness. It led to a vast amount of research. This research supports the view that stress does affect the body's systems and may lead to illness.
Selye's model is derived from research he did on rats and other animals. He exposed them to unpleasant stimuli (injections and other 'nocuous agents' such as extreme cold or severing limbs). All stressors produced a similar response, including the development of stomach ulcers.	This research was done with non-human animals and so emphasises *physiological* factors. Humans are capable of thinking about their situation, which is less true of non-human animals. This ability to think may mean that humans have the potential to control the extent to which an experience is stressful.	On the other hand, individuals who have no adrenal glands need to be given additional amounts of certain hormones in order to respond to stressors, otherwise they may die. This shows that part of the human stress response *can* be explained in terms of physiological systems.
Study 2 could be added if your essay is too short but there is enough here without further research.		

Effects of stress on cardiovascular disorders and the immune system

Specification extract

Research into the relationship between stress and cardiovascular disorders and the effects of stress on the immune system.

One approach to this question would be to list all the cardiovascular disorders you know but this would not amount to a full explanation. It would receive credit but not 3 marks.

Sometimes candidates find it difficult to think of enough to write about the aims of the study. It may help you to ask yourself 'what was it that the researcher wanted to test (the hypothesis)?'

Some candidates use the research by Holmes and Rahe but, in order for this to be creditworthy, the relationship with cardiovascular disorders has to be made explicit.

One way to criticise a study is to consider the methodology – you can be positive or negative about the methods used. 'Methods' includes the research method itself but also things such as sampling, experimental control or demand characteristics.

Some candidates include findings from Brady's study of ulcers in executive monkeys but this is not creditworthy.

Don't get sidetracked and start providing other details such as findings or criticisms. Some candidates forget themselves and start writing an AO2-type answer since this is what they have practised.

Keep your answer to 3 marks – you need to select the most important information to communicate.

Remember that criticisms do not have to be negative but can, for example, point out important applications.

This is an obvious question to ask after you have studied the topics in this section. Are you convinced by the evidence that stress is linked to cardiovascular disorders? Do you think there is evidence to confirm that stress actually *causes* cardiovascular disorders, or is it just a correlation? Is there evidence against the view that stress is linked with cardiovascular disorders? Since the question is on cardiovascular disorders it would not be creditworthy to include research on the effects of stress on the immune system unless this can be used as effective commentary (for example, 'stress also affects the immune system – it reduces its effectiveness – which may be part of the explanation of its effect on cardiovascular disorders').

Possible plan

	AO1 Description	AO2 Evaluation of the research	AO2 Possible commentary on what conclusions can be drawn
Study 1			Demonstrates a link
Study 2			Demonstrates that stress causes physical illness

AO1 questions

1. Explain what is meant by cardiovascular disorders.
    (3 marks)

2. Describe the aims and conclusions of **one** study that has investigated the relationship between stress and cardiovascular disorders. *(6 marks)*

3. Describe the procedures and findings of **one** study that has investigated the relationship between stress and cardiovascular disorders. *(6 marks)*

4. Give **two** criticisms of the study that you described in question 3.
    (3 marks + 3 marks)

5. Outline findings of research into the relationship between stress and cardiovascular disorders.
    (6 marks)

6. Outline conclusions of research into the relationship between stress and cardiovascular disorders. *(6 marks)*

7. Explain what is meant by the immune system. *(3 marks)*

8. Describe the aims and procedures of **one** study that has investigated the relationship between stress and the immune system.
    (6 marks)

9. Describe the findings of **one** study that has investigated the relationship between stress and the immune system, and give **one** criticism of this study.
    (3 marks + 3 marks)

10. Outline findings of research into the relationship between stress and the immune system.
    (6 marks)

11. Outline conclusions of research into the relationship between stress and the immune system.
    (6 marks)

AO1/AO2 question

Consider whether research (theories **and/or** studies) supports the view that stress is linked to cardiovascular disorders.

(18 marks)

1 Cardiovascular disorder refers to any disorder of the heart and circulatory system. These include hypertension (high blood pressure), coronary heart disease (CHD) caused by atherosclerosis and stroke.

You don't need the technical terms to score full marks here. Note that this is more than just a list of the disorders.

2 A study of the relationship between stress and cardiovascular disorders (Krantz et al., 1991).
Aims: This study aimed to investigate the extent to which mental stress could be shown to increase myocardial ischemia. An additional aim was to see if patients with coronary artery disease reacted differently to individuals with no cardiovascular problems.
Conclusions: These findings support the idea that there is a direct link between performing a mildly stressful cognitive task and physiological activity that could damage the cardiovascular system. However, not all cardiovascular patients responded in the same way, which leads us to conclude that there are important individual differences in responsiveness.

The findings have been used to provide conclusions, which is creditworthy.

3 A study of the relationship between stress and cardiovascular disorders (Krantz et al., 1991).
Procedures: Thirty-nine patients and 12 controls were studied while they performed three mental tasks: an arithmetic task, a Stroop task, and a task where they simulated public speaking. Each of these tasks was designed to create mild stress. Measurements were taken of the participants' blood pressure and of the extent to which blood vessels around the heart contracted (high, medium or low ischemia).
Findings: Patients who displayed greatest myocardial ischemia during the mental tasks also had the highest increases in blood pressure.
The control participants showed the lowest levels of both myocardial ischemia and blood pressure when performing the mental tasks.
There was an intermediate group of patients who had either mild myocardial ischemia or none at all when performing the mental tasks. They also had only moderate increase in blood pressure.

4 **Criticism 1:** A positive feature of this study is that it demonstrated a *direct* link between stress and behaviours associated with cardiovascular disorders. Other studies fail to discriminate between direct and indirect effects. For example, a link between work-related stress and cardiovascular problems may be due to the direct effects of stress on blood pressure or to indirect effects of stress on smoking.
Criticism 2: No controls were used to compare a patient's behaviour when stressed and not stressed. It is possible that the cardiovascular patients might show signs of muscle ischemia and raised blood pressure when relaxed as well as when mildly stressed. This would mean that stress was not the cause of the ischemia or raised blood pressure.

Although it isn't necessary to include examples, they offer a useful route to elaboration.

5 Krantz et al. (1991) found that patients who displayed greatest myocardial ischemia during stressful mental tasks also had the highest increases in blood pressure. The control participants showed the lowest levels of both myocardial ischemia and blood pressure when performing the mental tasks. There was an intermediate group of patients who had either mild myocardial ischemia or none at all when performing the mental tasks. They also had only moderate increase in blood pressure. Russek (1962) looked at heart disease in medical professionals and found that it was highest in those in high-stress occupations (GPs and anaesthetists) and lowest in low-stress occupations (pathologists and dermatologists). Of the GPs sampled, 11.9% had heart disease whereas 3.2% of the dermatologists surveyed had heart disease.

6 Krantz et al.'s findings support the idea that there is a direct link between performing a mildly stressful cognitive task and physiological activity that could damage the cardiovascular

patients responded in the same way, which leads us to conclude that there are important individual differences in responsiveness. Recent research suggests that the sympathetic branch of the ANS in some individuals is more reactive than in others (Rozanski et al., 1999). This would mean that some people respond to stress with greater increases in blood pressure and heart rate than others, and this would lead to more damage to the cardiovascular system in these hyperresponsive individuals.

7 The immune system is a system of cells (such as lymphocyctes) within the body that is concerned with fighting against intruders such as viruses and bacteria. It creates a barrier that prevents antigens from entering the body, and detects and eliminates those that have entered the body.

8 A study of the relationship between stress and the immune system (Kiecolt-Glaser et al., 1995).
Aims: This study sought to demonstrate the direct effects of stress on the immune system by looking at how fast wounds healed in a group of participants where high levels of chronic stress occur naturally.
Procedures: Participants were recruited by using advertisements in newspapers. Thirteen women aged 47–81 years were Alzheimer's carers and a further thirteen women were matched with the carers on the basis of age and income. All were given a wound ('punch biopsy'). The wounds were dressed and treated by a nurse in the same way for each participant, and the researchers assessed levels of cytokines in the participants. Participants were also given a ten-item perceived stress scale to check how stressed they actually felt.

The aims are not given in detail but this is balanced by very detailed procedures.

9 A study of the relationship between stress and the immune system (Kiecolt-Glaser et al., 1995).
Findings: First, complete wound healing took significantly longer in the carers than the controls. It took an average of 9 days (24%) longer in the carers. Second, it was also found that cytokine levels were lower in the carers than the control group. Third, on the perceived stress scale, the carers did actually indicate that they were feeling more stressed.
Criticism: These findings have important implications for treating people with infections, particularly in situations where people are recovering from surgery. Clearly it would be important to reduce stress as far as possible in such patients and thus speed their recovery.

10 In Kiecolt-Glaser et al.'s study of Alzheimer's carers, complete wound healing took significantly longer in the carers than the controls. It took an average of 9 days (24%) longer in the carers. Second, it was also found that cytokine levels were higher in the carers than the control group. Third, on the perceived stress scale, the carers did actually indicate that they were feeling more stressed. Riley (1981) experimented with mice, inducing stress by placing the mice on a rotating turntable. Within 5 hours this led to a lowered lymphocyte count. Some mice were implanted with cancer cells. After 3 days of 10 minutes of rotation per hour, mice were more likely to develop tumours than control mice given no stress.

11 The findings in Kiecolt-Glaser et al.'s study of Alzheimer's carers support the view that chronic stress depresses the functioning of the immune system, because wound healing was slower in individuals who experienced chronic stress. The lower levels of cytokines in chronically stressed individuals supports the view that stress lowers immune response directly. In Riley's study of mice (Riley, 1981), the findings show that stress reduced immune activity (lymphocyte count) and was related to illness (more tumours). Evans et al.'s finding that levels of the antibody sIgA increased during acute stress situations but decreased during situations of chronic stress suggests that stress appears to have two effects on the immune system: upregulation for very short-term acute stress and downregulation for chronic stress.

AO1 Description	AO2 Evaluation	AO2 Conclusions
Outline of Krantz et al. (1991) – see answer to question 5	A positive feature of this study is that it demonstrated a *direct* link between stress and behaviours associated with cardiovascular disorders. Other studies fail to discriminate between direct and indirect effects. For example, a link between work-related stress and cardiovascular problems may be due to the direct effects of stress on blood pressure or to indirect effects of stress on smoking.	These findings support the idea that there is a direct link between performing a mildly stressful cognitive task and physiological activity that could damage the cardiovascular system. However, not all cardiovascular patients responded in the same way, which leads us to conclude that there are important individual differences in responsiveness.
Rosenman and Friedman (1959) found that men classed as Type A personality were more likely to die of cardiovascular problems and had higher blood pressure than Type B individuals. Type As are people who are very stressed (ambitious with a competitive drive and a chronic sense of time urgency).	Type As were also more likely to smoke and have a family history of CHD, both of which would increase their risk and might explain the higher incidence of CHD rather than stress alone. This means that we cannot really conclude from this study that stress causes CHD.	The findings support the view that stress may be associated with CHD and indicate how individual differences may modify the effects of stress. Whereas Type A personality is linked to negative effects there are other personality characteristics (e.g. the hardy personality) which reduce the effects of stress.

End of section review

Sample exam question

a. (i) Outline the stages of Selye's general adaptation syndrome. *(3 marks)*

(ii) Give **one** criticism of this model. *(3 marks)*

b. Describe the procedures and findings of **one** study into the relationship between stress and cardiovascular disorders. *(6 marks)*

c. Outline and evaluate psychological research (theories and/or studies) on the relationship between stress and the immune system. *(18 marks)*

See page viii for an explanation of how questions are marked.

Student answer	Examiner's comments
(a) (i) The three stages of Selye's model are: alarm reaction, resistance and exhaustion. In the first stage, the body responds to a stressor with ANS activity. In the second stage, the body adapts to stress by returning to a normal level of functioning. In the third stage, if the stressor persists, the body's resources become exhausted and the individual is susceptible to becoming ill. (ii) One criticism of this model is that it is just about the body. It relates to nothing else but the way the body reacts.	(i) The stages have been given in the correct order and some detail provided for each stage, which is sufficient for **3/3 marks**. (ii) This is a valid criticism but little explanation has been provided, just a repetition of the same point. Basic **1/3 marks**.
(b) One study of stress and cardiovascular disorders was by Russek. They sent questionnaires to various different medical professionals who were high stress (such as GPs) and who were examples of having little stress in their professional lives (e.g. dermatologists). They found that people in the high-stress occupations were more likely to have developed a cardiovascular disorder compared to the low-stress occupations.	This is a competent description of Russek's research. Although this could be taken as a study of work stress, this candidate does make the link with cardiovascular disorders, so it is perfectly acceptable here. The details for both procedures and findings are brief, so **3/6 marks** (limited and less detailed than for the top band).
(c) One study that investigated the relationship between stress and the immune system was done by Keicolt-Glaser. Participants had a hole made in their arm and this was observed while it was healing. One group of participants were more stressed than the others because they were caring for sick relatives. This group of participants had slower healing than the others. This shows that more stress produces a weaker immune system because the participants' blood was tested and lower quantities of cytokines were found. This suggests a direct link. It may be asked whether the participants really were stressed but they were also given a questionnaire to assess how stressed they felt. Keicolt-Glaser also investigated university students and tested levels of killer T-cells. These were higher before they took the exams and lower afterwards. They were lowest in the students who said they had less social support. This suggests that social support is an important factor in reducing the effects of stress. The importance of this research is that it shows why people who are more stressed are more likely to become ill. It is because their immune systems are not functioning as well. For example, Cohen did research on colds and found that people who said in a questionnaire that they were more stressed were more likely to get a cold. All of this research is supported by studies of non-human animals. For example, Riley studied mice and found that those on a rotating turntable had a lower count of white cells, presumably due to stress. We should be careful about generalising from studies with non-human animals. [264 words]	The AO1 component of this question requires a description of studies on the immune system. Four studies have been included. Brady's study is not related to immune system activity and so receives no credit. Those by Kiecolt-Glaser are given in reasonable detail and, overall, the breadth of the descriptive material results in **6/6 marks for AO1**. If anything, there is less commentary than description in this answer. The second half of the first paragraph is commentary and quite effective. The same is true of the last sentence of the second paragraph. There is one further piece of commentary about generalising from non-human animals. Taken overall, the commentary is basic but probably closer to the band above than being 'superficial' and 'rudimentary', thus **6/12 marks for AO2**, a **total of 12/18 marks**.
	Total for whole question is **19 marks**, equivalent to a weak Grade A, possibly a Grade B.

This module is divided into

Stress as a bodily response

The body's response to stressors

Stress and physical illness: Cardiovascular disorders and the immune system

End of section review

Sources of stress

Life changes

Workplace stressors

Individual differences: Personality and gender

End of section review

Critical issue: Stress management

Physiological methods of stress management

Psychological methods of stress management

End of section review

COGNITIVE PSYCHOLOGY:
HUMAN MEMORY

DEVELOPMENTAL PSYCHOLOGY:
ATTACHMENTS IN DEVELOPMENT

PHYSIOLOGICAL PSYCHOLOGY:
STRESS

INDIVIDUAL DIFFERENCES:
ABNORMALITY

SOCIAL PSYCHOLOGY:
SOCIAL INFLUENCE

RESEARCH
METHODS

Life changes

Specification extract
Research into sources of stress, including life changes (e.g. Holmes and Rahe).

research methods Q

a) What is a correlation coefficient?

b) What does a correlation coefficient of 0.4 tell us with a sample of 20 participants?

c) What does a correlation coefficient of 0.4 tell us with a sample of 200 participants?

A psychology class decides to write their own life events scale and in order to do this they want to ask people questions about what kinds of things stress them.

d) Describe **two** considerations they should bear in mind when designing their questionnaire.

e) How might they prevent respondents guessing the true purpose of the questionnaire?

f) Why might it be a good idea to conduct a pilot study in this study?

Make sure you know the difference between life changes and life events, and don't explain the latter instead of the former. Don't list life events.

Daily hassles are not life changes. The latter are the outcome of major, life events whereas hassles are minor events which may, of course, be more stressful. You can use research on hassles as a form of evaluation but not as a substitute for life changes.

Make sure you stick to procedures and findings only, and don't include information about aims, conclusions or criticisms as these will receive no credit. It is always tempting to write everything you know about a topic area but it is vital to be selective in what you write.

Criticisms must be contextualised in order to obtain high marks.

Some candidates write an answer to this question that is very similar to their answer to question 3. It is fairly obvious, in such cases, that such a candidate has failed to understand what it means to 'focus on the requirements of the question'.

You keep answering questions about conclusions, but do you know what a conclusion is? It is an interpretation of the findings; making generalisations about all people.

It may help you to answer this question if you consider what things create stress. You can provide a rather broad answer such as positive changes as one way and negative changes as another, or you can focus on two specific life changes and explain how they create stress.

Most students will feel quite comfortable considering and evaluating Holmes and Rahe's life events scale and related research. A good answer will go beyond this and consider other research as well. You may use the hassles scale as a means of evaluation, i.e. to claim that life changes are not a realistic measure of stress.

AO1 questions

1. Explain what is meant by life changes. *(3 marks)*

2. Describe the aims and conclusions of **one** study that has investigated life changes. *(6 marks)*

3. Describe the procedures and findings of **one** study that has investigated life changes. *(6 marks)*

4. Give **two** criticisms of the study that you described in question 3.
   (3 marks + 3 marks)

5. Outline findings of research into life changes. *(6 marks)*

6. Outline conclusions of research into life changes.
   (6 marks)

7. Describe **two** ways in which life changes are a source of stress.
   (3 marks + 3 marks)

AO1/AO2 question

To what extent does research into life changes indicate that these are a source of stress?
(18 marks)

Possible plan

	Description **(A01)**	Criticisms **(A02)**	Conclusions (does this indicate that life changes are a source of stress?) **(A02)**
Life events scale (SRRS)			
Study/studies using SRRS			

1 Life changes are those events in a person's life (such as divorce or bereavement) that necessitate a significant adjustment in various aspects of their life. As such, they can be seen as significant sources of stress.

> *Examples offer useful elaboration and in this case they help to make sure of full marks.*

2 A study of life changes as a source of stress (Rahe et al., 1970).
Aims: Rahe et al. used the SRRS to test Holmes and Rahe's hypothesis that the number of life events a person experienced would be positively correlated with illness. Rahe et al. aimed in particular to study a 'normal' population as distinct from the populations previously studied of individuals who were already ill in hospital.
Conclusions: The findings support the hypothesis of a link or positive correlation between life changes/events and physical illness. It is possible that the link is stress: life changes cause stress and we know that stress causes illness. Therefore life changes are sources of stress. Both positive and negative events are included in the SRRS, so we see that it is change rather than negativity that is important. It is the overall amount of 'psychic energy' required to deal with an event that creates stress.

> *Aims and conclusions can be quite short, so make sure you have enough material if this is the combination asked for.*

3 A study of life changes as a source of stress (Rahe et al., 1970).
Procedures: A military version of the SRRS was given to all the men aboard three US navy cruisers, a total of over 2,700 men. The men filled in the questionnaire just before a tour of duty, noting all the life events experienced over the previous 6 months. An illness score was calculated on the basis of the number, type and severity of all illnesses recorded during the tour of duty (about 7 months).
Findings: An LCU score and an illness score was calculated for each man. Rahe et al. found a positive correlation between these scores of +0.118. This is not a very strong correlation between stressful life events and incidence of physical illness. However, given the number of participants involved, it is significant.

> *The opposite problem may be evident with this combination, so make sure you can be sufficiently concise.*

4 **Criticism 1:** The LCUs were calculated by asking the men to recall life changes over the previous months. It is possible that they didn't remember these events accurately. For example, a man might repress the memory of an event that was a negative experience or might not recall exactly when it took place.
Criticism 2: Many psychologists have suggested that the SRRS is not a valid measure of stress. The main complaints that have been made are that the scale focuses on acute life events rather than ongoing (chronic) stressors, it does not distinguish between desirable and undesirable events, and does not take social resources into account which may moderate the effects of stress.

> *Remember the three-point rule. Try to say three things in each criticism (e.g. identify, elaborate, conclude).*

5 In the Rahe et al. study, an LCU score and an illness score was calculated for each man. Rahe et al. found a positive correlation between these scores of +0.118. Jacobs and Charles (1980) investigated a possible link between life events and cancer in children. They found that children who developed cancer had families with a higher life change rating than a control group of children being treated for non-cancerous illnesses. Stone et al. (1987) analysed the 10 day period prior to an episode of illness and compared this to another 10 day period where there was no illness for that participant. They found that wherever there was an episode of illness there had been a significant increase in both undesirable and desirable events in the previous 4 days.

6 In the Rahe et al. study, the findings support the hypothesis of a link or positive correlation between life changes/events and physical illness. It is possible that the link is stress: life changes cause stress and we know that

a) A correlation coefficient is a mathematical representation (between +1 and −1) of the relationship between measurements of two variables.

b) This is a moderate relationship between the covariables, but with just 20 participants it is unlikely to be significant.

c) This is still a moderate relationship between the co-variables, but with 200 participants it is likely to indicate a significant relationship between the variables.

d) Questions need to be written so that the reader (respondent) understands what is being asked. There should be no ambiguity. Questions need to be written so that the answers provided are easy to analyse.

e) Some irrelevant questions may be included to mislead the respondent from the main purpose of the survey. This acts as a single blind.

f) A pilot study could be carried out to see if a small sample of people were confused by any of the questions about life events. This means that the questions could be refined in response to any difficulties encountered.

stress causes illness. Therefore life changes are sources of stress. Both positive and negative events are included in the SRRS so we see that it is change rather than negativity that is important. It is the overall amount of 'psychic energy' required to deal with an event that creates stress. DeLongis et al. (1988) found no relationship between life events and health, or between uplifts and health, but did find a significant positive correlation between hassles and next-day health problems, suggesting that daily hassles rather than major life changes cause stress-related health problems.

> *Remember that material on hassles and uplifts does not count as life changes research, but can be used to make a critical point or to offer a conclusion concerning the adequacy of such research.*

7 **Way 1:** Post-traumatic stress disorder (PTSD) can occur after exposure to a traumatic event in which grave physical harm occurred or was threatened. People with PTSD may re-experience their ordeal in the form of flashbacks, nightmares or frightening thoughts. People with PTSD may also experience emotional numbness and sleep disturbances, depression, anxiety and outbursts of anger.
Way 2: The death of a spouse is regarded as the most stressful life event. The stressful impact of bereavement is more pronounced if the death is sudden or violent, or if the relationship was one in which one or both partners were very dependent.

Description (AO1)	Criticisms (AO2)	Conclusions (AO2)
Life events scale (SRRS) Brief outline of Rahe et al. study – see answers to questions 2 and 3	The LCUs were calculated by asking the men to recall life changes over the previous months. It is possible that they didn't remember these events accurately. For example, a man might repress the memory of an event that was a negative experience or might not recall exactly when it took place.	The findings support the hypothesis of a link or positive correlation between life changes/events and physical illness. It is possible that the link is stress: life changes cause stress and we know that stress causes illness. Therefore life changes are sources of stress.
Study/studies using SRRS Brief outline of Jacobs and Charles (1980) and Stone et al. (1987) study – see answer to question 5	The SRRS may not be a valid measure of stress. The scale focuses on acute life events rather than ongoing stressors. It does not distinguish between desirable and undesirable events, and does not take into account social resources which may moderate the effects of stress.	DeLongis et al. (1988) found no relationship between life events and health, or between uplifts and health, but did find a significant positive correlation between hassles and next-day health problems, suggesting that daily hassles rather than major life changes cause stress-related health problems.

Workplace stressors

Specification extract
Research into sources of stress, including workplace stressors (e.g. Johansson and Marmot).

research methods

Q

A psychologist is asked to conduct a questionnaire survey of workplace stress. He will interview people from a number of different workplaces and find out what factors make them feel stressed.

a) *Describe the aim of this study.*

b) *Suggest **two** ways that the psychologist might operationalise the concept of stress.*

c) *Write **one** question for this questionnaire and explain **one** feature of the question which makes it a 'good' question.*

AO1 questions are always worth a total of 3 marks, which means that you would never be asked for one definition alone. It is most likely that you would be asked to explain a second key term (these are listed on page ix) or you may be asked, for example, to describe the findings of a related research study for the additional 3 marks.

Johansson's sawmill study is frequently chosen by candidates as a study of workplace stressors. Better answers provide detail by making reference to the measurement of adrenaline and noradrenaline, as well as identifying key differences between the control and experimental groups, and reporting the findings in terms of stress-related illness.
Weak candidates get sidetracked on to general issues of workplace stress, whereas others don't refer to any particular study. Studies of non-human animals (such as Brady) receive credit only if they are related to the study of workplace stressors.

Make sure you focus on findings only for the first part of the question. Candidates find it hard to mention findings without mentioning procedures.

The same advice applies again here as for question 3.

Remember that you can focus on the conclusions from one study only if you know enough to provide 6 marks' worth of detail. You should know about more than one study of workplace stress in enough detail to be able to describe the conclusions (what did the findings show us about stress?).

Candidates can name ways that workplace stressors are a source of stress but have difficulty providing details about why they were stressful.

This is an opportunity to use the findings and conclusions of research studies (or theories) to argue whether workplace stressors do create problems or whether they don't. What do you think? Is workplace stress important? Describe (AO1) studies of workplace stress and use them (AO2) to consider whether workplace stress is or isn't a source of stress. AO2 marks can also be gained for any other commentary on the research studies, such as methodological issues or applications of this research (a positive criticism).

AO1 questions

1. Explain what is meant by workplace stressors.
(3 marks)

2. Describe the aims and procedures of **one** study that has investigated workplace stressors.
(6 marks)

3. Describe the findings of **one** study that has investigated workplace stressors and give **one** criticism of this study.
(3 marks + 3 marks)

4. Outline findings of research into workplace stressors.
(6 marks)

5. Outline conclusions of research into workplace stressors.
(6 marks)

6. Describe **two** ways in which the workplace may be a source of stress.
(3 marks + 3 marks)

AO1/AO2 question

'Not everyone is stressed by the work that they do.' Consider whether psychological research (theories **and/or** studies) supports the view that the workplace is a major source of stress.
(18 marks)

Possible plan

	Description (AO1)	What does this tell us about workplace stressors as a source of stress? (AO2)	Other commentary on the research (AO2)
Study 1			
Study 2			
Study 3			

1 Workplace stressors are some aspect of our working environment (such as work overload) that we experience as stressful, and which causes a stress reaction in our body.

Adding the second sentence gives the necessary elaboration to ensure full marks.

These might be divided into *physical stressors* (such as noise) and *psychosocial stressors* (such as role responsibility).

2 A study of the workplace as a source of stress (Marmot *et al.*, 1997).
Aims: Marmot *et al.* sought to test the *job strain model*. This model proposes that the workplace creates stress and illness in two ways: (1) high demand and (2) low control. Marmot *et al.* suggested that this could be tested in the context of civil service

There are a number of aspects of this study that could constitute aims and likewise a number of points that would constitute conclusions.

employees where the higher grades would experience high job demand, and low-grade civil servants would experience low job control.
Conclusions: The main conclusion is that low control appears to be linked to higher stress and also linked to cardiovascular disorder, whereas high job demand is not linked to stress and illness. This does not fully support the job strain model because it does not show that high demand is linked to illness, but lack of control does appear to be linked to stress and illness.

3 A study of the workplace as a source of stress (Marmot *et al.*, 1997).
Findings: It was found that participants in the higher grades had developed the fewest cardiovascular problems. Participants in the lower grades expressed a weaker sense of job control and also had poorest social support. It was also found that

The fact that those who developed cardiovascular disease were more likely to be smokers and be overweight is also a finding. Sometimes you do not have time to include all the findings you know.

cardiovascular disease could in part be explained in terms of risk factors such as smoking (i.e. people who developed cardiovascular disease were more likely to be smokers and to be overweight).
Criticism: The sample (civil servants) was biased. The responses of such individuals may not be typical of all adults as they are urban dwellers who are probably quite job-oriented and ambitious, in contrast with rural inhabitants whose jobs may play a less significant role in their lives. This means you can't generalise the conclusions to all people.

4 In the Marmot *et al.* study, it was found that participants in the higher grades of the civil service had developed the fewest cardiovascular problems. Participants in the lower grades expressed a weaker sense of job control and also had poorest social support. It was also found that

Although merely using the word 'found' over and over again does not necessarily make everything you write a 'finding', it does help to discipline you in what you include in your response.

cardiovascular disease could in part be explained in terms of risk factors such as smoking (i.e. people who developed cardiovascular disease were more likely to be smokers and be overweight). Schaubroeck *et al.* (2001) found that some workers respond differently to lack of control – they are *less* stressed by having no control or responsibility. They found that some people had higher immune responses in low-control situations.

research methods **A**

a) The aim of this study is to discover which particular features of the working environment are perceived as being most stressful.

b) Way 1: The psychologist can ask respondents to rate their levels of stress on a scale to give a subjective measurement of stress.
Way 2: Levels of stress hormones such as cortisol can be taken to give a physiological measurement of stress.

c) *Work is stressful*

Strongly agree ☐   Agree ☐   Not sure ☐
Disagree ☐   Strongly disagree ☐

This question would allow the researcher to quantify respondents' responses on a range of questions relating to the relationship between the workplace and stress.

5 In the Marmot *et al.* study, the main conclusion was that low control appears to be linked to higher stress and also linked to cardiovascular disorder, whereas high job demand is not linked to stress and illness. This does not fully support the job strain model because it does not show that high demand is linked to illness, but lack of control does appear to be linked to stress and illness. In contrast to

It is acceptable to include some mention of findings, but only to prepare a context for the conclusions that follow.

the Marmot *et al.* study, Johansson *et al.*'s study found evidence of a direct link between job demand, stress hormones and illness, which suggests that a sense of control *increases* stress. Schaubroeck *et al.* (2001) concluded that some people view negative work outcomes as being their fault. For these employees control can actually exacerbate the unhealthful effects of stress.

6 **Way 1:** 'Role ambiguity' refers to the lack of definition given to a worker's job. This leads to a sense of frustration and makes it hard to achieve a sense of satisfaction. Kahn *et al.*

It is creditworthy to include details of a research study to elaborate a point being made.

(1964) surveyed workers and found that 35% felt unclear about their job responsibilities and also unclear about what they actually had to do.
Way 2: There are many environmental factors in the workplace that increase stress. Such factors include overcrowding, heat, poor lighting and noise. Glass *et al.* (1969) suggested that random noise is particularly difficult because we can 'tune out' constant stimuli, but unpredictable stimuli require continued attention, and this reduces our ability to cope with stress.

Description (AO1)	What does this tell us? (AO2)	Other commentary (AO2)
Outline of Marmot *et al.* study (1997) – see answer to question 4	In this study, the main conclusion was that low control appears to be linked to higher stress and also linked to cardiovascular disorder, whereas high job demand is not linked to stress and illness. This does not fully support the job strain model because it does not show that high demand is linked to illness, but lack of control does appear to be linked to stress and illness.	The conclusions of this study are based on the sample studied – civil servants. The responses of such individuals may not be typical of all adults as they are urban dwellers who are probably quite job-oriented and ambitious, in contrast with rural inhabitants whose jobs may play a less significant role in their lives.
Outline of Schaubroeck *et al.* (2001) study – see answer to question 4	Schaubroeck *et al.* (2001) concluded that some people view negative work outcomes as being their fault.	Schaubroeck *et al.* showed that for these employees, control can actually exacerbate the unhealthy effects of stress.
Johansson *et al.* (1978) found evidence of a direct link between job demand, stress hormones and illness.	This study suggests that a sense of control *increases* stress in contrast with the study by Marmot *et al.*	However, the findings from this study *do* agree with Brady's findings that monkeys who developed ulcers were the ones who had to control the shocks.

Individual differences: Personality and gender

The phrase 'modifying the effects of stressors' requires you to consider whether personality is related to differences in the way an individual copes with stress, i.e. do some personality types cope better or differently from others?

~~~~~~~~~~~~~~~~~~

Specification extract
Individual differences in modifying the effects of stressors, including the roles played by personality (e.g. Friedman and Rosenman) and gender.

In this question you can use your answers to question 1 and this time restate them as conclusions. What do the findings show us?

Take care to clearly distinguish between personality types such as A and B. Candidates don't often have much to say about type B.

A psychology class plan to conduct a survey on stress. They plan to compare the answers from men and women in order to find out more about gender differences in coping with stress.

It is probably easier to identify conclusions of specific studies rather than discuss research more generally. A general discussion tends to be rather vague and lacking detail.

a) Give **one** advantage of using a questionnaire survey in the context of this study.

Take care not to represent a dated and stereotyped view of gender roles. And make sure your answer is psychologically informed such as looking at evolutionary explanations, differences in coping strategies and/or differences in physiological reactivity.

b) Give **one** disadvantage of using a questionnaire survey in the context of this study.

c) Write a leading question that might be included in this study.

Just to remind you that you might be asked about personality, culture and gender in this form. Any of the answers for questions 3, 6 and 9 would be suitable.

d) Rewrite this question so it is more suitable.

You may restrict your answer to a consideration of any of the three individual differences named in the specification and provided in the quotation (personality, culture and gender), or you may cover all three. The danger with the latter approach is that you may have too much to write, and may focus too much on describing various relevant studies rather than including sufficient AO2 material.

Possible plan

	AO1 Description	AO2 Criticisms of the study	AO2 Conclusions regarding individual differences
Studies relating to personality			
Studies relating to gender			

AO1 questions

1. Outline findings of research into the role played by personality in modifying the effects of stressors. *(6 marks)*

2. Outline conclusions of research into the role played by personality in modifying the effects of stressors. *(6 marks)*

3. Describe **two** ways in which personality may modify the effects of stressors.
   (3 marks + 3 marks)

4. Outline findings of research into the role played by gender in modifying the effects of stressors. *(6 marks)*

5. Outline conclusions of research into the role played by gender in modifying the effects of stressors. *(6 marks)*

6. Describe **two** ways in which gender may modify the effects of stressors.
   (3 marks + 3 marks)

7. Describe **two** ways that individual differences may modify the effects of stressors.
   (3 marks + 3 marks)

AO1/AO2 question

Consider whether research (theories **and/or** studies) shows that individual differences can modify the effects of stressors. *(18 marks)*

1 Friedman and Rosenman (1959) found that twice as many type A participants died of cardiovascular problems than non type A. Type As also had higher blood pressure and higher cholesterol, and were also more likely to smoke and have a family history of CHD, both of which increased their risk. The link between repressed emotion (type C) and cancer was demonstrated in a study by Morris *et al.* (1981). Women whose breast lumps were found to be cancerous also reported that they both experienced and expressed far less anger than those women whose lumps were found to be non-cancerous.

There is a lot of material to choose from here, so it pays to practise constructing a representative selection of it. The answer here is 150 words, more than is required for a 6 mark answer.

2 Friedman and Rosenman concluded that type A personalities possessed a number of physiological characteristics (such as higher blood pressure and higher cholesterol) and psychological characteristics (such as being aggressive and ambitious with a competitive drive and a chronic sense of time urgency) that increased the risk of them developing CHD. Morris *et al.*'s research supports the idea of a link between cancer and the suppression of anger. Temoshok (1987) suggests that such individuals cope with stress in a way that ignores their own needs, even physical ones, in order to please others, and this has negative physiological consequences. All stresses are suppressed but eventually such stresses take their toll.

3 **Way 1:** Type A personalities are aggressive and ambitious with a competitive drive and a chronic sense of time urgency. These characteristics mean they respond to stress in a different way to type Bs, who will not develop raised blood pressure or higher hormone levels when exposed to stressful situations (Friedman and Rosenman, 1959).

Many students forget that they can use 'hardiness' in relation to workstress because it 'belongs' to a different section. It is perfectly relevant here as well.

Way 2: Kobasa (1979) suggested that some people are more psychologically 'hardy' than others. Hardiness enables people to cope better with stress. Hardy individuals demonstrate higher levels of control and commitment and see life changes as challenges to be overcome rather than as threats or stressors. All three of these characteristics will result in a reduced physiological arousal to potential stressors.

4 Taylor *et al.* (2000) suggest that women may be biologically programmed to be less affected by stress, because of the action of the hormone oxytocin. Individuals with high levels of oxytocin are calmer, more relaxed, more social and less anxious. In terms of social support, research shows that women are more likely to have confidantes and friends then men, and women report making use of social support networks more than men (Carroll, 1992). Stone *et al.* (1989) looked at the effects of two stressors, a video game and cigarette smoking, using six measures of stress. On five out of six measures, females had a higher cardiovascular reactivity to both stressors.

'Research' can be a theory instead of a study, as in Taylor's suggestion that women have evolved different responses to stress.

 research methods **A**

a. *Questionnaires do not require specialist administrators, therefore they could be used and scored by members of the psychology class.*

b. *There may be a social desirability bias, with perhaps one gender not being truthful about how they cope with stress.*

c. *Why do you think women are more likely than men to talk to friends when stressed?*

d. *Are women or men more likely to talk to friends when stressed?*

5 Taylor *et al.*'s research might explain why, under stressful situations, women seek the support of others, which further serves to reduce their stress levels. Men also secrete oxytocin, but its effects appear to be reduced by male hormones, so oxytocin may have reduced effects on men's behaviour under stress. Carroll (1992) concluded that as well as making use of social support networks more than men, women engage in fewer unhealthy behaviours than men. Carroll also concluded that gender differences are changing, which would lead us to expect a narrowing of the gender gap in CHD mortality rates. Carroll reports that this has been happening.

6 **Way 1:** Social explanations focus on the fact that males have less social support, more unhealthy habits (such as smoking and drinking) and more stressful occupations. All of these factors can explain why men are more prone to cardiovascular disorders than women.

Way 2: It is possible that men react more than women to stressful events. However, Stone *et al.* (1989) looked at the effects of two stressors, a video game and cigarette smoking, using six measures of stress. On five out of six measures, females had a higher cardiovascular reactivity to both stressors, still showing that gender modifies stress responses.

Select any two from the six available.

7 See answer to question 3 or 6.

AO1 Description	AO2 Criticisms of the studies	AO2 Conclusions
Outline of research studies relating to personality – see answer to question 1	It may be that anxiety or depression is the *result* of stress rather than the cause. However, one study showed that the cancer-prone behaviour patterns can be reversed to reduce illness. Greer *et al.* (1979) found women with a 'fighting spirit' were more likely to recover from cancer. This suggests that such behaviour patterns are a cause of health or illness, rather than an effect.	There appears to be evidence that some aspects of personality are linked to CHD and other illnesses. This may be because some aspect of personality actually causes the immune system to underperform and/or causes blood pressure to increase. Or it may be that personality has an indirect effect, such as making it more likely that an individual would smoke and this would increase the likelihood of CHD.
Outline of research studies relating to gender – see answer to question 4	The findings from Taylor *et al.* suggest that oxytocin reduces stress in women. Men also secrete oxytocin, but its effects appear to be reduced by male hormones, so oxytocin may have reduced effects on men's physiology and behaviour under stress. Eagley (2000) disagrees with the claim that gender differences in individuals' reactions to stress have an evolutionary basis. It is possible that differences in the way that males and females deal with stress have nothing to do with biological factors but are simply a part of the gender-role socialisation that males and females experience as they grow up.	The findings from Stone *et al.* lead us to conclude that there may be certain stressful situations where women react *more* rather than *less* than men. Carroll (1992) concluded that as well as making greater use of social support networks than men, women engage in fewer unhealthy behaviours than men. Carroll also concluded that gender differences are changing, which would lead us to expect a narrowing of the gender gap in CHD mortality rates. Carroll reports that this has indeed been happening.

End of section review

See page viii for an explanation of how questions are marked.

Sample exam question

a. Describe **two** sources of workplace stress. *(3 marks + 3 marks)*

b. Outline findings of **one** study that has investigated life changes and give **one** criticism of this study. *(3 marks + 3 marks)*

c. Consider whether psychological research has shown that either personality and/or gender modifies the effects of stressors. *(18 marks)*

Student answer	Examiner's comments
(a) Sources of stress in the workplace include role ambiguity, too much control, too little control, responsibility, noise and work overload. I will write about two of these. Too much noise has been shown to lead to stress. One study found that uncontrolled and random noise was the worst. Too much responsibility (and too much control) also leads to stress. This was shown in Brady's study of monkeys where the executive suffered from an ulcer at the end whereas the yoked control, who had no responsibility (and no control), had no ulcer. It may not be reasonable to generalise these findings to human behaviour.	The first sentence is a waste of time (and marks). All that is required by this question is details of two sources of workplace stress. The first (too much noise) is basic. Reference to the study is not entirely relevant as it concerns the uncontrollability of noise rather than the volume. The second source is supported by reference to relevant research which is detailed and accurate. The final sentence (a criticism) is irrelevant. Total of **1/3 + 3/3 marks**.
(b) Rahe *et al.* tested thousands of naval men using the SRRS. They found a small but significant positive correlation between life changes and physical illness while the men were on a six-month tour of duty. One criticism of this study is that the men may not have recalled their life changes accurately over the previous six months. They may have repressed memories of negative changes and this would affect their life change score.	One finding has been given but in reasonable detail which is worth at least **2/3 marks**. The criticism provided is justified and explained clearly (the three-point rule) for **3/3 marks**.
(c) Friedman and Rosenman proposed that there was a type of personality (type A) in men that made them more prone to the effects of stress and led to higher rates of CHD. They studied 3,000 men over a period of time. After about eight years they checked to see how many had developed CHD and found that of those who had developed CHD about 70% had originally been classified as having a type A personality. This suggests that personality may cause CHD.

This research shows that personality modified the effect of stress. However, Friedman and Rosenman didn't take into account any individual differences or confounding variables. For example, how do we know that CHD is caused by personality rather than any other factors? Research has found that stressed people smoke more, drink more alcohol and take less exercise. These practices can all have a detrimental effect on health and cause CHD and not other individual differences. Friedman and Rosenman have also been criticised in that correlation doesn't mean causation. Just because there seems to be a link between stress and illness doesn't mean that stress causes illness. Friedman and Rosenman's study also only investigated the effect of stress and personality in men. This is because, at the time of the study, few women held executive positions. Can these results be generalised to women?

Overall Friedman and Rosenman showed a link between stress and personality but they did not take other factors into account, e.g. if someone has an external locus of control, they may then feel more stressed because they feel that life is throwing things at them and they can't control it. This is also an aspect of personality. Friedman and Rosenman were only investigating one aspect of personality and to get a true picture of whether personality modifies the effects of stressors we would have to look at all aspects of personality. [316 words] | In order to consider whether personality and/or gender modifies the effects of stressors, you need to identify the relevant research (AO1) and then comment on it (AO2). Only one study has been described which could be sufficient for the full 6 AO1 marks if it were given in sufficient detail. There is a good amount of detail but not quite enough for full marks. This is supported by the fact that the first paragraph is about 80 words whereas 100 words would be a more appropriate length for the AO1 component, thus a generous **5/6 marks**.

The AO2 is clearly better (because there is more than twice as much). Notice how each point that is made is then also explained/expanded. This is important for making *effective* AO2 points. There is not quite enough to count this as 'informed' but it is very close to the top band, a somewhat mean **10/12 marks for AO2, a total of 15/18 marks**. |
| | Total for whole question is **24 marks**, equivalent to a Grade A. |

COGNITIVE PSYCHOLOGY:
HUMAN MEMORY

DEVELOPMENTAL PSYCHOLOGY:
ATTACHMENTS IN DEVELOPMENT

**PHYSIOLOGICAL PSYCHOLOGY:
STRESS**

INDIVIDUAL DIFFERENCES:
ABNORMALITY

SOCIAL PSYCHOLOGY:
SOCIAL INFLUENCE

RESEARCH
METHODS

This module is divided into

Stress as a bodily response

The body's response to stressors

Stress and physical illness: Cardiovascular disorders and the immune system

End of section review

Sources of stress

Life changes

Workplace stressors

Individual differences: Personality and gender

End of section review

Critical issue: Stress management

Physiological methods of stress management

Psychological methods of stress management

End of section review

Physiological methods of stress management

Specification extract
Methods of managing the negative effects of stress, including physiological (e.g. drugs, biofeedback). The strengths and weaknesses of methods of stress management.

research methods

Q

a) What is a sampling technique?

b) Why are sampling techniques necessary?

c) What is a 'target population'?

d) Name **three** methods of sampling a target population.

e) For each method describe **one** advantage and **one** disadvantage.

This question is not the same as asking you to describe *examples* of physiological approaches to stress management. You are required to explain the overarching concept but can use examples to assist you.

You do not have to describe one of the examples provided in the question (taken from the specification), but they are the most popular choices. When candidates describe drugs as a method of stress management, they tend to be rather confused about the difference between benzodiazepines and beta blockers. For good marks you should provide a detailed and accurate answer.

Both strengths and weaknesses are included in the specification so you should be prepared for this question. Better candidates go beyond simply saying what the strength (or weakness) is and are able to provide good detail of the mechanisms of action. Strengths can include reference to research studies.

This question is an example of where you could be asked to provide a shortened description of one method (3 marks' worth).

There are no tricks in this question except that you must cover two methods of stress management, which must be physiological methods. If you describe only one method there will be a partial performance penalty of a maximum of 4 marks for AO1 and 8 marks for AO2. Don't spend too much time describing the two methods as there are only 6 marks for this. You need to present a short but detailed description of each. A total of 100 words would be appropriate.

When evaluating each model there is no requirement to provide strengths as well as limitations but including them does give a nice sense of balance to your evaluation.

Psychological methods would only be creditworthy as commentary.

Possible plan

	AO1 Description	AO2 Strengths	AO2 Limitations
Method 1			
Method 2			

AO1 questions

1. Explain what is meant by physiological approaches to stress management.
   (3 marks)

2. Describe **one** physiological approach (e.g. drugs, biofeedback) to stress management. *(6 marks)*

3. Explain **one** strength and **one** weakness of **one** physiological approach to stress management.
   (3 marks + 3 marks)

4. Explain **two** physiological approaches to stress management.
   (3 marks + 3 marks)

5. Briefly outline **one** physiological approach to stress management and give **one** criticism of this approach.
   (3 marks + 3 marks)

AO1/AO2 question

Outline and evaluate **two** physiological methods of stress management.

(18 marks)

1 Physiological approaches to stress management focus on alleviating the emotions associated with the stressful situation. They include the use of drugs that reduce the anxiety associated with stress, and biofeedback, which involves learning how to control some aspects of the body's stress reaction.

> This is a 3 mark explanation, not a 2 mark definition, so it needs that extra bit of detail.

2 Biofeedback is a method by which an individual learns to exert voluntary control over involuntary (autonomic) behaviours by being made aware of what is happening in the ANS. It involves four processes:

> How can you remember the four processes? Think of a silly sentence from the letters FROT (e.g. 'Frogs rarely offer tips'). It is acceptable to use bullet points in your answer, but if the points are not elaborated, they will be given little credit.

- **Feedback.** The patient is attached to machines that provide information (feedback) about various ANS activities.
- **Relaxation.** The patient is taught techniques of relaxation, which have the effect of reducing activity of the sympathetic nervous system and activating the parasympathetic nervous system.
- **Operant conditioning.** Relaxation leads to a target behaviour, e.g. heart rate is decreased. This is rewarding, which increases the likelihood of the same behaviour being repeated.
- **Transfer.** The patient then needs to transfer the skills learned to the real world.

3 **Strength:** Biofeedback is not an invasive technique. In other words, it does not alter the body in any permanent way as drugs do. The only effects or side effects are increased relaxation, which can only be desirable.

> For the weakness, try to say more than just 'it is expensive'. You need elaboration for this point to have impact.

Weakness: The technique requires specialist equipment, which means that it is expensive and can only be undertaken with specialist supervision. If the success of biofeedback is mainly due to relaxation rather than feedback and conditioning, then there is no need for these expensive and time-consuming procedures.

4 **Approach 1:** Drugs used to treat anxiety include benzodiazepines (BZs) and beta blockers. Benzodiazepines slow down the activity of the central nervous system and imitate the activity of GABA (the body's natural form of anxiety relief) thus reducing arousal of the nervous system and reducing anxiety. Beta blockers reduce the activity of the sympathetic nervous system and reduce the associated undesirable symptoms.

> It is a tall order to précis a huge topic such as anxiolytic drugs into a 3 mark answer, so practise doing just that for all methods of stress management. Don't leave it to the exam.

Approach 2: In biofeedback, the patient is connected to a machine that provides information about ANS activity. They learn to relax to control this activity. Successful behaviours are repeated because they are rewarding, and the patient then transfers this to everyday situations.

 research methods **A**

a) A sampling technique is a way of selecting participants such that they can be considered to be representative of the population being selected from.

b) You cannot test an entire population but if a representative sample is selected (rather than being biased in some way), then the researcher is able to generalise results back to that population.

c) A target population is the group of people from whom the sample is drawn, and to which the researcher intends to generalise the results once the study is completed.

d) Random sample, opportunity sample and volunteer sample.

e) Random sample: An advantage is that it is potentially unbiased, but a disadvantage is that it must be drawn from a large population in order to be unbiased.

Opportunity sample: An advantage is that it is easy to get an opportunity sample (people who are available at the time), but a disadvantage is that this often makes the sample extremely biased (e.g. people who happen to be in that location at that time).

Volunteer sample: An advantage is that this gives access to a variety of participants without the need for coercion, but a disadvantage is that this may result in volunteer bias (they may have different psychological characteristics to non-volunteers).

5 **Approach:** as for Approach 1 in Question 4.

> In this topic, you might be asked for strengths or weaknesses, but 'criticisms' allows for either.

Criticism: Drugs may be very effective at treating symptoms but this only lasts as long as you take the drugs. As soon as you stop taking the drugs, the effectiveness ceases. This means that it may be preferable to seek a treatment that addresses the problem itself rather than one that deals only with the symptoms.

AO1 Description	AO2 Strengths	AO2 Limitations
Outline of drugs (use approach 1 from question 4 above)	Anxiolytic drugs work, e.g. Kahn *et al.* (1986) followed patients over 8 weeks and found that BZs were significantly superior to a placebo. One of the great appeals of using drug treatments is that they require little effort from the user. This is much easier than the time and effort needed to use other stress management techniques.	Drugs may be very effective at treating symptoms but this only lasts as long as you take the drugs. As soon as you stop taking the drugs the effectiveness ceases. This means that it may be preferable to seek a treatment that addresses the problem itself rather than one that deals only with the symptoms.
Outline of biofeedback (use approach 2 from question 4 above)	Biofeedback is not an invasive technique, i.e. it does not alter the body in any permanent way as drugs do. The only effects or side effects are increased relaxation, which can only be desirable. Biofeedback has been found to be successful in treating a wide assortment of behaviours (e.g. high blood pressure) and disorders (curvature of the spine).	If the success of biofeedback is mainly due to relaxation rather than feedback and conditioning, then there is no need for these expensive and time-consuming procedures. Biofeedback does not treat the source of stress, such as workplace tension. However it does provide the patient with a potentially long-lasting means of dealing with stress symptoms – by applying relaxation techniques.

Psychological methods of stress management

PHYSIOLOGICAL PSYCHOLOGY: STRESS

Specification extract

Methods of managing the negative effects of stress, including psychological approaches (e.g. stress-inoculation, increasing hardiness). The strengths and weaknesses of methods of stress management

A psychologist wishes to compare the effectiveness of two approaches to stress management. One method is physiological (a form of biofeedback) and the other is a psychological method (a form of hardiness training).

a) Describe the aims of this study.

b) What method of research could be used?

c) Describe **one** advantage of using this method in the context of this study.

d) Identify a suitable sampling method that might be used.

e) Describe how you would carry out this sampling procedure.

f) Give **one** advantage and **one** disadvantage of this sampling technique in the context of this study.

This question is not the same as asking you to describe *examples* of psychological approaches to stress management. You are required to explain the overarching concept but can use examples to assist you.

Examples are given to help you but they are not compulsory. For high marks you should describe the techniques *plus* give some account of the theoretical background; for example, stress inoculation therapy has clear stages and also has a rationale – a set of principles to explain why the method should work.

Candidates who use hardiness as a psychological method of stress management often get sidetracked into a discussion of the effects of personality and forget to link hardiness to stress management.

Biofeedback is accepted as a psychological approach but, in order to receive credit, the psychological element(s) need to be made clear. Candidates who choose relaxation or meditation or yoga usually provide little detail and get low marks.

Candidates often waste time describing the method. Some candidates choose methods not related to stress, for example psychoanalysis. They may gain some credit if the strengths/weaknesses are related to stress management.

This question is an example of where you could be asked to provide a shortened description of one method (3 marks' worth).

Possible plan

	AO1 Description	AO2 Strengths	AO2 Limitations
Method 1			
Method 2			

AO1 questions

1. Explain what is meant by psychological approaches to stress management.
(3 marks)

2. Explain **one** psychological approach (e.g. stress inoculation, increasing hardiness) to stress management. *(6 marks)*

3. Outline **one** strength and **one** weakness of **one** psychological approach to stress management.
(3 marks + 3 marks)

4. Outline **two** psychological approaches to stress management.
(3 marks + 3 marks)

5. Briefly outline **one** psychological approach to stress management and give **one** criticism of this approach.
(3 marks + 3 marks)

AO1/AO2 question

Outline one or more psychological methods of stress management and evaluate in terms of strengths and weaknesses. *(18 marks)*

1 Psychological approaches to stress management involve the use of techniques that are designed to help people cope better with stressful situations or to alter their perception of the demands of a stressful situation. Examples include relaxation, hypnosis and specific cognitive–behavioural techniques (such as stress inoculation).

2 Meichenbaum suggested that an individual should develop a form of coping before the problem arises. Stress inoculation has three phases:

> *What else begins with the letters CSA that would help you remember? The Child Support Agency may help!*

- Conceptualisation phase. The therapist and client establish a relationship, and the client is educated about the nature and impact of stress. This enables the client to reconceptualise their problem.
- Skills acquisition phase (and rehearsal). Coping skills are taught and practised primarily in the clinic and then gradually rehearsed in real life. These include positive thinking, social skills, using social support systems and time management.
- Application phase (and follow-through). Clients are given opportunities to apply the newly learned coping skills in different situations, which become increasingly stressful. Various techniques may be used such as imagery, modelling and role-playing.

3 **Strength:** Stress inoculation offers a two-pronged attack: skills to cope with current problems and also skills and confidence to cope with future problems. The focus on skills acquisition provides long-lasting effectiveness.

> *There is a subtle distinction between merely making a descriptive point and offering a critical point (as here).*

Skills are taught, practised and followed through. They are also dealt with on a cognitive and behavioural level, and tailored to the needs of the individual.
Weakness: The training programme involved in stress inoculation requires a lot of time and effort, motivation and money. Its strengths are also its weaknesses. It is effective because it involves learning and practising many new skills, but this complexity makes it a lengthy therapy which would suit only a limited range of determined individuals.

4 **Approach 1:** Stress inoculation has three phases: In the conceptualisation phase, therapist and client establish a relationship, and the client is educated about the nature and impact of stress. In the skills acquisition phase, coping skills are taught and practised. In the application phase, clients are given opportunities to apply the newly learned coping skills in situations which become increasingly stressful.
Approach 2: The aim of hardiness training is to increase self-confidence and sense of control so that individuals can more successfully navigate change. Hardiness can be increased by training in three phases – focusing (recognising signs of stress and identifying the sources), relieving stress encounters (to help understand current stressors and coping strategies), and self-improvement, where insights gained can be used to move forwards and learn new techniques.

5 **Approach:** as for Approach 1 in Question 4.
Criticism: The focus on skills acquisition in stress inoculation provides long-lasting effectiveness. Skills are taught, practised and followed through. They are also dealt with on a cognitive and behavioural level, and tailored to the needs of the individual.

> *It is always a good idea to try and say three things when there are three marks available. This ensures sufficient elaboration for the full three marks.*

research methods **A**

a) The aim of this study is to see which of the two methods being compared is more effective as a form of stress management.

b) An experiment could be used in this research.

c) An advantage is that the researcher will be able to control other potential confounding variables, such as the nature of the individual participants, and their existing levels of stress.

d) A volunteer sample could be used.

e) Advertisements could be placed in a local newspaper, asking for people who believe they may be suffering from stress, but who are not currently under treatment for their stress.

f) Advantage: This would remove the problems of coercing people to take part in the study, as people would respond to the newspaper advertisement of their own free will.

Disadvantage: The sample would be restricted only to those people who read that particular newspaper, and so may reflect just a narrow socio-economic range of participants.

AO1 Description	AO2 Strengths	AO2 Limitations
Outline of stress inoculation (see approach 1 in question 4 above)	The focus on skills acquisition in stress inoculation provides long-lasting effectiveness. Skills are taught, practised and followed through. They are also dealt with on a cognitive and behavioural level, and tailored to the needs of the individual. Stress inoculation has been shown to be successful with acute and chronic stressors, including occupational stress (e.g. combat), and stressful events (such as dealing with rape).	The strengths of this technique are also its weaknesses – it is effective because it involves learning and practising many new skills, but this complexity makes it a lengthy therapy which would suit only a limited range of determined individuals. It may be that its effectiveness is due to certain elements of the training rather than all of it, meaning that one could reduce the range of activities without losing much of the effectiveness.
Outline of hardiness training (see approach 2 in question 4 above)	Hardiness training, like stress inoculation training, teaches an individual to manage all stressors in their lives not just a particular set of symptoms related to a particular problem. This makes it a much more adaptable and effective therapy than using drugs. Skills acquisition leads to longer-term effectiveness.	It is possible that hardiness is no more than being in control, and commitment and challenge matter less. Funk (1992) argues that low hardiness is the same as being negative, and it is negativity rather than lack of hardiness that leads to the ill effects of stress.

End of section review

Note that this entire question has been drawn from different sections of the module on stress. This is acceptable. It is also acceptable to set an entire question on one section only.

Sample exam question

a. Explain what is meant by the terms cardiovascular disorder and immune system. *(3 marks + 3 marks)*

b. Describe **one** physiological approach to stress management. *(6 marks)*

c. 'Many people now believe that stress is an important cause of physical illness.' Consider whether research (theories **and/or** studies) does show a relationship between stress and physical illness. *(18 marks)*

See page viii for an explanation of how questions are marked.

Student answer	Examiner's comments
(a) A cardiovascular disorder is something that affects the heart. It is when stress or what you eat makes it difficult for the heart to function and this leads to a heart attack. The immune system is the body's system of defence against infection. Things like white blood cells attack invaded organisms.	The first explanation is at best 'generally accurate'. The candidate knows that cardiovascular disorders are to do with the heart and that this may lead to a heart attack, thus **2/3 marks**. The second explanation is both accurate and detailed, so **3/3 marks**.
(b) Biofeedback involves holding a monitor to record your blood pressure and heart rate. Whenever you start to feel aroused you can see this on the machine. You are then taught how to decrease your blood pressure and heart rate by relaxation techniques such as deep breathing. Biofeedback is good because a person can see when they are in control and see when they have made a difference to their heart rate. This is very encouraging because the person feels they are helping themselves. Biofeedback was very popular in the 1970s. Dworkin and Dworkin used it to treat curvature of the spine. They used it to help the muscle tension and improve the posture of sufferers.	The first few sentences offer a reasonable explanation of how biofeedback works but the middle part is really an evaluation of the method (though it adds some detail to the description). To some extent the research by Dworkin and Dworkin counts as further description insofar as it includes an explanation of how the method worked with curvature of the spine. If we cut out the irrelevant parts, we are left with a reasonably detailed and accurate account, **5/6 marks**.
(c) Most research suggests that there is a relationship between stress and physical illness. The study by Friedman and Rosenman showed that people who were type A personalities (more prone to the effects of stress) were more likely to develop CHD. A study by Russek and Zohman found that people in high-stress jobs were more likely to get heart disease. These studies do show that there is a relationship but they don't tell us if stress actually caused the physical illness. An alternative explanation might be that some other factor was responsible. For example, people who are stressed also smoke and drink more, and these may be the factors that cause physical illness. Research on life changes also shows a relationship between stress and physical illness. Rahe *et al.* studied men in the navy. The men recorded all the major life events that occurred to them over the previous six months and then the researchers correlated this with the navy's record of ill health while the men were on a tour of duty. They found a small positive correlation between number of life changes and illness. The more life changes a person experiences, the more stress they are supposed to have experienced. However, the reason why the correlation was so low may have been because the men didn't accurately recall their life events (they might have repressed the unpleasant ones) but also it may be that life changes do not accurately reflect the stress a person experiences. There are more recent life events scales such as LISRES and there is also the daily hassles scale which suggests that stress and physical illness are linked. The classic study by Brady found that stress was associated with the development of ulcers. The monkey that was stressed got ulcers and died. We also should be careful about generalising from animals to human behaviour, though studies found similar results when studying human ulcers. [298 words]	Lots of research has been described here, all relevant to the topic of stress and physical illness, thus **6/6 marks for AO1**. The answer moves nicely from AO1 to AO2 in each paragraph, providing effective commentary (using useful phrases like 'An alternative explanation is …' and 'However, …'). Despite the quality of the commentary there is perhaps rather too little of it. There is about the same amount of AO1 and AO2 (whereas there should be twice as much AO2). It might have been better to write less description and/or offer more commentary. The commentary is limited/slightly limited (about 160 words of AO2 – less than half the answer) = **9/12 marks for AO2**, a total of **15/18 marks**.
	Total for whole question is **25 marks**, equivalent to a Grade A.

INDIVIDUAL DIFFERENCES: ABNORMALITY

Individual differences are those aspects of each of us that distinguish us from others, such as personality and intelligence. Each of us also differs in the extent to which we are 'normal'. For the most part, deviation from normal is not a problem, but in some circumstances it is. How do we know when abnormality is unacceptable?

This module is divided into

Defining psychological abnormality

Definitions of abnormality

End of section review

Biological and psychological models

Biological (medical) and psychodynamic models

Behavioural and cognitive models

End of section review

Critical issue: Eating disorders

Biological explanations of eating disorders

Psychological explanations of eating disorders

End of section review

COGNITIVE PSYCHOLOGY: HUMAN MEMORY

DEVELOPMENTAL PSYCHOLOGY: ATTACHMENTS IN DEVELOPMENT

PHYSIOLOGICAL PSYCHOLOGY: STRESS

INDIVIDUAL DIFFERENCES: ABNORMALITY

SOCIAL PSYCHOLOGY: SOCIAL INFLUENCE

RESEARCH METHODS

Definitions of abnormality

Specification extract

Attempts to define abnormality in terms of statistical infrequency, deviation from social norms, a failure to function adequately, and deviation from ideal mental health. Limitations associated with these definitions of psychological abnormality (e.g. cultural relativism).

research methods

Q

a) What is a measure of dispersion?

b) Identify **two** measures of dispersion.

c) For each measure of dispersion state **one** advantage and **one** disadvantage.

Consider the numbers below and in each case state what measure of dispersion would be most suitable to use and explain why.

d) 8, 9, 10, 11, 13, 14, 16, 19, 28

e) 11.2, 15.1, 16.3, 17.4, 18.9, 21.2

Many candidates find it difficult to distinguish between these, perhaps because they both involve the concept of norms. Statistical infrequency refers to deviation from statistical norms (not often) whereas deviation from social norms concerns bizarre or deviant behaviour (not acceptable).

The specification only mentions limitations but you would also need to know strengths as well in order to answer an AO2 question.
Again, candidates get confused and provide limitations of deviation from social norms instead of statistical infrequency. Many candidates also don't know a second limitation for statistical infrequency.

Weak candidates fail to provide detail – they just about manage to mention cultural differences or eccentricity. Using examples is a good way to provide detail in your answers but take care here to provide examples that are related to abnormality rather than, for example, mentioning cultural differences in queuing behaviour.

Here again candidates tend to be muddled about which phrase goes with which definition. Good answers outline failure to function by mentioning a range of behaviours such as personal distress, bizarre behaviour or causing distress to others.

If your answer to part (i) is wrong then you lose all the marks for this question, a disaster.

You might answer this question by considering all the four definitions in the specification, and their strengths and limitations. However, in reality you are unlikely to have time to cover all of this. You are not expected to write the perfect answer, especially as you have only 15 minutes. It is quite acceptable to be selective, which will help ensure that you have time to present sufficient AO2 material. You could always use other definitions (or classification schemes such as DSM) as a means of evaluation/contrast/commentary.
Remember that there is never one correct answer. There are no correct answers in psychology, only well-argued answers that are psychologically informed. The 'model' answers on the right of each spread are intended as examples only.

Possible plan

	AO1 Description	**AO2** Strengths	**AO2** Limitations
Definition 1			
Definition 2			
Definition 3			

AO1 questions

1. Explain what is meant by the statistical infrequency definition of abnormality and the deviation from social norms definition of abnormality.
   (3 marks + 3 marks)

2. Give **two** limitations of the definition of abnormality in terms of statistical infrequency.
   (3 marks + 3 marks)

3. Give **two** limitations of the social norms definition of abnormality.
   (3 marks + 3 marks)

4. (i) Outline the failure to function adequately definition of abnormality.
   (3 marks)

   (ii) Give **one** limitation of the failure to function adequately definition of abnormality.
   (3 marks)

5. (i) Outline the deviation from ideal mental health definition of abnormality.
   (3 marks)

   (ii) Give **one** limitation of the deviation from ideal mental health definition of abnormality. *(3 marks)*

AO1/AO2 question

'Psychologists have various ways to define abnormality but none of these is totally successful.' To what extent are attempts to define psychological abnormality successful? *(18 marks)*

1 The statistical infrequency definition relies on the idea of a statistical norm. A 'norm' is something that is usual or regular or typical. If we can define what is most common or normal, then we also have an idea of what is not common, i.e. abnormal. Any behaviour that departs from this 'typical' behaviour would be regarded as abnormal.

Deviation from social norms defines abnormality in terms of behaviour that is antisocial or undesirable. In any society there are social norms – standards of acceptable behaviour that are set by the social group. Departure from these norms constitutes abnormal behaviour.

2 **Limitation 1:** There are many abnormal behaviours that are quite desirable. For example, very few people have an IQ over 150 yet we would not want to suggest that this is undesirable behaviour. Equally there are some normal behaviours that are undesirable. For example, depression is relatively common yet it is undesirable.

Limitation 2: Behaviours that are statistically infrequent in one culture may be statistically more frequent in another. For example, one of the symptoms of schizophrenia is claiming to hear voices. However, this is an experience regarded as normal and even desirable in some cultures. Revered religious leaders often claim to have heard the voice of God.

3 **Limitation 1:** The main difficulty with the concept of deviation from social norms is that it varies as times change. What is socially acceptable now was not socially acceptable 50 years ago. For example, today homosexuality is acceptable but in the past it was included under sexual and gender identity disorders.

> *As always you should look for three things to say for 3 marks; for example, identify, elaborate, and provide an example.*

Limitation 2: Attempting to define abnormality in terms of social norms is obviously bound by culture because social norms are defined by the culture. Classification systems, such as DSM and ICD, are almost entirely based on the social norms of the dominant culture in the West (white and middle class) and yet the same criteria are applied to people from different subcultures living in the West.

4 (i) From an individual's point of view, abnormality can be judged in terms of not being able to cope. For example, feeling depressed might be tolerated as long as it doesn't interfere with day-to-day living. As soon as depression interferes with such things the individual might then be prepared to label their own behaviour as 'abnormal', and perhaps wish to seek treatment.

(ii) Definitions of adequate functioning are related to cultural ideas of how one's life should be lived. The failure to function criteria are likely to result in differential diagnoses when applied to people from different cultures because the standard of one culture is being used to measure another.

research methods **A**

a) A measure of dispersion is a measure of how dispersed or spread out the numbers in a set of data are.

b) Range and standard deviation.

c) *Range:* The range is easy to calculate, but is affected by extreme values.

Standard deviation: The standard deviation is a more precise measure of dispersion because all values are taken into account, but it is harder to calculate.

d) The standard deviation would be most suitable as the range would be affected by the presence of an extreme score (28).

e) The range would be most suitable as it would be easy to calculate and there are no extreme scores.

5 (i) Jahoda (1958) conducted a review of what others had written about mental health and identified six categories that were commonly referred to. These included being independent and self-regulating, and having an accurate perception of reality. This model proposes that the absence of these criteria indicates abnormality, and potential mental disorder.

(ii) According to these criteria, most of us are abnormal and possibly mentally disordered. Jahoda presented them as ideal criteria and they certainly are. We also have to ask how many of the three need to be lacking before a person would be judged as abnormal.

> *For (ii) you are asked to provide **one** limitation. It could be argued that two limitations have been provided here but there is sufficient link to regard the second sentence as an elaboration of the first.*

AO1 Description	AO2 Strengths	AO2 Limitations
See the first part of the response to question 1	In some situations it is appropriate to use a statistical criterion to define abnormality. For example, mental retardation is defined in terms of the normal distribution using the concept of standard deviation to establish a cut-off point for abnormality.	Choose one limitation from the response to question 2
See the second part of the response to question 1	The social deviancy model takes into account the effect that behaviour has on others. Deviance is defined in terms of transgression of social rules and (ideally) social rules are established in order to help people live together.	Choose one limitation from the response to question 3
See the first part of the response to question 5	The deviation from mental health is a positive approach to the definition of abnormality; it focuses on what is desirable rather than what is undesirable.	See the second part of the response to question 5

End of section review

Sample exam question

a. (i) Outline the failure to function adequately definition of abnormality. (3 marks)

(ii) Outline the deviation from ideal mental health definition of abnormality. (3 marks)

b. Give **two** limitations of the definition of abnormality as a deviation from social norms. (3 marks + 3 marks)

c. Outline **two or more** definitions of abnormality and consider the limitations of such definitions. (18 marks)

> Note that this entire question has been drawn from the one section (defining psychological abnormality). This is acceptable. It is also acceptable to set an entire question on two or three sections.

See page viii for an explanat[ion] of how questions are marked

Student answer	Examiner's comments
a) The failure to function adequately definition suggests that a person can't do things like maintain a relationship and a job. The deviation from mental health model suggests that we can define mental illness by looking at what is mental health, such as being in control and self-actualising.	There really isn't enough detail in the first explanation to award it any more than **1/3 marks**. The second outline is slightly more detailed, so **2/3 marks**.
(b) One limitation of the definition of abnormality as a deviation from social norms is that it is hard to know how far the deviation has to be. Some problems are actually fairly normal, like feeling depressed, but are actually a problem that should be treated. Another limitation is the question of how you define what is socially normal and what is abnormal. This varies from one culture to another and this means this definition doesn't work.	The first limitation may look lengthy but about one-third is a repetition of the question itself. The rest of the response does little more than name rather than explain the limitation. The second limitation is better explained but there is still some lack of clarity = **1/3 + 2/3 marks.**
(c) One definition of abnormality is called the statistical infrequency definition which says that abnormality is defined by a statistical norm. A 'norm' is something that is usual or regular or typical. If we can define what is most common or normal, then we also have an idea of what is not common, i.e. abnormal. Any behaviour that departs from this 'typical' behaviour would be regarded as abnormal. Another definition is the deviation from social norms definition. Abnormality is defined as any behaviour that is antisocial or undesirable. In any society there are social norms – standards of acceptable behaviour that are set by the social group. Departure from these norms constitutes abnormal behaviour. A third definition is the failure to function adequately. From an individual's point of view, abnormality can be judged in terms of not being able to cope. For example, feeling depressed is acceptable as long as it doesn't interfere with day-to-day living. As soon as depression interferes with such things then the individual might be happy to label their own behaviour 'abnormal', and would wish to seek treatment. All of these definitions have limitations especially in terms of being culturally relative. This means that the problem with the definition is that it is related to a particular culture and doesn't take into account the fact that different cultures see things differently. For example, the statistical infrequency model assumes that certain behaviours have the same frequency in different cultures. In fact this isn't true. One of the symptoms of schizophrenia is claiming to hear voices but this is an experience regarded as normal and even desirable in some cultures. This means that such behaviour isn't always abnormal. [278 words]	This candidate has made the rather obvious mistake of putting in too much AO1 material (presumably because these definitions had been memorised and it seemed a shame to waste them!). If the AO1 content had been limited to two definitions, the AO1 mark would have been **6 marks**. As it is, it is worth **6+**, but it can still only achieve **6/6 marks for AO1**. The AO2 commentary is good – it is reasonably effective and shows some analysis. It is creditworthy to consider what is meant by cultural relativism – in another context this explanation might be credited as AO1 but here it is part of the commentary and thus receives AO2 credit. This illustrates the important point that no material is simply 'AO2' – it's how you use it that determines whether something is AO1 or AO2. While the final paragraph is informed, the amount that is there is restricted. Therefore this would be given **5/12 marks** for AO2, a total of **11/18 marks**.
	Total for whole question is **17/30 marks**, probably equivalent to a Grade B.

This module is divided into

Defining psychological abnormality

Definitions of abnormality

End of section review

Biological and psychological models

Biological (medical) and psychodynamic models

Behavioural and cognitive models

End of section review

Critical issue: Eating disorders

Biological explanations of eating disorders

Psychological explanations of eating disorders

End of section review

COGNITIVE PSYCHOLOGY:
HUMAN MEMORY

DEVELOPMENTAL PSYCHOLOGY:
ATTACHMENTS IN DEVELOPMENT

PHYSIOLOGICAL PSYCHOLOGY:
STRESS

INDIVIDUAL DIFFERENCES:
ABNORMALITY

SOCIAL PSYCHOLOGY:
SOCIAL INFLUENCE

RESEARCH
METHODS

Biological (medical) and psychodynamic models

Specification extract
Assumptions made by biological (medical) and psychological (including psychodynamic) models of abnormality in terms of their views on the causes of abnormality.

Candidates often write extremely vague assumptions such as 'something wrong with the brain'. Some candidates confuse biological and behavioural models, and some include irrelevant material, for example on implications for treatment. Detail can be provided by setting the assumption in context, such as relating it to a specific mental disorder (depression or schizophrenia).

In answering this question you can use any of the material from the question above. Take care to focus on the biological model of abnormality as distinct from the biological *approach* in psychology.

This is a slight variation on question 1.

Candidates often write rather general answers about the role of childhood experiences, or the significance of unconscious/repressed material, or conflicts between the id/ego/superego. It is often difficult to identify two clear assumptions in such answers. For good marks these assumptions need to be distinct and detailed.

Remember to focus on the psychodynamic model in relation to *abnormality* rather than just providing an outline of Freud's theory.

Try, as far as possible, to avoid giving a shopping list of the criticisms. It is more elegant to offer criticisms in relationship to points you make about the model. For example, you might identify one feature of the model (assumes that mental illness is due to physical causes) and then criticise this (there is only limited research support for this view).

AO1 questions

1. Outline **two** assumptions made by the biological model in relation to the causes of abnormality.
(3 marks + 3 marks)

2. Outline the biological model of abnormality. *(6 marks)*

3. Describe **one** assumption of the biological model of abnormality and give **one** criticism of this model.
(3 marks + 3 marks)

4. Outline **two** assumptions of the psychodynamic model in relation to the causes of abnormality.
(3 marks + 3 marks)

5. Outline the psychodynamic model of abnormality.
(6 marks)

6. Describe **one** assumption of the psychodynamic model of abnormality and give **one** criticism of this model.
(3 marks + 3 marks)

AO1/AO2 question

Outline and evaluate the biological (medical) model of abnormality. *(18 marks)*

You could try answering the same question on the psychodynamic model of abnormality.

Possible plan

AO1	AO2 strengths	AO2 limitations
Description of the model	Strength 1 (e.g. success of therapy)	Limitation 1 (e.g. limitation of therapy)
	Strength 2 (e.g. research support for therapy)	Limitation 2 (e.g. contrast with another model)
	Strength 3 (e.g. lack of blame)	Limitation 3 (e.g. ethical issues)

1 **Assumption 1:** The biological model assumes that all mental disorders are related to some change in the body. Mental disorders are like physical disorders, i.e. they are illnesses. Such changes or illnesses may be caused by one of four possible factors: genes, biochemical substances, neuroanatomy and micro-organisms.
Assumption 2: Genes also determine the structure of the brain (neuroanatomy). Some research has indicated that schizophrenics have large holes (ventricles) in their brains. The biological model assumes that such abnormalities are inherited and cause mental illness.

2 The biological model assumes that all mental disorders are related to some change in the body. Mental disorders are like physical disorders, i.e. they are illnesses. Such changes or illnesses may be caused by one of four possible factors: genes, biochemical substances, neuroanatomy and micro-organisms. It makes sense that if all mental disorders have a physical cause, then they should be treated physically by using drugs or some other treatment of the body. It also follows that mental disorders should be approached in the same way as physical disorders. That is, you record symptoms, identify a syndrome and diagnose a disorder. Following a diagnosis, one can prescribe a suitable treatment and also describe the likely course of the illness.

Notice how the same material has been used in both answers. It shows you how a little knowledge can go a long way when used effectively. There may be many different questions that can be set but you can often use the same material to inform your answer.

3 **Assumption:** Genes determine the structure of the brain (neuroanatomy). Some research has indicated that schizophrenics have large holes (ventricles) in their brains. The biological model assumes that such abnormalities are inherited and cause mental illness.
Criticism: Historically, the emergence of the medical model in the eighteenth century led to more humane treatment for mental patients. Until then mental illness was blamed on demons or evil in the individual. The medical model offered a different source of blame, the illness, which was potentially treatable. This was a more humane approach.

This is a good example of a positive criticism.

4 **Assumption 1:** Conflicts between the id, ego and superego create anxiety. The ego protects itself with various defence mechanisms (ego defences). These defences can be the cause of disturbed behaviour if they are overused. For example, repression is the blocking of unpleasant thoughts and placing them in the unconscious.
Assumption 2: Ego defences, such as repression, exert pressure through unconsciously motivated behaviour. Freud proposed that the unconscious consists of information that is either very hard or almost impossible to bring into conscious awareness. However, it exerts a powerful effect on behaviour which cannot be controlled until brought into conscious awareness.

5 An individual's abnormal behaviour is determined by underlying psychological conflicts of which they are largely unaware (i.e. *unconscious* forces). Psychodynamic theorists focus mostly on past experiences, notably early parent–child relationships, because they believe the majority of psychological conflicts are rooted in these relationships. Conflicts between the id, ego and superego create anxiety. The ego protects itself with various defence mechanisms, which can be the cause of disturbed behaviour if they are overused. In childhood the ego is not developed enough to deal with traumas and therefore they are repressed. Ego defences, such as repression, exert pressure through unconsciously motivated behaviour. Freud proposed that the unconscious exerts a powerful effect on behaviour which cannot be controlled until brought into conscious awareness.

*You are required to consider only **two** assumptions for this question.*

6 **Assumption:** Conflicts between the id, ego and superego create anxiety. The ego protects itself with various defence mechanisms (ego defences). These defences can be the cause of disturbed behaviour if they are overused. For example, repression is the blocking of unpleasant thoughts and placing them in the unconscious.
Criticism: The fact that the treatment focuses on the past means that present conflicts may be overlooked. The cause of an individual's difficulty may be a mixture of something relatively recent as well as early experience, so there is a danger in focusing exclusively on the past.

AO1 Description	AO2 strengths	AO2 limitations
See response to question 2	Historically, the emergence of the medical model in the eighteenth century led to more humane treatment for mental patients. The medical model offered a source of blame, the illness, which was potentially treatable. This was a more humane approach.	More recent critics have claimed that the medical model is inhumane. Szasz (1972) argued that mental illnesses did not have a physical basis. He suggested that the concept of mental illness was 'invented' as a form of social control.
	A strength of this approach lies in the success of its treatments. If physical causes can be found then it is possible to offer suitable treatments that control or eradicate mental illness. The use of drug therapies has gone some way to achieving this but not without limitations.	It is not clear whether abnormal biochemistry or abnormal neuroanatomy is a cause of abnormal behaviour, or whether it is an effect. If it is an effect of the disorder, such changes may perpetuate the disorder.
	If the cause of a mental disorder is genetic, then we can use genetic testing before birth to detect foetuses with possible disorders. This model therefore offers the possibility of eradicating many mental disorders that have a genetic basis.	There is no evidence that mental disorders are purely caused by biology. Concordance rates are never 100%. It is likely that, in the case of certain disorders, individuals inherit a susceptibility for the disorder but the disorder only develops if the individual is exposed to stressful life conditions.

Behavioural and cognitive models

Specification extract

Assumptions made by psychological (including behavioural and cognitive) models of abnormality in terms of their views on the causes of abnormality.

A surprising number of candidates confuse the behavioural model with the biological model or other models. The behavioural model focuses on *behaviours* that we can observe, the biological model is concerned with biology (the physical systems of the body). Good answers can distinguish classical conditioning and operant conditioning, and use Pavlov and Little Albert effectively to illustrate classical conditioning.

This question offers you the opportunity to write whatever you wish about the behavioural model as long as you stick to abnormality *and* as long as you limit yourself to 6 marks' worth *and* to description (not evaluation).

In this case you have to reduce your outline of the behavioural model and cover only a few key points. Identify and explain one criticism only.

Of the four models, candidates find this one the most difficult. They often present muddled accounts of memory as an example of the cognitive approach. Cognitive = thinking; this might help you start describing the key assumption.

Select from key points from your answers to question 4 and weave them into a 6 minute/mark outline of the model.

The task of reducing a 6 mark version to a 3 mark version should increase your understanding of the model, because you must try to select the key points to conclude and in making your selection you will be processing the information deeply. The levels of processing model of memory says this is what creates long-term memories.

The question is essentially asking for an evaluation of the behavioural model as a model of abnormality, which should clearly focus you on abnormality rather than considering the behavioural model more generally (a trap some candidates fall into). How can you evaluate the model? You might show how it produces successful therapies which confirm the basic assumptions (though the success of the therapies may be due to different factors), you might contrast the behavioural model with other models and you can look at the limitations of the model (e.g. the danger of overlooking a real physical cause).

AO1 questions

1. Outline **two** assumptions made by the behavioural model in relation to the causes of abnormality.
   (3 marks + 3 marks)

2. Outline the behavioural model of abnormality.
   (6 marks)

3. Describe **one** assumption of the behavioural model of abnormality and give **one** criticism of this model.
   (3 marks + 3 marks)

4. Outline **two** assumptions of the cognitive model in relation to the causes of abnormality.
   (3 marks + 3 marks)

5. Outline the cognitive model of abnormality. *(6 marks)*

6. Describe **one** assumption of the cognitive model of abnormality and give **one** criticism of this model.
   (3 marks + 3 marks)

AO1/AO2 question

To what extent does the behavioural model successfully explain abnormality? *(18 marks)*

Possible plan

AO1	AO2 Strengths	AO2 Limitations
Description of the model	Strength 1	Limitation 1
	Strength 2	Limitation 2
	Strength 3	Limitation 3

1 **Assumption 1:** All behaviour is learned through experience, and abnormal behaviour is no different in this respect from normal behaviour. We can use the principles of classical and operant conditioning to explain all behaviour, therefore these principles also apply to the acquisition of abnormal behaviour.
Assumption 2: Behaviourists assume that the mind is an unnecessary concept, only behaviour is important. It is therefore sufficient to explain behaviour in terms of what can be observed. There are no such things as mental illnesses, only maladaptive behaviours.

> *In each case useful elaboration of the main point has been provided to make the answers worth 3 marks each.*

2 Behaviourists believe that our actions are determined largely by the experiences we have in life, rather than by underlying pathology or unconscious forces. Abnormality is seen as the development of behaviour patterns that are considered maladaptive for the individual. Such patterns develop through classical and operant conditioning, or through observational learning. Most learned behaviours are adaptive, helping people to lead happy and productive lives, but maladaptive (and therefore undesirable) behaviours can be acquired in the same way. When determining treatment for abnormal behaviour, behaviourists believe that we need only concern ourselves with a person's actions – there is no need to search for the mind or analyse thoughts and feelings.

> *You can use details about treatment methods as part of the description of the model, as has been done here.*

3 **Assumption:** All behaviour is learned through experience, and abnormal behaviour is no different in this respect from normal behaviour. We can use the principles of classical and operant conditioning to explain all behaviour, therefore these principles also apply to the acquisition of abnormal behaviour.
Criticism: The simplicity of the model makes it easy to conduct research to test how association and rewards affect behaviour. An example of such research can be seen in experimental studies (such as Little Albert) that have shown how abnormal behaviours can be learned, giving support to the model.

4 **Assumption 1:** The cognitive model assumes that thinking, expectations and attitudes direct behaviour. Mental illness is the result of disordered thinking. The issue is not the problem itself but the way you *think* about it. Faulty and irrational thinking prevents the individual behaving adaptively.
Assumption 2: In other models of abnormality, the prevailing view is that an individual's behaviour is controlled by forces outside one's own control – physiological, genetic, unconscious or environmental factors. The cognitive model portrays the individual as being in control because the individual controls their own thoughts. Abnormality, therefore, is faulty control.

> *Only two assumptions have been covered here but the elaboration of each of these provides plenty of detail for a 6 mark answer.*

5 The cognitive model assumes that thinking, expectations and attitudes direct behaviour. Mental illness is the result of disordered thinking. Faulty and irrational thinking prevents the individual behaving adaptively. The cognitive model portrays the individual as being in control because the individual controls their own thoughts. Abnormality, therefore, is faulty control. It follows that if mental illness is the result of disordered thinking, then what needs to be changed is the way you think. This can be done by challenging belief systems and changing self-beliefs and motivations. It follows from the assumption that behaviour is self-controlled, that the client needs to be actively involved in therapy.

6 **Assumption:** The cognitive model assumes that thinking, expectations and attitudes direct behaviour. Mental illness is the result of disordered thinking. The issue is not the problem itself but the way you *think* about it. Faulty and irrational thinking prevents the individual behaving adaptively.
Criticism: It is not clear which comes first. Do thoughts and beliefs really cause disturbance, or does mental disorder lead to faulty thinking? It may be that, for example, a depressed individual develops a negative way of thinking *because* of their depression rather than the other way around.

A01 Description	A02 Strengths	A02 Limitations
See response to question 2	The simplicity of the model makes it easy to conduct research to test how association and rewards affect behaviour. Experimental studies (such as Little Albert) have shown how abnormal behaviours can be learned, giving support to the model.	Learning theory can account for some aspects of normal and abnormal behaviour, but much of human behaviour is more complex than this. The way we *think* about things affects our experiences, yet behaviourism disregards thoughts and emotions as causes of abnormal behaviour.
	Behavioural therapies have been found to be effective for behaviours such as phobias. These therapies have the advantage of being quick and requiring little effort from the client.	Behavioural therapies may not work with certain disorders because the symptoms are only the tip of the iceberg. If the symptoms are removed, the cause still remains, and the symptoms will simply resurface, possibly in another form (symptom substitution).
	Behavioural explanations are clearly part of the story, but it is likely that a more complete explanation involves a combination of learning theory, biological explanations plus elements from the other models.	A problem arises over who chooses what would be 'more desirable' behaviour? In the past, homosexuals have been subjected to behavioural therapy because others felt that their behaviour was abnormal. This is clearly not acceptable.

End of section review

Sample exam question

a. Outline **two** assumptions of the cognitive model in relation to the causes of abnormality. *(3 marks + 3 marks)*

b. Give **two** criticisms of the psychodynamic model of abnormality. *(3 marks + 3 marks)*

c. 'For many psychologists the biological model offers the best explanation of abnormality and the best form of treatment.'

Outline and evaluate the biological (medical) model of abnormality. *(18 marks)*

See page viii for an explanation of how questions are marked.

Student answer	Examiner's comments
(a) The cognitive model of abnormality assumes that abnormality is something within our thinking. A phobia would be considered abnormal yet not for the sufferer who has irrational thoughts about the phobia, e.g. bees, water or fear of heights. The cognitive model also assumes that an injury to the brain can cause abnormality.	Most candidates find the cognitive model more difficult than the other models of abnormality. The first assumption is appropriate to the cognitive model and there is an attempt to link this to causes but it is lacking clarity. The second assumption is wrong, thus **2/3 + 0/3 marks.**
(b) The first criticism is a positive one. Freud's explanation of abnormality has been very influential. He introduced the idea that physical symptoms could be explained in terms of psychological causes. Many of his explanations have become so much part of our culture that we are not even aware of them, such as unconsciously motivated behaviour. The second criticism is that there was too much emphasis on sex in his theory, for example suggesting that certain adult behaviours were due to too much oral satisfaction. This may have been more appropriate at the time he was writing because sex was repressed and it may have motivated behaviour. Today people are not so repressed.	Both criticisms are appropriate and detailed and therefore deserve full marks = **3/3 + 3/3 marks**. Notice how in each case the criticism is named and then explained by referring to aspects of the theory. Finally there is an attempt to explain or interpret the positive or negative criticism (i.e. the three-point rule).
(c) The biological model of abnormality believes that abnormality is caused by physical problems. It is a physical illness and therefore should be treated medically. However, this is not always the case. All abnormality cannot be caused physically as in the case of Anna O. There was no physical reason why she could not drink, she was just unable to because of problems in her unconscious. On the other hand, the biological approach can sometimes be right. The medical model focuses on genetics, neuroanatomy and psychosurgery as a treatment. One study found that concordance rates for anorexia in identical twins was 55% compared with 7% in non-identical twins. This shows that genetics can sometimes be a factor in abnormality. But if it was the only factor then concordance rates would be 100%. The biological model also more or less rules out individual differences. It assumes that everyone is the same in their physiology. This is not a good idea. [158 words]	The first paragraph consists of some description and some evaluation. The second paragraph is mainly descriptive even though it starts with 'on the other hand'. The last two sentences of this paragraph are effective commentary. The final paragraph is reasonably effective commentary though somewhat superficial. This makes the AO1 content rather limited, worth a generous **3/6 marks for AO1** as it is not muddled or flawed. The commentary is a mixture of 'effective' and only 'reasonably effective' but overall is basic in its scope, so perhaps a harsh **5/12 marks for AO2**, a total of **8/18 marks**.
	Total for whole question is **16 marks,** probably equivalent to a Grade C.

COGNITIVE PSYCHOLOGY:
HUMAN MEMORY

DEVELOPMENTAL PSYCHOLOGY:
ATTACHMENTS IN DEVELOPMENT

PHYSIOLOGICAL PSYCHOLOGY:
STRESS

INDIVIDUAL DIFFERENCES:
ABNORMALITY

SOCIAL PSYCHOLOGY:
SOCIAL INFLUENCE

RESEARCH
METHODS

Biological explanations of eating disorders

Some candidates are not clear about the difference between a characteristic of anorexia and a *clinical* characteristic of anorexia. Only the latter will receive marks. Don't make the mistake of saying that anorexia is a loss of 85% of body weight – it is loss of 15% or more of one's body weight *or* a drop below 85% of the individual's normal weight.

🖊🖊🖊🖊🖊🖊🖊🖊🖊🖊

Specification extract
The clinical characteristics of anorexia nervosa and bulimia nervosa. Explanations of eating disorders in terms of biological models of abnormality, including research studies on which these explanations are based.

In order to provide sufficient detail you need to go beyond statements such as 'poor body image' and elaborate these by, for example, mentioning cognitive/perceptual disturbances in body image.

Some candidates answer this question by listing the characteristics of each without addressing the requirement to describe *differences*.

Some candidates give more than one answer, in which case only the best one is credited. Some candidates present too much detail on symptoms though these can be linked to an explanation.

research methods
Q

a) *Explain what is meant by qualitative data.*

b) *What is the difference between qualitative data and quantitative data?*

A study of anorexia involves interviewing ten young girls about their eating habits.

c) *Identify **one** way a researcher might analyse this data.*

d) *Describe this method in detail.*

Learning how to present and explain criticisms is very important preparation for **AO1/AO2** questions.

Sometimes candidates find it difficult to think of enough to write about the aims of the study – what was it that the researcher wanted to test? In other words, what was the hypothesis?

Weak answers provide general reviews of research with no identifiable studies. Remember the **three-point rule** when writing criticisms.

The AO1 component will be a description of research supporting the biological model. This can be theory (explanations) or studies. Studies may be used as AO1 or can be used as a means of evaluating (AO2) explanations *if* an appropriate link is made (e.g. 'This shows that …'). Psychological explanations can also be used as evaluation but again description would not be creditworthy; there is only credit for the extent to which they inform us about the value of the biological approach. Again effective links must be made. Evaluation can also be achieved by examining facts/arguments, such as the fact that the incidence of anorexia has increased in recent years and is found mainly in women of teenage years.

Make sure you write only about findings here and not about procedures or conclusions.

Possible plan

	AO1 Description	**AO2** Commentary on research	**AO2** Conclusion relating to whether or not it is a biological disorder
Theory/study 1			
Theory/study 2			
Theory/study 3			

AO1 questions

1. Outline **three** clinical characteristics of anorexia nervosa. *(2 marks + 2 marks + 2 marks)*

2. Outline **three** clinical characteristics of bulimia nervosa. *(2 marks + 2 marks + 2 marks)*

3. Describe **three** differences in the clinical characteristics of anorexia nervosa and bulimia nervosa. *(2 marks + 2 marks + 2 marks)*

4. Describe **one** biological explanation of eating disorders. *(6 marks)*

5. Give **two** criticisms of the explanation that you have outlined in question 3. *(3 marks + 3 marks)*

6. Describe the aims and procedures of **one** study into biological explanations of eating disorders. *(6 marks)*

7. Describe the findings of **one** study into biological explanations of eating disorders and give **one** criticism of this study. *(6 marks)*

8. Outline findings of research into biological explanations of eating disorders. *(6 marks)*

AO1/AO2 question

'It may well be that eating disorders are biological rather than psychological disorders.' To what extent does research (theories **and/or** studies) support the view that eating disorders have biological explanations? *(18 marks)*

1
- People with anorexia are not simply obsessed with weight but fearful of weight gain.
- Weight loss is considered abnormal when it drops below 85% of the individual's normal level, based on age and height.
- People with anorexia do not see their own thinness. They often continue to see themselves as fat despite the fact that their bones can be clearly seen.

It is sometimes a good idea to use bullet lists, as long as you don't just use a few words for each bullet point.

2
People with bulimia engage in recurrent episodes of secret binge eating. Bingeing involves eating an excessive amount of food within a short period of time and feeling a lack of control over eating during the episode.

Some candidates are confused about which characteristics belong with anorexia and which belong with bulimia.

After bingeing the individual with bulimia is likely to purge themselves to compensate for the overindulgence and in order to prevent weight gain.

In order to be diagnosed as suffering from bulimia, an individual should have been displaying binge eating and inappropriate compensatory behaviours, on average, at least twice a week for three months.

3
Difference 1: Extent of weight loss – in anorexia, the patient is severely underweight, whereas in bulimia they are slightly underweight or near normal weight.

Difference 2: Use of purging – in anorexia, the patient purges to maintain low weight whereas in bulimia, they purge to compensate for overeating.

Note the clear focus on differences as required by the question.

Difference 3: Maturity – in anorexia, the patient is more immature and likely to reject the feminine role, whereas in bulimia they are more mature and more likely to be sexually active.

4
It is possible that people with anorexia have problems with their neuroanatomy – both the hypothalamus and the hippocampus may be involved.

The hypothalamus is involved in the control of hunger – part of the hypothalamus produces feelings of hunger (the lateral hypothalamus, LH) whilst another part suppresses hunger (the ventromedial hypothalamus, VMH). If the LH is damaged the result is undereating because no feelings of hunger are produced and the VMH continues to send signals to suppress hunger. Prolonged stress leads to shrinkage of the hippocampus. The smaller the hippocampus, the more stress hormones are released. The more stress hormones released, the smaller the hippocampus may become. This could explain why people with anorexia get stuck in a vicious cycle and can't start eating again despite a desire to do so.

There are a number of other biological explanations but this one (the neuroanatomical explanation) is good because there is lots to say.

5
Criticism 1: Research has tended to rely on very small samples. Even in these small groups, there are individual differences (e.g. not all people with anorexia have a shrunken hippocampus). This means that no one biological mechanism has been pinpointed as the source of the disorder.

Criticism 2: Increasing research in this area is beginning to indicate which biological differences do exist between people with anorexia and normal individuals, which may explain why the disorder develops and also why it is so resistant to treatment. If neuroanatomy can be shown to be critical, then successful drug therapies could be developed.

6
A study into biological explanations of eating disorders (Kendler *et al.*, 1991).

Aims: Kendler *et al.* aimed to establish whether the increased incidence of bulimia nervosa in families was due to genetic or environmental

It is useful for you and for the examiner to identify the different parts of your answer.

research methods **A**

a) Qualitative data is data that expresses what people think or feel. Such data cannot be counted or quantified.

b) Quantitative data is concerned with 'how much' (i.e. quantities), whereas qualitative data is data that expresses what people think or feel.

c) The interviewer could use thematic analysis.

d) Themes or concepts (such as binge eating or refusing meals) are identified before starting the research. Then responses from an interview or questionnaire are organised according to the themes.

factors by comparing the incidence of bulimia in identical (MZ) and non-identical (DZ) twins, and so disentangle the relative causal influences of genes and environment.

Procedures: The study contacted over 1,000 pairs of twins (2,000 individuals) by using data from the Virginia twin registry. All twins were interviewed by trained interviewers. The same interviewer never interviewed both members of a twin pair.

7
A study into biological explanations of eating disorders (Kendler *et al.*, 1991).

Findings: In MZ twins there was 26% concordance for bulimia between twin pairs and 16% for DZ twins. Of the sample interviewed, there were 123 cases of bulimia. Most of these participants also reported other mental disorders at some time in their lives including anorexia (10% of them), depression (51%), phobia (42%) and anxiety disorder (11%).

Extra detail can be provided by any relevant elaboration of the main point, as has been done here.

Criticism: There may be reasons why twins are more prone to mental illness than non-twins and therefore the findings may not generalise to the rest of the population. It is possible that twins experience more stress or that they are genetically more vulnerable.

8
Holland *et al.* (1988) found significantly higher concordance rates for anorexia in MZ twins than in DZ twins. There was significantly more anorexia in relatives studied than found in the normal population. The measures of body mass, amenorrhea, drive to be thin, and body dissatisfaction indicated that these were heritable as there was greater similarity between MZ than DZ twins. Kendler *et al.* (1991) studied bulimia and found that in MZ twins there was 26% concordance between twin pairs and 16% for DZ twins. Of the sample interviewed, there were 123 cases of bulimia. Most of these participants also reported other mental disorders at some time in their lives including anorexia (10% of them), depression (51%), phobia (42%) and anxiety disorder (11%).

There are a lot of big words in this answer. Do not feel you have to provide such exact terms in order to get 6 marks but we thought it was preferable to include them here.

AO1 Description	AO2 Commentary	AO2 Conclusion
Holland *et al.* (1988) – see response to question 8 above	It may be that MZ twins are treated more similarly and this makes their environment more similar than DZ twins' environment. This would explain higher concordance rates for MZ twins compared to DZ twins.	The findings suggest that anorexia has a large genetic component. The figure of heritability may be as large as 80%. This high figure may be partly explained in terms of how genetic factors interact with the environment. What is inherited is a genetic sensitivity to environmental factors.
Kendler *et al.* (1991) – see response to question 8 above	There may be reasons why twins are more prone to mental illness than non-twins and therefore the findings may not generalise to the rest of the population. It is possible that twins experience more stress or that they are genetically more vulnerable.	This study suggests a reasonable genetic component in bulimia; however there appears to be a lower genetic influence than for anorexia. In contrast Bulik *et al.* (2000) concluded that bulimia is 83% genetically influenced and anorexia nervosa is 58% genetic, suggesting a greater genetic component for bulimia.
Lambe *et al.* (1997) found that people with anorexia whose weight returned to normal had reduced amounts of grey matter in their brain (which would impair their thinking abilities).	Becker *et al.* (2000) found a strong link between exposure to Western ideals of thinness and changed attitudes towards eating. This suggests that eating disorders are fundamentally psychosocial rather than biological in origin.	Research strongly supports biological explanations of eating disorders but psychological factors have a role to play as well as described by the diathesis–stress model.

Psychological explanations of eating disorders

Specification extract
Explanations of these eating disorders in terms of psychological models of abnormality, including research studies on which these explanations are based.

a) What is special about the clinical method?

b) Why is it called the 'clinical method'?

Candidates who give behavioural explanations often confuse classical and operant conditioning, and fail to specify the mechanisms in media influences (vicarious reinforcement).
Reference to research findings is an effective way of gaining greater detail/depth.

One way to provide a positive criticism is to think of an application of the explanation. A prime purpose of any research (theory or study) is to find ways to improve human lives – so applications are important.

There are two ways you could slip up here – only *aims and procedures* are required, and *psychological* not biological explanations.

There is no need here to worry about what will count as findings or conclusions because both are creditworthy in this question. If you don't have enough for 6 marks'-worth of material, don't be tempted to slip a few criticisms in, these won't be creditworthy.

Remember the **three-point rule**.

You may draw on the findings of one study only but this is not likely to be a very successful strategy. It is better to cover a variety of findings in detail to get 6 marks'-worth of material.

If you are unsure what to write for conclusions you can use what you know about findings to provide a springboard to conclusions. Think of what the findings mean, for example, in the real world.

It would be perfectly acceptable to focus on explanations of anorexia nervosa or of bulimia nervosa, or to cover both. You do not need to specify whether the explanation specifically relates to anorexia or bulimia. You should remember the formula AO1 = one-third, AO2 = two-thirds when constructing your response to this question. It is probably best to concentrate on just two explanations here, as the amount of detail you can include in each is fairly restricted.

Possible plan

	AO1 Outline of psychological explanations	**AO2** Commentary on explanations
Explanation 1		
Explanation 2		

AO1 questions

1. Describe **one** psychological explanation of eating disorders. *(6 marks)*

2. Give **two** criticisms of the explanation that you have outlined in question 1. *(3 marks + 3 marks)*

3. Describe the aims and procedures of **one** study into psychological explanations of eating disorders. *(6 marks)*

4. Describe the findings and conclusions of **one** study into psychological explanations of eating disorders. *(6 marks)*

5. Give **two** criticisms of the study that you described in question 4. *(3 marks + 3 marks)*

6. Describe the findings of research into psychological explanations of eating disorders. *(6 marks)*

7. Describe the conclusions of research into psychological explanations of eating disorders. *(6 marks)*

AO1/AO2 question

Outline **one or more** psychological explanations of eating disorders. *(18 marks)*

1 Many people with eating disorders report abuse in childhood. McLelland *et al.* (1991) found that 30% of patients with eating disorders had reported abuse in childhood. Such experiences may be repressed and then expressed through the symptoms of bulimia. Bulimia is a means of punishing the body, and expressing self-disgust. The notion of bulimia as a coping mechanism could explain gender differences because, it could be argued, females are taught to be self-critical whereas males are taught to blame others. Thus an abused female turns the blame inwards and is more likely to develop bulimia. An abused male becomes hostile towards others and is less likely to develop bulimia.

> *One common weakness when providing a psychodynamic explanation is failing to explain why a person might want to repress things.*

2 **Criticism 1:** By no means all people with bulimia have experienced abuse, therefore this cannot explain all cases. And even in cases where an individual has suffered abuse, focus on this may distract attention away from other important factors.
Criticism 2: Equally, issues of merger and autonomy are not apparent in all people with bulimia. This suggests that psychodynamic explanations may only be relevant to certain individuals.

3 A study into psychological explanations of eating disorders (Cutts and Barrios, 1986).
Aims: Many researchers have suggested that fear of weight gain underlies both anorexia and bulimia yet few have tested this belief empirically. This study aims to investigate whether fear of weight gain is more prevalent in people with bulimia than in 'normal' controls.
Procedures: Thirty females aged 18–25 were assigned to a 'bulimic' or the control group on the basis of questionnaires and interviews. They listened to two descriptions: one of a neutral scene and one depicting weight gain. Both scenes were described by a man, and participants were asked to imagine themselves in this situation. Their accompanying physiological responses were recorded by measuring facial muscle activity, heart rate and skin resistance. They were also asked to report their own reactions using a self-report checklist.

> *It is useful to identify the different parts of your answer so that you ensure you answer the question and the examiner can clearly see the key parts of your answer.*

4 A study into psychological explanations of eating disorders (Cutts and Barrios, 1986).
Findings: Both groups of participants showed similar responses to the neutral scene but different responses to the weight gain scene. People with bulimia had higher physiological activity when imagining the weight gain. They also reported greater subjective distress and their overt behaviour was rated as showing higher levels of stress.
Conclusions: The findings support the view that fear of weight gain may be a factor in bulimia. Such faulty perceptions could trigger biological responses and/or a behavioural cycle of reinforcement. If an individual fears weight gain, he or she diets and starvation leads to changes in neurotransmitters. If an individual starts dieting and loses weight, this leads to increased attention and attractiveness, encouraging further weight control.

5 **Criticism 1:** The concept of faulty cognitions may also offer us a form of treatment for the disorder (by dealing with fear of weight gain) and also may

a) It is special because it is a semi-structured approach (rather than a structured or unstructured interview). The questions start off as pre-determined (and easily codeable) and then become freer. 'Freer' questions usually require qualitative analysis.

b) It is 'clinical' because it's the kind of method used by doctors and clinicians when interviewing patients.

offer ideas about how to detect potential people with bulimia (by using checklists of faulty cognitions). This is a benefit of this research.
Criticism 2: It may be that certain personality characteristics co-vary with faulty perceptions. For example, an individual who holds maladaptive assumptions may also have a more rigid cognitive style. It could be the rigid cognitive style rather than the faulty perceptions that is the cause of bulimia. This means the conclusion drawn is mistaken.

> *One of the lofty aspirations of psychological research is to produce solutions to problems, so considering applications of research is an excellent way to make a positive critical point.*

6 Sui-Wah (1989) reported that anorexia is rare in black populations in Western and non-Western cultures, and in China. Hoek *et al.* (1998) examined the records of 44,192 people admitted to hospital between 1987 and 1989 in Curacao, a non-Westernised Caribbean island, and found only six cases of anorexia. Becker *et al.* (2000) found that following the introduction of television in Fiji, girls' attitudes to eating changed significantly. Girls were now more likely to report that they vomited to control weight, and a higher proportion gained a high score on an eating questionnaire, indicating risk of disordered eating. When interviewed, many of the girls said they wanted to look like the girls on TV.

7 Becker *et al.*'s findings indicate a strong link between exposure to Western ideals of thinness and changed attitudes towards eating. The girls' desire to be slim is one sign that young Fijians are striving to conform to Western cultural standards. These changed attitudes are likely to lead to the development of eating disorders such as anorexia. This study supports the view that the media introduces social norms, which contribute to increases in anorexia. Nasser (1988) reviewed a number of cross-cultural studies and concluded that increases in eating disorders are positively associated with increased Westernisation. Identification with Western norms leads to an increase in weight consciousness and risk of developing eating disorders. This suggests that eating disorders are fundamentally psychosocial rather than biological in origin.

> *If you are describing what happened to the participants, then you are describing findings. If you are making generalisations about people's behaviour, then you are (probably) describing conclusions.*

	AO1 Outline	AO2 Commentary
Explanation 1	In the behaviourist explanation, dieting and the quest for thinness may be seen as a habit, with the individual associating thinness with the admiration of others or with feelings of positive well-being. A person may strive to achieve the 'idealised' body that they see modelled in the media through dieting and exercise. As body weight drops below a critical point, eating disorders such as anorexia nervosa may be triggered.	The behavioural view is appealing because it can explain many observed facts. It can explain gender differences (female stereotypes more associated with dieting and thinness), increased rates of anorexia in males (male thinness stereotypes are increasing), increased rates of anorexia in general (due to increasing emphasis on thinness), and cultural differences (different attitudes to eating and different social norms). However, the behavioural model cannot explain individual differences. All of us in the West are exposed to thin models but very few develop anorexia. Equally many people diet but very few develop anorexia. This means that behavioural explanations on their own are insufficient. It may require the addition of one of the other biological and/or psychological explanations to account for the development of the disorder in particular individuals.
Explanation 2	According to the cognitive model, an individual with anorexia is preoccupied with the way he or she looks – or thinks they look. People with anorexia often perceive themselves as unattractive and/or overweight. Only those with faulty belief systems are affected because they don't 'see' their excessive weight loss.	Distorted cognitions may be an effect rather than a cause of the illness. However, as with the other explanations, once an individual develops faulty cognitions one can see how these would help perpetuate the disorder. One strength of the cognitive approach is that it has the potential to lead to useful therapies, enabling clients to tackle self-defeating statements and therefore start eating again. Garner and Bemis (1982) point out that whatever the cause, the end result appears to be the desire to become thin. It is this cognition that should be the focus of therapy.

End of section review

Sample exam question

a. Explain what is meant by anorexia nervosa and bulimia nervosa. *(3 marks + 3 marks)*

b. Outline **two** assumptions of the psychodynamic model in relation to the causes of abnormality. *(3 marks + 3 marks)*

c. 'No single explanation of eating disorders can account for all the facts.'

With reference to **one or more** explanations of eating disorders, consider to what extent such explanations can account for the facts. *(18 marks)*

Note that this entire question has been drawn from *different* sections of the module on abnormality. This is acceptable. It is also acceptable to set an entire question on one section only.

See page viii for an explanation of how questions are marked.

Student answer	Examiner's comments
a) Anorexia and bulimia are both eating disorders. Anorexia is a disorder where the person is abnormally thin (less than 85% of normal body weight) and obsessive about not eating. A bulimic is less obsessive and maintains a low weight through purging after periods of bingeing. They usually have distorted perception.	A brief answer but accurate and sufficiently detailed for full marks, **3/3 + 3/3 marks**.
(b) An assumption of Freud's psychodynamic model is that if psychosexual development does not proceed smoothly, we can become fixated at one stage of development (such as the anal stage). This might happen if the child is exposed to a very strict toilet training regime. This might then result in obsessive behaviour later in life. Someone who is well adjusted has a good balance between the demands of their id and their superego. If these are in conflict, however, the person may become psychologically disturbed.	The first of these assumptions contains enough relevant information and is described with sufficient accuracy that it is worth full marks. The candidate does attempt to elaborate their answer by giving an appropriate example of the link between fixation and later abnormality. The second assumption lacks detail, but does indicate that an imbalance between id and superego may be damaging. This lacks clarity and although sufficient for 2 marks, it would not be sufficient for 3. The rather high marks also reflect the fact that the candidate has really tried to answer the question set rather than simply trotting out spurious detail about Freudian theory without tying it to an understanding of the causes of abnormal behaviour. Overall **3/3 + 2/3 marks**.
(c) Cultural pressures may influence the development of anorexia. People see lots of images of young, slim and beautiful girls in the media, and think that they also have to be like that. As a result they start slimming, and then the slimming gets out of hand. Once they drop below 85% of their ideal body weight then anorexia takes over. Another psychological explanation is that women may develop a weight phobia. This means they become fearful of putting on weight and so do everything they can to avoid getting fat. This is also linked to the images portrayed in the media. Psychoanalytic explanations of anorexia explain it in terms of ineffective parenting and the relationship that a girl has with her parents (particularly her mother). There are three different themes in psychoanalytic explanations of anorexia. Firstly, anorexia may be symptomatic of a desire to stay a child. In this way the anorexic could avoid the responsibilities of adulthood and the fears of sexual maturity. A second form of psychoanalytic explanation is that some parents are extremely controlling and the anorexic can control her body weight through dieting. This gives her at least some control over her life. Biological explanations of anorexia concentrate on the role of parts of the brain (hypothalamus). This controls eating and in anorexics there is the possibility that it might be damaged. Genetic explanations for anorexia claim that it runs in families and that if one twin becomes anorexic, there would be a high chance that the other one would as well. [256 words]	There is such a lot here, yet not one single evaluative comment is made. There is a great danger that questions such as this are seen (as here) as simply an invitation to write everything you know about explanations of eating disorders. This candidate has tried to cram as many different explanations as they can into the time available (not a particularly effective technique at the best of times). They have totally ignored the need to provide AO2 material, therefore **6/6 marks for AO1** and **0/12 marks for AO2**, a **total of 6/18 marks**.
	Total for whole question is **17/30 marks**, equivalent to a weak Grade B, possibly a Grade C.

SOCIAL PSYCHOLOGY: SOCIAL INFLUENCE

Social psychology is the study of social behaviour, which occurs when two or more members of the same species interact. Social psychology may be concerned with how people influence each other's behaviour (social influence) or about how our thoughts influence our social behaviour (social cognition).

This module is divided into

Majority and minority influence

Majority influence

Minority influence

End of section review

Obedience to authority

Obedience to authority

Resistance to obedience

Issues of validity

End of section review

Critical issue: Ethics in psychological research

Ethical issues

Dealing with ethical issues

End of section review

COGNITIVE PSYCHOLOGY: HUMAN MEMORY

DEVELOPMENTAL PSYCHOLOGY: ATTACHMENTS IN DEVELOPMENT

PHYSIOLOGICAL PSYCHOLOGY: STRESS

INDIVIDUAL DIFFERENCES: ABNORMALITY

SOCIAL PSYCHOLOGY: SOCIAL INFLUENCE

RESEARCH METHODS

Majority influence

Poor answers tend to be circular, for example 'majority influence is the influence of the majority'. This does not demonstrate any psychological knowledge or understanding and would receive no marks.

Specification extract

Research studies into majority (conformity) influence. Explanations of why people yield to majority influence.

The two most obvious studies are Asch and Zimbardo, but often candidates use the latter without making it clear in what way this is a study of conformity. If you use it as a study of conformity, you must make clear how it demonstrates conformity (to social roles). If you don't, you will score zero.
Candidates who write about Sherif and the autokinetic effect often provide a very muddled account of this study.

research methods Q

a) Give **two** reasons why researchers conduct debriefing.

b) What are standardised instructions and why are they used?

c) What are standardised procedures and why are they used?

Some candidates write about aims and conclusions anyway!

Most candidates can identify two criticisms though these often tend to be rather general and candidates are not able to apply them to the specific study. Remember the **three-point rule**.

Research on minority influence will gain no credit.

Remember that research can be theory or studies, so you could write about the conclusions of a 'theory' related to conformity, i.e. an explanation of why people conform.

Some candidates identify normative influence and then say 'as in Asch's study'. You need to say more than this in order for credit to be given. *How* does Asch's study illustrate normative influence?

The AO1 component of this question is straightforward, simply a matter of describing any aspect of research on conformity. For the AO2 marks, you need to look at the validity of any studies that you described. This can be internal validity (e.g. to what extent was the study well controlled?) or external validity (e.g. to what extent can we generalise the findings of this study to other settings or other people?).
It is perfectly acceptable to concentrate on different studies carried out by the same researcher; in this case the different variations in Asch's research would count as different 'studies'.

AO1 questions

1. Explain what is meant by majority (conformity) influence. *(3 marks)*

2. Describe the aims and conclusions of **one** study that has investigated majority (conformity) influence. *(6 marks)*

3. Describe the procedures and findings of **one** study that has investigated majority (conformity) influence. *(6 marks)*

4. Give **two** criticisms of the study that you described in question 2. *(3 marks + 3 marks)*

5. Outline findings of research into majority (conformity) influence. *(6 marks)*

6. Outline conclusions of research into majority (conformity) influence. *(6 marks)*

7. Outline **two** reasons why people yield to majority influence. *(3 marks + 3 marks)*

AO1/AO2 question

Outline research studies of majority (conformity) influence and consider whether these are valid. *(18 marks)*

Possible plan

	AO1 Description	**AO2** Comment on high or low validity	**AO2** Evidence to support comment
Study 1			
Study 2			

1 Majority influence is a form of social influence that results from exposure to the majority position. It is the tendency for people to adopt the behaviour, attitudes and values of other members of a reference group.

2 A study of majority influence (Asch, 1956).
Aims: The aim of this study was to find out how people would behave when given an unambiguous task. Would they be influenced by the behaviour of others, or would they stick firmly to what they knew to be right? How much conformity to majority influence would there be?

> It is acceptable to include, under the heading of 'aims', some of the research questions that Asch set out to answer.

Conclusions: The findings show a surprisingly strong tendency to conform to group pressures in a situation where the answer is clear. For Asch the important finding was that there was any conformity at all. However, Asch pointed out that there was clear evidence of resisting pressure to conform.

3 A study of majority influence (Asch, 1956).
Procedures: In total 123 male American undergraduates were tested. Asch showed a series of lines (the 'standard' line and the possible answers) to participants seated around a table. All but one of the participants were confederates of the researcher. The confederates were instructed to give the same incorrect answer on 12 critical trials. In total there were 18 trials with each participant. The true participant was the last or last but one to answer.
Findings: On the critical trials, 36.8% of the responses made by true participants were incorrect, i.e. conformed to the incorrect response given by the unanimous confederates.
Twenty-five per cent of the participants never gave a wrong answer; thus 75% conformed at least once. To confirm that the stimulus lines were unambiguous, Asch conducted a control trial with no confederates giving wrong answers. Asch found that people do make mistakes about 1% of the time.

4 A study of majority influence (Asch, 1956).
Criticism 1: Asking people to judge the length of the lines is a rather insignificant task and one where participants would probably be willing to conform to save face. On a more important task we would expect conformity levels to drop.
Criticism 2: It is possible that these findings are particular to one culture. The participants were all men, all American and the research was conducted in America in the 1950s, the era of McCarthyism, a highly conformist society, which may account for the findings in this study.

5 Asch (1956) found that on critical conformity trials, 36.8% of the responses made by true participants were incorrect, i.e. they conformed to the incorrect response given by the unanimous confederates. Twenty-five per cent of Asch's participants never gave a wrong answer; thus 75% conformed at least once. Perrin and Spencer (1980) repeated Asch's study in England in the late 1970s but found only one student conformed on 396 trials. However, when they used youths on probation as the participants, they found similar levels of majority influence to Asch. Burger and Cooper (1979) investigated the desire for personal control and found that those participants who measured high on desire for personal control were less likely to rate cartoons in the same way as a confederate.

> In answering this question, it is acceptable either to write about several different aspects of the same study (e.g. Asch), or to include brief findings of more than one study, as here.

6 Asch's study showed a surprisingly strong tendency to conform to group pressures in a situation where the answer is clear. For Asch the important finding was that there was any majority influence at all. However, Asch also saw the fact that on two-thirds of the trials his participants had remained independent, as clear evidence of how people could *resist* the pressure to conform. Perrin and Spencer concluded that Asch found such high levels of majority influence because his participants were all men, all American and the research was conducted in America in the 1950s, the era of McCarthyism, a highly conformist time in American history.

> What do each of the findings in the previous question tell us about majority influence? Remember there is an important distinction between findings and conclusions – one is fact, the other is interpretation.

7 **Reason 1:** Normative social influence. If we simply go along with the majority without really accepting their point of view, we are conforming in behaviour alone (compliance). In such cases people might conform out of a desire to be accepted by the group, who may make any deviation from the group position uncomfortable.
Reason 2: Informational social influence. Individuals may go along with the majority because they genuinely believe them to be right or when people are uncertain how to behave. As a result, they may do more than comply in behaviour alone, but also change their point of view in line with the majority viewpoint.

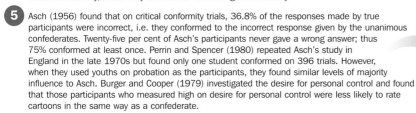

research methods **A**

a) Debriefing is especially vital when participants have been deceived in any way during the experiment.

Debriefing is also useful for finding out if the participant did believe in the original instructions, or whether they were simply 'playing along'.

b) Standardised instructions are a set of instructions that are the same for all participants. These help to avoid investigator effects.

c) Standardised procedures are a set of procedures that are the same for all participants. These enable replication of the study.

AO1 Description	AO2 Comment	AO2 Evidence
Asch (1956) found that on critical majority influence trials, 36.8% of the responses made by true participants were incorrect, i.e. they conformed to the incorrect response given by the unanimous confederates. Twenty-five per cent of Asch's participants never gave a wrong answer; thus 75% conformed at least once.	It is possible that these findings are particular to one culture. The participants were all men, all American and the research was conducted in America in the 1950s, the era of McCarthyism, a highly conformist society, which may account for the findings in this study, thereby threatening its external validity.	This conclusion is supported by the work of Perrin and Spencer (1980), who repeated Asch's study in England in the late 1970s but found only one student conformed on 396 trials. However, when they used youths on probation as the participants, they found similar levels of majority influence to Asch.
Asch (1956) found that the size of the opposing majority did affect conformity – up to a point. He found that as the size of the majority grew, so did the percentage of trials in which the naive participant conformed. There was a high percentage of conformity when a lone dissenter faced a unified majority of three people, but increasing the number of confederates beyond three did not raise conformity levels significantly.	Asking people to judge the length of the lines is a rather insignificant task and one where they would probably be willing to conform to save face. On a more important task we would expect majority influence levels to drop. This would threaten the internal validity of the research – the observed effect cannot be attributed to the experimental manipulation but to other factors.	These findings therefore only tell us about majority influence in special circumstances. For example, Williams and Sogon (1984) tested people who belonged to the same sports club and found that majority influence may be even higher with people you know.

Minority influence

Give the examiner enough material to award 3 marks – examiners want to give marks (honest) but they do need evidence of knowledge *and* understanding.

Specification extract
Research studies into minority influence. Explanations of why people yield to minority influence.

This is an alternative way to ask for an explanation of key terms. It also requires less detail because each component only gets 2 marks.

Some candidates use Milgram's study, displaying a lack of understanding that obedience (responding to a direct order) is different from minority influence (being influenced by the strength of someone's feelings or by their consistency).

Some candidates use the study by Clark (it is given as an example in the specification). They get confused about what actually took place in the study and what was in the film *Twelve Angry Men*.

research methods Q

a) Explain what is meant by demand characteristics.

b) What is an order effect?

c) Give an example of an order effect.

d) What are investigator effects?

Some candidates use the same criticisms every time (e.g. ecological validity and ethics) but sometimes they are not actually a criticism of the study! Take care when just saying 'It lacked ecological validity': maybe the study didn't lack ecological validity.
Some candidates say that a problem in minority influence studies is that they involved only a minority.

Candidates have found this question very difficult, because they didn't appear to know more than a couple of percentages from Moscovici's 'blue and green slide' study. There are more than two findings from this study and there is other research on minority influence.

As 'research' refers to theories as well as studies, it is permissible to report conclusions from research on explanations of minority influence, such as social cryptoamnesia.

Many candidates fail to provide enough detail in their answers to be awarded the full 3 marks.
Many candidates cannot sustain their answer beyond identifying the process (e.g. consistency). This betrays a fundamental lack of understanding about the nature of minority influence.

The term 'research' in this question indicates that you can draw upon both explanations *and* studies for your answer. Remember that research studies can also work effectively as AO2 commentary, so you need to think carefully how you use this material in your answer. Another route is to consider the value of explanations of minority influence. Do they provide useful insight into social influence? Is minority influence harder to explain than majority influence? Are explanations of minority influence more useful?

Possible plan

	AO1 Description	AO2 Commentary
Explanation/study 1		
Explanation/study 2		
Explanation/study 3		

AO1 questions

1. Explain what is meant by minority influence. *(3 marks)*

2. Explain what is meant by the terms majority influence and minority influence and give **one** difference between them.
(2 marks + 2 marks + 2 marks)

3. Describe the aims and conclusions of **one** study that has investigated minority influence. *(6 marks)*

4. Describe the procedures and findings of **one** study that has investigated minority influence. *(6 marks)*

5. Give **two** criticisms of the study that you described in question 4.
(3 marks + 3 marks)

6. Outline findings of research into minority influence.
(6 marks)

7. Outline conclusions of research into minority influence. *(6 marks)*

8. Outline **two** explanations of why people yield to minority influence.
(3 marks + 3 marks)

AO1/AO2 question

Outline and evaluate research (explanations **and/or** studies) into why people yield to minority influence. *(18 marks)*

1 Minority influence is a form of social influence where people reject the established norm of the majority of group members and move to the position of the minority. Minorities who advocate and defend their position consistently create uncertainty among members of the majority, and ultimately this may lead to social change.

2 Minority influence is a form of social influence where people reject the established norm of the majority of group members and move to the position of the minority.
Majority influence is a form of social influence that results from exposure to the majority position, being the tendency for people to adopt the behaviour, attitudes and values of other members of a reference group.
Majority influence tends to involve the need for social approval (normative influence), whereas minority influence involves the need for information about reality (informational influence).

> *Describing a difference requires an explicit comparison between the two forms of social influence rather than just stating definitions of each.*

3 A study of minority influence (Moscovici *et al.*, 1969).
Aims: This study aimed to investigate the process of innovation – the view that social influence occurs not just through conformity (or dependence on the views of others) but through a change to the previously held opinions of a group.
Conclusions: The findings show that minorities can influence majority opinion – not much, but an influence was demonstrated. The third experiment showed that consistency is a key element in this minority influence, because influence fell off sharply when confederates were not consistent. Minority influence was even greater on private opinion than publicly expressed opinion.

4 A study of minority influence (Moscovici *et al.,* 1969).
Procedures: In each of 32 groups of six females, four were real participants and two were confederates. The group was shown 36 blue-coloured slides. The two confederates answered first and second, or first and fourth, and consistently reported that the slides were green. In another part of this experiment, the confederates answered 'green' 24 times and 'blue' 12 times, i.e. they were not consistent.
Findings: Overall the participants agreed with the minority on 8.42% of the trials (i.e. they said the slides were coloured green). Thirty-two percent gave the same answer as the minority at least once. The physical position of the confederate (i.e. the order their responses were given) made no difference. When the confederates were inconsistent, agreement with the minority was reduced to 1.25%.

> *This is an involved study and description of all three 'experiments' would be a tall order. It is fine to focus on just some aspects of the study.*

5 A study of minority influence (Moscovici *et al.*, 1969).
Criticism 1: Since the study involved female undergraduates, we might question how much these results can be generalised. Females have been found to be more conformist than males (or at least have a greater desire to be oriented towards interpersonal goals), so we might expect females to be more affected by minority influence.
Criticism 2: It was necessary to deceive participants about the purpose of the experiment in order to investigate the hypothesis. Participants were told the true purpose at the end of the experiment, which serves to compensate for the deception. As the deception was relatively harmless and the task did not involve undue stress, we might judge this study to be ethically acceptable.

6 In the Moscovici *et al.* study, participants agreed with the minority on 8.42% of the trials (i.e. they said the slides were coloured green). Thirty-two per cent gave the same answer as the minority at least once. The physical position of the confederate (i.e. the order their responses were given) made no difference. When the confederates were inconsistent, agreement with the minority was reduced to 1.25%.
Moscovici and Nemeth (1974) demonstrated that seating position can affect minority influence. When a confederate (in a group of five people) was assigned a seat then position did not matter, but if the confederate chose to sit at the head of the table then he exerted more influence.

7 In the Moscovici *et al.* study, the findings showed that minorities can influence majority opinion – not much, but an influence was demonstrated. The third experiment showed that consistency is a key element in this minority influence because influence fell off sharply when confederates were not consistent. The consistent minority had an even greater influence on private opinion than publicly expressed opinion. Nemeth *et al.* pointed to confidence as a key factor and showed that unreasonable consistency was not effective. Likewise, Mugny (1984) showed that unreasonable confidence was also counterproductive. Moscovici and Nemeth's finding that seating position can affect minority influence shows that where you sit may be as important as what you say, or how consistently/confidently you say it.

8 **Explanation 1:** Social categorisation.
Influence occurs when the minority are members of our 'in-group' – the people we identify with. This in-group provides a group identity and thus exerts a group influence even though they are a minority.

> *You should have enough elaboration to ensure the full 3 marks for each explanation.*

Explanation 2: There is a point in any group where, after some members have started to agree with the minority, the minority then turns into a majority (the snowball effect). The minority position gains power as more people express the same opinion. Eventually minority influence changes to majority influence.

research methods **A**

a) Demand characteristics are features of an experiment that elicit a particular response from participants.

b) In a repeated measures design, an order effect is a confounding variable arising from the order in which conditions are presented.

c) An example of an order effect is a practice effect, i.e. participants do better on condition B because they have already practised on condition A.

d) Investigator effects are unconscious cues from an investigator that encourage certain behaviours from participants, leading to a fulfilment of the investigator's expectations. They include anything the investigator does which has an effect on a participant's performance in a study other than what was intended.

AO1 Description	AO2 Commentary
Description of Moscovici *et al.*'s (1969) study – see answer to question 4	Criticisms – see response to question 5
Maass *et al.* (1982) arranged for a group of 'straight' participants to hear arguments about gay rights. If the minority group were gay, they had less influence on the participants than if they were straight, presumably because the participants were better able to identify with the straight minority and this led to greater influence.	This challenges Moscovici's view that deviant minorities (or out-groups) are fundamental in innovation. As in-group minorities share the same group identity as the majority, they are more likely to succeed in their attempts at social influence. Out-groups, on the other hand, are more likely to be discriminated against and less likely to be influential in changing the minds of the majority (Pennington *et al.*, 1999).
Moscovici and Nemeth (1974) have argued that a *majority* is influential because it is consistent in its position, both among its members and over time. In other words, their position must be right because everyone always goes along with it. Without this consistency, a majority would lose its credibility.	However, flexibility rather than consistency has been found to be more important. Nemeth and Brilmayer (1987) found that a minority of one who refused to change his position had no effect on others, whereas a minority member who changed his opinion and moved in the direction of the majority did exert an influence on majority opinion.

End of section review

Sample exam question

a. Describe the findings of **one** study that has explored minority influence and give **one** criticism. *(3 marks + 3 marks)*

b. Outline **two** reasons why people yield to majority influence. *(3 marks + 3 marks)*

c. Consider whether the findings from research on majority (conformity) influence can justify the methods used to obtain such findings. *(18 marks)*

Note that this entire question has been drawn from the one section (conformity and minority influence). This is acceptable. In other cases questions are drawn from more than one section of the module. It is also acceptable to set an entire question on two or three sections.

See page viii for an explanation o how questions a marked.

Student answer	Examiner's comments
(a) Moscovici is a psychologist who studied minority influence. He found that when the confederates were consistent, and claimed the slides were green, on all the trials there was over 8% conformity of the majority to this view. However, when on 12 of the trials the confederates stated the correct answer, conformity dropped to around 5%. One criticism of this study is that it was an arbitrary task. It was not something of any great importance to the participants, so they wouldn't feel as strongly about resisting conformity.	The first finding is accurate and detailed (8% is close enough to the actual figure of 8.42%). The second finding is very muddled, but positive marking means that we ignore this and award **2/3 marks** for the first finding. The criticism is appropriate but needs a bit more detail. In what sense was it an 'arbitrary' task? The participants were not resisting 'conformity' but minority influence, thus **2/3 marks**.
(b) The two reasons why people yield to majority influence are first to fit in and be accepted by the group. Conforming makes their lives easier. They don't necessarily change their views but just want to avoid ridicule. The second reason is when someone is unsure of their opinion or about what fork to use. The group provides information. This may lead to a change of opinion.	Both explanations are accurate but the full 3 marks require the extra detail that would be provided by saying normative and informational influence, respectively. **2/3 + 2/3 marks**.
(c) Zimbardo used deception in his research, which the participants weren't very happy about. He didn't tell them they would be arrested in their homes, but the findings do justify this to some extent. This made the research on conforming to social roles more realistic and probably helped to get better results. Zimbardo had to withdraw all his participants because they went too far into their roles. These results were good because they showed abuse of power. Withdrawal was justified. Asch also used deception in his research, otherwise the study wouldn't have worked. He had to tell the real participants that all the others were also real participants, though they were confederates. He did debrief the participants afterwards. The participants also didn't suffer very much from the deception, so it could be justified, though some of them did dig their nails into their hands and sweated. Perrin and Spencer repeated this study even though they knew what kind of distress it might cause, but this study can be justified because they were investigating whether Asch's study was a child of its time. In conclusion, research into majority influence is unethical but it has clearly produced some very important findings. Good debriefing has ensured that no participants have experienced any long-term damage as a result of taking part in this research, so in this sense it can be justified. [227 words]	AO1 marks are awarded for any description of research that is included. Zimbardo's study is only credited insofar as it relates to majority influence, which it does here. The paragraph on Asch contains almost no description of the study. The **AO1 mark would be 3/6** because it is 'limited' but closer to 'basic' than 'accurate and detailed'. Both of the first two paragraphs contain relevant commentary on Zimbardo's research, indicating how the procedures could be justified. Some comments lack elaboration such as 'withdrawal was justified'. The same applies to Asch's research and there is some confusion as well – the comment about nails and sweating belongs to Milgram's study. The comments on the study by Perrin and Spencer are rather weak. The conclusion is really a repetition of the points already made and therefore receives little credit. **AO2 mark is 7/12** as overall the commentary is just about 'reasonable' rather than 'basic', a total of **10/18 marks**.
	Total for whole question is **18 marks**, equivalent to a Grade B.

This module is divided into

Majority and minority influence

Majority influence

Minority influence

End of section review

Obedience to authority

Obedience to authority

Resistance to obedience

Issues of validity

End of section review

Critical issue: Ethics in psychological research

Ethical issues

Dealing with ethical issues

End of section review

COGNITIVE PSYCHOLOGY:
HUMAN MEMORY

DEVELOPMENTAL PSYCHOLOGY:
ATTACHMENTS IN DEVELOPMENT

PHYSIOLOGICAL PSYCHOLOGY:
STRESS

INDIVIDUAL DIFFERENCES:
ABNORMALITY

SOCIAL PSYCHOLOGY:
SOCIAL INFLUENCE

RESEARCH
METHODS

Obedience to authority

You can use Milgram's research as an effective way to answer this question, but make sure you use it to explain obedience, not to engage in a lengthy description of the study. Don't lose sight of the question you have been asked.

Specification extract
Research studies into obedience to authority. Explanations of why people obey.

You may be asked to explain a term for 3 marks or you may be asked to explain the same term for 2 marks. In the latter case you should reduce the information included in your explanation and use appropriate material for explaining the difference. Don't reuse the same material for the explanations and the difference. If you understand both terms, you should know how they are different.

The greatest danger exists for candidates who know lots and lots about Milgram's procedures and can't resist recording most of them. The very best version will only receive 4 marks (you have to do aims as well), and you probably will restrict the time you have for other questions on the paper.

research methods **Q**

Milgram studied obedience and found that some people stopped when the shocks became intense, others continued to extreme intensity and still others continued to the maximum level.

a) *Would you use a bar chart or a histogram to display this data? Explain your answer.*

b) *How might demand characteristics have affected participants in this study?*

Candidates who include Zimbardo here should take care to discuss the findings and conclusions that relate to obedience rather than conformity.

If you select a criticism such as 'demand characteristics', make sure you know what you are talking about. There is very little credit for just naming the criticism.

Don't get sidetracked and start providing other details such as procedures or criticisms, especially when describing Milgram's findings. You can restrict yourself to this study alone if you know enough findings, or include findings from other studies.

Candidates often miss out on receiving full marks because their answers are unnecessarily brief and lack detail. Or their answers are somewhat speculative, such as 'people obey famous people such as pop stars because they are famous' without any explanation of why or how this might come about.

There are only 6 marks available for AO1 (description) and you must provide details of at least two studies. This means you must restrict your descriptions, probably minimising the procedural details included. The more studies you include, the more material available for evaluation (AO2), though you could use some studies as a form of evaluation.

AO1 questions

1. Explain what is meant by obedience to authority.
   (3 marks)

2. Explain what is meant by the terms majority (conformity) influence and obedience to authority and give **one** difference between them.
   (2 marks + 2 marks + 2 marks)

3. Describe the aims and procedures of **one** study that has investigated obedience to authority. *(6 marks)*

4. Describe the findings and conclusions of **one** study that has explored obedience to authority. *(6 marks)*

5. Give **two** criticisms of the study that you described in question 3.
   (3 marks + 3 marks)

6. Outline findings of research into obedience to authority.
   (6 marks)

7. Outline **two** reasons why people obey.
   (3 marks + 3 marks)

AO1/AO2 question

Outline and evaluate **two or more** studies of obedience to authority. *(18 marks)*

Possible plan

	AO1 Description on methodology	AO2 Commentary	AO2 Comparison with other research findings
Study 1			
Study 2			

1 Obedience refers to a type of social influence whereby somebody acts in response to a direct order from a figure with perceived authority. There is also the implication that the person receiving the order is made to respond in a way that they would not otherwise have done.

The second sentence adds the necessary elaboration to turn this 'definition' into an 'explanation'.

2 Majority influence is a form of social influence that results from exposure to the majority position, being the tendency for people to adopt the behaviour, attitudes and values of other members of a reference group. Obedience refers to a type of social influence whereby somebody acts in response to a direct order from a figure with perceived authority. Majority influence is increased with the size of group and the status of members, whereas obedience is unrelated to group size but is affected by an individual's perceived authority.

3 A study that has investigated obedience to authority (Milgram, 1963). **Aims:** Milgram set out to investigate whether ordinary people will obey a legitimate authority even when required to injure another person, i.e. obedience to unjust authority. He was also interested in situational influences on obedient behaviour.

As with the Moscovici study on the previous spread, this is a very involved study, so you need to select the important details.

Procedures: Milgram recruited 40 male participants by advertising for volunteers for a study of how punishment affects learning. There were two confederates: an experimenter, and a 'learner'. The participant acted as the 'teacher' and was told that he must administer increasingly strong electric shocks to the learner each time he got a question wrong. The learner received his (fake) shocks in silence until they reached 300 volts (very strong shock). At this point he pounded on the wall and then gave no response to the next question. He repeated this at 315 volts and from then on said or did nothing.

4 A study that has investigated obedience to authority (Milgram, 1963). **Findings:** Prior to the actual study, Milgram asked psychology students to say how far they thought participants would go. They estimated that less than 3% would go to the maximum level. The main finding was that 65% of the participants continued to the maximum voltage, far beyond what was marked 'Danger: severe shock'. Only 5 participants (12.5%) stopped at 300 volts, the point when the learner first objected. **Conclusions:** The findings suggest that ordinary people are astonishingly obedient to authority when asked to behave in an inhumane manner. This suggests that it is not evil people who commit evil crimes but ordinary people who are just obeying orders. It appears that an individual's capacity for making independent decisions is suspended under certain situational constraints, namely being given an order by an authority figure.

5 **Criticism 1:** It is possible to explain the unexpectedly high level of obedience in terms of demand characteristics (e.g. the 'prods' to continue). Most people found these hard to resist but this does not mean they would always be so obedient to unjust authority. Subsequent replications showed that obedience rates drop when these demand characteristics are changed.

You could also include commentary on the ethical issues of this study as one or both of the criticisms.

Criticism 2: Individual differences. Some of the participants showed no emotion and were 'happy' to go along with what they were told to do. Others showed clear signs of being very uncomfortable. Some participants stopped relatively early on, whereas a number went all the way.

research methods **A**

a) The x axis would be the level of shocks and the y axis would be the number of people continuing to this point. This means that the x axis would have continuous data, so a histogram would be appropriate.

b) The fact that the experimenter wore a white coat communicated certain expectations to participants, which meant they responded in predictable ways.

6 The main finding in the Milgram (1963) study was that 65% of the participants continued to the maximum voltage, far beyond what was marked 'Danger: severe shock'. Only 5 participants (12.5%) stopped at 300 volts, the point when the learner first objected. Milgram found that the closer the subject was to the teacher, the more likely they were to refuse the experimenter's command. Milgram also discovered that obedience levels were lower when the experimenter was not physically present and gave orders over the phone. Smith and Bond (1993) reviewed a number of studies that replicated Milgram's baseline experiment in different countries. Rates of obedience varied from 85% in Germany to 16% for female Australians.

You could include findings from the one study or findings from different studies, but ensure that you have sufficient detail to gain full marks.

7 **Reason 1:** In Milgram's proximity study, both teacher and learner stayed in the same room, and in the touch-proximity study, teachers had to hold the learner's hand on a plate in order to deliver the shocks once the learner had refused to co-operate. Obedience rates dropped, suggesting that physical presence and contact made teachers empathise more strongly with the learner's suffering and made it harder to deny or ignore.

These answers are inverted in that the elaboration comes first and the 'reason' second. This is an effective way of answering such questions provided you are clear about the reason you are working towards.

Reason 2: In another variation the experimenter left the room before the 'learning' session and continued to give instructions by telephone. Here only 9 out of 40 (23%) participants went to the maximum shock level, showing that the authority's direct supervision is a crucial factor in determining obedience in this setting.

8 **Process 1:** Once participants are actually part of the experiment, *binding factors* begin to operate. Once they have begun their role as 'participant', various cues (the experimenter's status and manner, the volunteer status of the participant, the learner's apparent willingness to be shocked) increase the pressure on the participant to continue. The participant is 'bound into' his or her social role within the social hierarchy of the experiment. **Process 2:** Milgram argued that people shift back and forth between an *agentic* state and an *autonomous* state, the latter referring to the state a person is in when he 'sees himself acting on his own'. Upon entering an authority system, Milgram claimed, the individual no longer views himself as acting out of his own purposes but rather comes to see himself as an agent for executing the wishes of another.

AO1 Description	AO2 Commentary on methodology	AO2 Other commentary
The main finding in the Milgram (1963) study was that 65% of the participants continued to the maximum 450 volts. Only 5 participants (12.5%) stopped at 300 volts, the point when the learner first objected. Milgram found that the closer the subject was to the teacher, the more likely they were to refuse the experimenter's command.	See response to question 5 (Criticisms 1 and 2).	Baumrind (1964) attacked Milgram's study for the severe distress it created. Milgram defended himself in several ways. For example, he asked participants afterwards if they had found the experience distressing and interviewed them again a year later; 84% felt glad to have participated, and 74% felt they had learned something of personal importance.
Hofling *et al.* (1966) conducted a study in a hospital. Nurses were telephoned by a 'Dr Smith' who asked that they give 20 mg of a drug to a patient. This order contravened hospital regulations in a number of ways, but 21 out of 22 nurses (95%) did as requested.	Rank and Jacobson (1975) also asked nurses to carry out an irregular order, but this time 16 out of 18 (89%) refused. The difference was that on this occasion the drug was familiar (Valium) and the nurses were allowed to consult with peers.	Although Hofling's study *appears* to provide support for the ecological validity of obedience research, Rank and Jacobson suggest that Hofling's findings would not apply to real-life hospital situations, and therefore lack ecological validity.

Resistance to obedience

Being able to respond to this question is fundamental to understanding this whole area of research. There is more to resisting obedience than just saying no.
Don't provide a circular answer. Consider this answer: 'Resistance to obedience means not doing what someone tells you.' Not much evidence of psychological knowledge and understanding. Can you write something better?

Specification extract
How people might resist obedience.

Candidates tend to give rather anecdotal answers, for example saying that one way to resist is to say no. Such answers receive no marks.
You can approach this question by considering what you know about obedience to authority and situations where this is low. Use such situations to tell you about the factors that lead people to resist obedience.

This is essentially the same question. The reasons why people resist are because they can resist under certain circumstances.

research methods
Q

Explain the difference between each of the following:

a) A laboratory experiment and a field experiment.

b) A field experiment and a field study.

c) A field experiment and a natural experiment.

d) Which kind of experiment cannot demonstrate a causal link?

e) Which kind of experiment tends to suffer most from investigator effects?

f) In what kind of circumstances is it necessary to conduct a natural experiment?

This is a legitimate question even though the term 'research' is not linked in the specification to 'how people might resist obedience'. It is assumed that, in every area of the specification, you can be asked about relevant psychological research, which can be theory or studies.

AO1 questions

1. What is meant by resistance to obedience? *(3 marks)*

2. Explain **two** ways in which people might resist obedience. *(3 marks + 3 marks)*

3. Outline **two** reasons why people might resist obedience. *(3 marks + 3 marks)*

4. Outline findings of research on resistance to obedience. *(6 marks)*

Much of the research on obedience appears to indicate that people are highly obedient, yet even in Milgram's baseline study one-third of the participants were not fully obedient. This question requires you to consider the evidence regarding resistance to obedience. A balanced answer will look at evidence for and against the proposal that people can resist obedience. Since the question asks 'To what extent ...' this means you should not be looking to give the answer yes or no but to consider the circumstances when people do resist and when they don't.
'Counterevidence' counts as commentary (AO2) if it is used effectively as a critical comment upon AO1 material. If you are *describing* further evidence, it will be credited as AO1.

AO1/AO2 question

To what extent has psychological research (theories **and/or** studies) shown that people can resist obedience to authority? *(18 marks)*

Possible plan

Possible kinds of research to look at	Description of study or other source of evidence (AO1)	Commentary on methodology, etc. (AO2)	Conclusion about resisting obedience (AO2)
Research that shows that people are resistant to authority			
Research that shows that people are not resistant			
Research that highlights the situations where people are resistant			
Research that highlights the situations where people are not resistant			

1 Resistance to obedience refers to the act of defying an order from an authority figure despite pressures to obey. In Milgram's study, a high proportion of participants gave the maximum 450 volts, yet others defied the experimenter's instructions and withdrew before this point.

The first sentence would be enough for a 2 mark definition, but more detail (as here) is needed for a 3 mark explanation.

2 **Way 1:** During the process of obedience, individuals shift the responsibility for their actions onto the authority figure. They can, however, be reminded that is *they* who are responsible for their actions, not the authority figure. Hamilton (1978) found that under these conditions, agentic shift was reversed and sharp decreases in obedience could be obtained.
Way 2: The presence of disobedient models can also serve to reduce obedience. In Milgram's research the presence of two disobedient peers was sufficient to override all the binding and agentic shift dynamics that usually produce an obedient response. The presence of 'rebels' therefore helps the person see resistance as legitimate.

It is easy to get confused over the ways that people might resist obedience and the reasons for resisting obedience. Think 'how' and 'under what conditions'.

3 **Reason 1:** In variations to his original baseline study, Milgram moved the learner progressively closer to the teacher. As a result, obedience rates dropped, suggesting that physical presence and contact made teachers empathise more strongly with the learner's suffering and therefore made it easier to resist orders.
Reason 2: In another variation, the experimenter gave instructions by telephone. Here, only 9 out of 40 participants went to the maximum shock level. This shows that, in the laboratory setting at least, people find it easier to resist obedience in the absence of direct supervision by the authority figure.

Working out what is a reason for resisting obedience is quite tricky, hence the last part of each answer to put this response in the right context.

4 Milgram discovered that the closer the subject was to the teacher, the more likely they were to refuse the experimenter's command. He also discovered that resistance was greater when the experimenter was not physically present and gave orders over the phone. The most significant reduction of obedience occurred when two peers (actually stooges) defied the experimenter early in the experiment. When Milgram's study was moved to a downtown office, more people felt able to resist authority. Gamson et al. (1982) showed that in certain conditions, people will not obey orders from authority – individuals who are members of groups are more likely to disobey because of the possibility of collective action.

In order to answer this question and the following question, it may be necessary to think what you know about those conditions where obedience levels dropped. Lower levels of obedience mean higher levels of resistance.

research methods A

a) A laboratory experiment takes place in the controlled conditions where participants are aware of being studied, whereas a field experiment takes place in a more natural setting where participants are not aware that they are being studied.

b) A field study is any piece of research that takes place outside the laboratory and within the context in which the behaviour typically occurs, whereas a field experiment is a field study with an identifiable independent variable that is manipulated by the experimenter.

c) In a field experiment, the IV is manipulated by the experimenter, whereas in a natural experiment it has been caused to change as a result of real-life factors.

d) It is more difficult to demonstrate a causal link in a natural experiment because there are many confounding variables that cannot be controlled. Also the fact that the IV has not been purposely manipulated means that one cannot claim that the IV has caused the DV to change.

e) A laboratory experiment suffers most from investigator effects because participants are aware that they are taking part in a study and are most likely to be influenced by the behaviour of the investigator.

f) It is necessary to conduct a natural experiment where the IV cannot be manipulated, and where the investigator wishes to study 'real-life' problems.

Description of study or other source of evidence (AO1)	Commentary on methodology, etc. (AO2)	Conclusion about resisting obedience (AO2)
Gamson et al. (1982) showed that people, under certain conditions, will not obey orders from authority. Individuals who are members of groups are more likely to disobey because of the possibility of collective action.	During the debriefing in this study, many participants reported that they found the experience quite stressful. However, the researchers did stop the study prematurely, ending halfway through the number of groups they intended to test.	It was observed in this study that once sufficient individuals had taken a rebellious stance, the whole group conformed to this. This may be an example of minority influence, and a possible way in which people might resist blind obedience.
The main finding in the Milgram (1963) study was that 65% of the participants appeared unable to resist an authority figure and continued to the maximum 450 volts.	It is possible to explain the unexpectedly high level of obedience in terms of demand characteristics (such as the fact they were part of a scientific experiment). Most people found these hard to resist but this does not mean they would always be so obedient to unjust authority.	Subsequent replications showed that obedience rates drop when these demand characteristics are changed, therefore situational factors may not be as important in determining obedience (or resistance to obedience) as claimed by Milgram.
Milgram found that the closer the participant was to the teacher, the more likely they were to refuse the experimenter's command. He also discovered that resistance was greater when the experimenter was not physically present.	When the experiment was repeated with different people it was found that educated participants were less obedient, and military participants were more obedient.	What all of this tells us is that the simple conclusion that situational factors cause obedience is wrong. Dispositional factors are important as well because not everyone obeys.
Milgram established that once participants became part of the experiment, binding factors (e.g. the experimenter's status) began to operate. As participants had already given lower-level shocks, it became hard to resist the experimenter's requirement to subsequently increase the shocks.	Baumrind (1964) attacked Milgram's study for the severe distress it created. Milgram defended himself in several ways. For example, he asked participants afterwards if they had found the experience distressing and interviewed them again a year later; some 84% felt glad to have participated, and 74% felt they had learned something of personal importance.	Milgram's research suggested that destructive obedience may be evoked in the majority of people by purely situational factors, but many did choose to reject the experimenter's commands, providing a powerful affirmation of human ideals (Milgram, 1974).

Issues of validity

Some candidates use a study to explain their answer yet fail to attract marks because no explanation is embedded in the study description.

Specification extract
Issues of internal and external validity associated with obedience research.

In this question you are asked to describe a study but some candidates offer lengthy descriptions of a study which are largely irrelevant to the question set. It is important first to establish whether a study is high or low in internal validity and then to describe what it is that makes the study high/low in internal validity.

One way to explain a concept is to discuss it in the context of a research study. In this question you are required to take this approach. It still means that you must use the study to explain the concept not just describe the study.

research methods

Q

a) What is validity?

b) What is internal validity?

c) What is external validity?

d) Is ecological validity an example of internal or external validity?

e) What is population validity?

f) Give an example of a study that is high in internal validity.

g) Give an example of a study that is high in ecological validity.

A team of researchers study obedience by arranging for confederates to ask passers by to pick up a piece of paper. The confederate was dressed in a suit or dressed as a student.

h) What method was used in this study?

i) Give one *advantage* of this method in the context of this study.

j) *Explain* one feature of the study that might affect the validity of the data being collected.

k) *Name* one way that investigator effects might threaten the validity of this study and suggest a way to overcome this problem.

l) What is reliability?

A study aimed to assess obedience by observing behaviour at a manned pedestrian crossing. The researchers decided to have three observers recording the pedestrians' behaviour.

m) *Identify* one way in which you could ensure reliability among the different observers.

n) *Explain* how you might put this into practice.

AO1 questions

1. Explain what is meant by internal validity and external validity.
(3 marks + 3 marks)

2. Explain the concept of internal validity with reference to **one** study of obedience. *(6 marks)*

3. Explain the concept of external validity with reference to **one** study of obedience.
(6 marks)

Unlike the question on page 84 this question restricts your discussion to external validity rather than validity in general. Although it can be argued that a study that lacks internal validity cannot be generalised to other settings, you would need to make this link explicit in order to gain credit for commentary on external validity. AO1 credit will be given to any description of studies of obedience. But the main focus of your answer needs to be a consideration of whether any study did or did not have external validity. It may be best to describe selected aspects of a study (such as procedures) and commenting on whether these indicate external validity. For example, you might outline Hofling's study and then mention that the findings were not replicated in another study (Rank and Jacobson) which suggests a lack external validity (ecological validity) – however features of the Rank and Jacobson study mean that the two studies are not directly comparable.

AO1/AO2 question

Consider the extent to which studies of obedience have external validity. *(18 marks)*

Possible plan

Obedience studies	Description of appropriate aspects of the study (AO1)	Commentary about high or low external validity in the study (AO2)	Further consideration of this commentary (AO2)
Study 1			
Study 2			
Study 3			

1 Internal validity in an experiment concerns the extent to which an observed effect can be attributed to the experimental manipulation rather than some other factor (in which case the wrong conclusion might have been drawn).

The answers may be short but are detailed.

External validity refers to the ability to generalise a study beyond the specific situation in which the study took place (i.e. to other people, other settings and over time – population, ecological and historical validity respectively).

2 Internal validity is the extent to which the study has tested what it set out to test. Orne and Holland claimed that demand characteristics in Milgram's study explained participants' behaviour rather than the independent variable. This means changes in the dependent variable (obedience) may not be due to changes in the independent variable (increasing shocks) and the conclusion is not valid.

As the question asks you to explain the concept of internal validity, it is wise to include a brief definition followed by an illustration in the context of a study.

3 External validity refers to the ability to generalise the findings of a study to other people, other settings and over time. Orne and Holland (1968) claimed that Milgram's research was actually measuring the experimenter–participant relationship rather than other authority–subject relationships, and so it was not reasonable to generalise the findings beyond this specific setting to obedience behaviour generally.

research methods **A**

a) Validity refers to the legitimacy of a study, the extent to which the findings can be applied to real life as a consequence of either internal or external validity.

b) Internal validity is the extent to which the study is 'legitimate' or valid within itself, i.e. the extent to which the observed effect is due to the experimental manipulation.

c) An experiment is externally valid if the results can be generalised beyond this specific situation (i.e. to other people, other settings and over time).

d) Ecological validity is an example of external validity.

e) This is one aspect of external validity. An experiment has population validity if the results can be generalised to other groups of people besides those who took part in that study.

f) Asch (1956) – to prevent participants from guessing the true nature of the experiment, Asch arranged for the confederates to give the right answer some of the time but not all of the time so they would seem more plausible. This way he ensured that he measured what he intended to measure rather than measuring participants' responses to demand characteristics.

g) Cross-cultural research lends further support to the idea that Milgram's findings have good ecological validity, i.e. they apply to a variety of settings.

h) This was a field experiment.

i) The field experiment would avoid some participant effects in that passers-by would be more likely to behave naturally, not knowing they were part of a study.

j) Participants might guess that they were part of a psychological study and so behave accordingly; this would threaten the internal validity of the investigation.

k) The investigator may speak differently to each passer-by, thus influencing their behaviour. Greater use of standardised procedures would decrease this effect.

l) Reliability refers to whether something (e.g. a procedure or a measurement) is consistent.

m) The investigator could ensure reliability by using standardised observation procedures, and training observers in their use.

n) A set of behavioural categories could be drawn up (e.g. stopped, paused, did not stop). A pilot study could then be used and observations using these categories compared. Any discrepancies between the observers could be discussed before the study proper.

Description of appropriate aspects of the study (AO1)	Commentary about high or low ecological validity in the study (AO2)	Further consideration of this commentary (AO2)
The main finding in the Milgram (1963) study was that 65% of the participants appeared unable to resist an authority figure and continued to the maximum 450 volts.	Orne and Holland (1968) claimed that Milgram's research was actually measuring the experimenter–participant relationship rather than other authority–subject relationships, and so it was not reasonable to generalise the findings beyond this specific setting to obedience behaviour generally.	Milgram's response was that real life was no different. Experiments are like social situations – the experiment is a reflection of life. The relationship between an experimenter and a participant is no different to that between any authority figure and someone in a subservient position.
Smith and Bond (1993) reviewed a number of studies that replicated Milgram's baseline experiment in different countries. Rates of obedience varied from 85% in Germany to 16% for female Australians.	Although Smith and Bond found evidence of differing rates of obedience in different cultures, all produced rates of obedience greater than originally predicted in Milgram's study, adding support to the claim of ecological validity for this research.	However, one can't be sure how equivalent the studies are to each other, for example the conditions and nature of the participants were often slightly different.
Hofling et al. (1966) conducted a study in a hospital. Nurses were telephoned by a 'Dr Smith', who asked that they give 20 mg of a drug to a patient. This order contravened hospital regulations in a number of ways, but 21 out of 22 nurses (95%) did as requested.	Although this research was carried out in a more naturalistic setting than Milgram's study, it is not reasonable to generalise from a doctor–nurse authority relationship to all other kinds of obedience. It is part of a nurse's job to obey the orders of doctors.	In addition, one subsequent attempt to replicate this study (Rank and Jacobson) in more realistic hospital settings found a complete reversal of findings, so we can conclude that Hofling's study lacks ecological validity.

End of section review

Sample exam question

a. Outline **two** reasons why people might resist obedience. *(3 marks + 3 marks)*

b. Outline conclusions of research on obedience to authority. *(6 marks)*

c. To what extent can obedience research (theories **and/or** studies) be said to lack validity? *(18 marks)*

See page viii for an explanation of how questions are marked.

Student answer	Examiner's comments
(a) One reason why people might resist obedience is that they have social support from others. For example, in Milgram's study, when there was another participant present, obedience levels dropped. Another reason why people might resist obedience is if they don't like the orders they are given. This is also illustrated in Milgram's study when one participant who had lived through the Nazi regime refused to carry out the orders given, because she didn't want to inflict any pain as she had seen what happened when people did this.	Using an example from a study is an effective means of elaboration. What is missing is an answer to the question why? Because the agreement of others increases one's confidence. The second explanation does include an explanation of why, thus **2/3 + 3/3 marks**.
(b) Milgram's study showed that legitimate authority was a reason why people obeyed someone else. The person giving orders is obeyed if they appear to have authority. This was the case in Milgram's study where the experimenter wore a white coat. Milgram's research also showed how buffers may increase obedience to authority. If a person is placed in a remote location to the victim, they are more likely to obey orders from the authority. In some experiments the teacher did not actually see the learner but when they could see the learner their obedience levels dropped.	Two conclusions are provided in detail. The candidate has elaborated each conclusion by describing procedures (in the first paragraph) and by reference to findings in the second paragraph. In this way, other information is credited as part of a conclusion. There is some temptation to call this answer 'limited' therefore **5/6 marks** rather than the full 6 marks.
(c) Some obedience studies have been criticised for their lack of internal and external validity. Milgram's study was artificial because it is a laboratory experiment, and thus has no ecological validity. He asked participants to administer electric shocks to a 'learner' and found high levels of obedience in this restricted setting. In other settings, levels of obedience dropped but the fact that obedience did persist shows that the findings could be applied to other settings. Hofling *et al.*'s study aimed to see the effect of an authority figure in a real-life situation. His field study confirmed that nurses were likely to obey an order from a fictitious doctor given over the telephone. This supports Milgram's findings, and shows that his study does have ecological validity, and that there are high levels of obedience in real life. However, Milgram's research did include prods and thus high levels of stress in the teachers. This would prevent participants feeling they had the right to withdraw. But Milgram claimed that prods are also used in everyday life in order to get people to obey authority (e.g. in an office environment). Some suggest that the entering of a social contract by paid volunteers considerably reduced the value of the study. Only a certain type of individual is likely to volunteer and thus the samples do not represent the whole of society. The fact that they were paid may encourage participants to act in the way they feel the experimenter expects. They may also feel that failure to do this may result in them not being paid. [275 words]	The AO1 mark is based on any descriptions of obedience research. The brief descriptions of Milgram and Hofling's research are sufficiently detailed for an **AO1 mark of 4/6**. There is greater focus on AO2 commentary, as is appropriate. The AO1 material has been well linked to AO2 points about validity; for example, the end of the first paragraph uses the description of the study to show that in fact it did have ecological validity. The same is true at the end of the second paragraph. The final two paragraphs are all AO2, presenting effective arguments for and against validity. The final paragraph considers population validity. This answer is better than 'limited' but not in the top band because of the slightly limited amount of material covered, thus **9/12 marks for AO2**, a total of **13/18 marks**.
	Total for whole question is **23 marks**, equivalent to a Grade A.

SOCIAL PSYCHOLOGY: SOCIAL INFLUENCE

This module is divided into

Majority and minority influence

Majority influence

Minority influence

End of section review

Obedience to authority

Obedience to authority

Resistance to obedience

Issues of validity

End of section review

Critical issue: Ethics in psychological research

Ethical issues

Dealing with ethical issues

End of section review

COGNITIVE PSYCHOLOGY:
HUMAN MEMORY

DEVELOPMENTAL PSYCHOLOGY:
ATTACHMENTS IN DEVELOPMENT

PHYSIOLOGICAL PSYCHOLOGY:
STRESS

INDIVIDUAL DIFFERENCES:
ABNORMALITY

SOCIAL PSYCHOLOGY:
SOCIAL INFLUENCE

RESEARCH
METHODS

Ethical issues

Specification extract
Ethical issues surrounding the use of deception, informed consent and the protection of participants from psychological harm, including the relevance of these issues in the context of social influence research.

research methods

Q

A psychology class decides to ask pupils in the school playground to estimate the number of beans in a jar and record their answers on an answer sheet where previous answers have already been recorded. In one condition the previous answers are high. In a second condition the previous answers are low. They intend to compare participants' behaviour in the high and low estimate conditions to see how the estimates affected behaviour.

a) *Describe the aims of this study.*

b) *Write a suitable non-directional hypothesis.*

c) *Identify **two** ethical issues in this study.*

Many candidates find it difficult to provide any detail for their explanations and just say 'deception means deceiving participants' or 'protection from psychological harm means preventing psychological harm'. These are circular answers.
Better answers explain what the participants are being deceived about or protected from, and examine some of the consequences; for example, deception prevents participants from being able to give truly informed consent.

Many candidates get confused between ethical issues and ethical guidelines, thinking they are the same. You won't receive marks for describing ethical guidelines which are ways of resolving ethical issues. For example, debriefing is not an ethical issue, it is a way of dealing with various issues such as deception and confidentiality.
Some candidates fail to achieve high marks because they make no link to a study or they describe a study but don't clearly link this to an ethical issue. Good answers demonstrate both why an issue was problematic and the degree to which it was evident in social influence research.

Don't simply describe the study, but show how it illustrates the ethical issue of informed consent.

Sometimes candidates find it difficult to think of enough to write about the aims of the study – what was it that the researcher wanted to test (the hypothesis)?

Many candidates can describe two issues but cannot lodge these issues in their previous study. Some candidates try to provide detail by saying how the issue was resolved, which receives no marks. The **three-point rule** can be applied here: name it, explain it and state why it is an issue here.

Some candidates answer a question such as this by just describing everything that Milgram and Zimbardo did. Such responses can receive AO1 credit but lose out on a large slice of AO2. Merely describing the ethical issues that arise from such studies will do little to boost your mark, because you are required to consider whether they can be justified. One way to do this is to consider ethical issues as they arise in two or more studies, and then use this information to consider whether, on balance, these studies were justified.

AO1 questions

1. Explain what is meant by 'deception' and 'protection of participants from psychological harm' in the context of psychological research.
(3 marks + 3 marks)

2. Outline **two** ethical issues that have arisen in social influence research.
(3 marks + 3 marks)

3. i Explain what is meant by 'informed consent' in the context of psychological research. *(3 marks)*

ii Illustrate your answer to part (i) with reference to **one** study of social influence. *(3 marks)*

4. Describe the aims and procedures of **one** study of social influence. *(6 marks)*

5. Describe **two** ethical issues that were a feature of the study you described in question 4.
(3 marks + 3 marks)

AO1/AO2 question

Outline **two or more** ethical issues arising in studies of social influence and consider whether such studies can be ethically justified. *(18 marks)*

Possible plan

	Outline of ethical issues in studies (**AO1**)	Commentary on ethical issues (**AO2**)	Can the study be justified? (**AO2**)
Issue 1			
Issue 2			
Issue 3			

1 Deception involves the withholding of information or the misleading of research participants. Baumrind (1985) argued that deception is morally wrong on the basis of the right of informed consent, the obligation of researchers to protect the welfare of the subject, and the responsibility of researchers to be trustworthy. Protection of participants from psychological harm means that research participants should be protected from undue risk during an investigation. This might include embarrassment, loss of dignity or threats to a person's self-esteem as a result of participation. Lack of such protection denies important rights to the participants.

There are a number of ways that you can elaborate a 2 mark definition into a 3 mark explanation. Ideally you should explain why each of these is an issue.

2 Deception involves the withholding of information or the misleading of research participants. Asch told his participants that the study was about visual perception. Milgram told his participants that they were involved in a study of the effects of punishment on learning. They both used deception, arguing that the experiment would be meaningless otherwise.
Informed consent means that research participants should be allowed to agree or refuse to participate in a research investigation based on comprehensive information concerning the nature and purpose of the research and their role in it. In Zimbardo *et al.*'s study, the participants did give a limited degree of informed consent, yet this did not provide a full understanding of what was to happen next.

3i Informed consent means that research participants should be allowed to agree or refuse to participate in a research investigation based on comprehensive information concerning the nature and purpose of the research and their role in it. Such consent is not always possible from the researcher's viewpoint because it may undermine the validity of the study.

Offering an explanation of a concept requires a little more detail than a straightforward definition.

3ii In Zimbardo *et al.*'s study, the participants did give a limited degree of informed consent, yet this did not provide a full understanding of what was to happen next. This illustrates how informed consent does not guarantee true understanding, nor does it protect participants from harm.

It is important to remember that this answer requires description of informed consent within the context of a study.

4 A study of social influence (Zimbardo *et al.*, 1973).
Aims: The aim of this study was to explore the validity of a dispositional explanation of aggressive behaviour.
If you place 'ordinary' people in a prison environment and designate some of them as guards and others as prisoners, how would they behave? Would they too behave aggressively, thus showing situational influences (social conformity to roles)?

You could have chosen any study of social influence, but Zimbardo's study has been chosen here as it neatly illustrates ethical issues that can be covered in response to question 6.

Procedures: Twenty-four male volunteers were randomly assigned to being a prisoner or a guard. The 'prisoners' were unexpectedly 'arrested' at home. On entry to 'prison' they were put through a delousing procedure, given a prison uniform with ID number, nylon stocking caps, and an ankle chain. The 'guards' only referred to the prisoners by number. The guards had uniforms, clubs, whistles, handcuffs and reflective sunglasses (to prevent eye contact).

5 The 'prisoners' were arrested unexpectedly in their own homes, though otherwise they were not deceived in this experiment.
The 'guards' were under the impression that the study was primarily about the behaviour of prisoners; Zimbardo did not correct this false impression. Such 'deceptions' may be regarded as acceptable.
Participation in this study must have caused all participants emotional distress. Five of the prisoners had to be released because of 'depression, crying, rage and acute anxiety' as well as one who had developed a 'psychosomatic rash'. One defence is that the extremes of behaviour could not have been anticipated at the outset. In addition, Zimbardo did conduct debriefing sessions for several years afterwards and concluded that there were no lasting negative effects.

There is no need to name these issues, although that might make your intention clearer to the examiner!

research methods **A**

a) The aims of this study are to see whether participants are likely to conform to previous estimates.

b) There will be a difference in the estimates given by participants in the high and low conditions when estimating the number of beans in a jar.

c) One potential ethical issue in this study is deception, as participants were not told this was a study of conformity.

A related ethical issue is informed consent, as the use of deception made it impossible for participants to agree or refuse to participate in the light of comprehensive information concerning the nature and purpose of the research.

Outline of ethical issues in studies (AO1)	Commentary on ethical issues in these studies (AO2)	Can these studies be ethically justified? (AO2)
Milgram told his participants that they were involved in a study of the effects of punishment on learning, which denied them the right to provide informed consent.	Milgram argued that the experiment would be meaningless without some degree of deception. Deception was vital for the internal validity of the study.	Milgram claimed that his research was criticised because of the findings rather than the procedures used. His research effectively 'opened our eyes' to the possibility that each of us was capable of 'destructive obedience'.
Zimbardo's 'guards' were under the impression that the study was primarily about the behaviour of prisoners.	Zimbardo felt that lack of full disclosure of procedural details was justifiable given the nature of the study.	Zimbardo did conduct debriefing sessions for several years afterwards and concluded that there were no lasting negative effects.
Milgram's participants were told that they could leave at any time, although 'prods' from the experimenter made this quite difficult.	Milgram argued that one-third of participants left before the final stages of the experiment and this was testimony to the fact they felt they had the right to withdraw.	Mandel (1997) claimed that Milgram offered little more than an 'obedience alibi' for the behaviour of Holocaust perpetrators. This demonstrates how the misapplication of research findings can have an ethical impact far beyond their immediate research setting.
Zimbardo had to release four prisoners because of their extreme psychological reaction to participation, and ended the study early.	Zimbardo agrees that he was 'trapped' in his role as prison superintendent, making him impervious to the suffering of his participants.	Zimbardo's experiment cannot be justified in terms of changes in prisons or even in guard training programmes as a result of the study. Prisons have been radically transformed in the United States in the last 25 years with the result that they are *less* humane.

Dealing with ethical issues

Specification extract
Ways in which psychologists deal with ethical issues (e.g. through the use of ethical guidelines, ethical committees).

research methods

Q

There are six research methods named in the specification (laboratory experiment, field experiment, natural experiment, investigations using a correlational analysis, naturalistic observation and questionnaire survey/interview).

For each of these, identify **one** example from your studies, and identify **one** potential ethical issue in this study and suggest how this issue might have been resolved.

Many candidates write far too much in answer to this question, using up precious time when it is not necessary. You will get very little credit for just listing ethical guidelines. You will get no credit for just identifying ethical issues. Some candidates write about how certain issues were dealt with in the context of certain studies. This is a reasonable approach but the danger is that you get sidetracked onto a wider description of the study.
Some candidates evaluate the ways of dealing with the issues, which would gain no credit. Some candidates write anything they can think about that is related to ethics and appear not to have read the question carefully. This 'machine-gun approach' gains minimal credit.

The ethical issue must be described in the context of an identifiable study of social influence.

You must make sure that you clearly answer the two parts of this question, distinguishing between the ethical issue and how it could have been dealt with.

Many students believe that the mere existence of ethical guidelines (or other attempts to deal with ethical issues) is sufficient resolution of ethical issues. You should be prepared to offer criticisms (positive and/or negative) of such attempts.

The AO1 content of this essay will be the description of how ethical issues have been resolved in social influence research. This might be done by looking at particular studies. The AO2 content will be an evaluation of these ways of resolving ethical issues. Evaluation may involve any commentary – positive or negative – as well as a look at alternative methods of resolving ethical issues. A weak answer will simply include anything about ethical issues. A good answer will be structured and focus specifically on what is required – an assessment of whether guidelines (or other methods) work.

AO1 questions

1. Describe some of the ways in which psychologists have attempted to deal with ethical issues that may occur in psychological research. *(6 marks)*

2. Describe **one** ethical issue that has arisen in a study of social influence and explain how it was dealt with. *(3 marks + 3 marks)*

3. Describe **one** ethical issue and explain **one** way of dealing with it. *(3 marks + 3 marks)*

4. Give **two** criticisms of **one** way of dealing with ethical issues. *(3 marks + 3 marks)*

AO1/AO2 question

'Ethical issues in social psychology can be resolved using ethical guidelines.' Consider whether psychologists have been successful in resolving the ethical issues raised by social influence research. *(18 marks)*

Possible plan

	How ethical issues are resolved **(AO1)**	Negative criticisms (e.g. impossible to debrief participants) **(AO2)**	Other commentary **(AO2)**
Approach 1			
Approach 2			

1 All professions draw up rules which 'guide' the behaviour of their members. These guidelines tend to present minimal 'bottom line' information for what is considered acceptable and unacceptable behaviour when carrying out research with human participants. Each guideline is matched to an underlying ethical issue (e.g. advice about maintaining confidentiality). All institutions where research takes place have an ethical committee which must approve any study before it begins. They look at all possible ethical issues and at how they have been dealt with, weighing up the value of the research against the possible costs in ethical terms. A third method of dealing with ethical issues is the process of socialisation within any professional group. Part of learning about psychology is learning to take on their ethical attitudes.

> *This question might have asked for two ways, but here there is a more open invitation to write about 'some of the ways'. It is okay to address specific issues, or to respond more generally as here. You must, however, describe at least two ways for full marks.*

2 Baumrind (1964) criticised Milgram on the basis that participants would suffer permanent psychological harm from the study, including a loss of dignity and self-esteem, and distrust of authority. She also suggested that Milgram had not done enough to remove any of the trauma the participants had felt after taking part in the study.
Milgram arranged for a psychiatrist to interview the participants a year after the initial study. He reported that there was no evidence of emotional harm arising from participation in the study. Participants claimed to have learned important lessons about how social influence can affect behaviour, and about how to resist such influences.

> *Baumrind's criticisms identify an appropriate ethical issue, and Milgram's responses show how he dealt with that particular issue.*

3 **Ethical issue:** Deception involves the withholding of information or the misleading of research participants. Baumrind (1985) argued that deception is morally wrong on the basis of the right of informed consent, the obligation of researchers to protect the welfare of the subject, and the responsibility of researchers to be trustworthy.
A way to compensate for deception is to inform participants, after the research has taken place, of the true nature of the study. This is called debriefing. In general the aim of debriefing is to restore the participant to the state they were in at the start of the experiment.

> *Having an ethical issue and a way of dealing with it (typically an ethical guideline) highlights the important distinction between an issue and a guideline. This is a distinction you should be very clear about.*

4 One way of dealing with ethical issues is the use of guidelines.
Criticism 1: Diana Baumrind (1959) argued that the cost–benefit approach of ethical guidelines solves nothing because the intention is to develop a means of solving ethical dilemmas but, in fact, one is left with another set of dilemmas (i.e. weighing up the potential costs against the potential benefits).
Criticism 2: Although professional bodies provide guidelines for acceptable conduct in research, their regulatory powers are limited. Unlike other professions, there is no obligation to take up membership and the sanctions of exclusion (e.g. from the BPS) are fairly weak. As a result, although ethical guidelines threaten sanctions for ethical infringements, in reality they have no teeth.

research methods **A**

Laboratory experiment (e.g. Loftus and Palmer's study of eyewitness testimony) – this could result in psychological harm, particularly if the participant is deceived. One way of dealing with this is by prior general consent (participants provide consent for a variety of studies, including a study which would involve deception).

Field experiment (e.g. Bickman's study of obedience) – there is a difficulty of debriefing in field experiments, therefore the investigator could use presumptive consent (i.e. if it is not possible to gain full informed consent from participants, it can be gained by others on their behalf).

Natural experiment (e.g. Hodges and Tizard's study of privation) – there is a problem of confidentiality in natural experiments (they often deal with sensitive issues such as institutional care). It is important to protect individual identities and the identity of the institution.

Investigations using a correlational analysis (e.g. Rahe et al.'s study of stress and illness) – there may be misunderstanding of findings (the public perception is often that a cause rather than a link has been identified and this may lead to erroneous understanding of important social issues). The investigator should make it clear what the findings show, and what they don't show.

Naturalistic observation (e.g. Schaffer and Emerson's study of attachment in infants) – there is a risk of invasion of privacy. One way of dealing with this is to observe behaviour only in public places.

Questionnaire survey/interview (e.g. Rahe et al.'s study of stress and illness used both techniques) – there is the problem of confidentiality, particularly in questions about sensitive issues. It is necessary, therefore, to protect individual identities by making them anonymous.

How ethical issues are resolved (AO1)	Negative criticisms (AO2)	Other commentary (AO2)
All professions draw up rules that 'guide' the behaviour of their members. These guidelines tend to present 'bottom line' information for what is considered acceptable and unacceptable behaviour when carrying out research with human participants. Each guideline is matched to an underlying ethical issue (e.g. advice about maintaining confidentiality).	Diana Baumrind (1959) argued that the cost–benefit approach of ethical guidelines solves nothing because the intention is to develop a means of solving ethical dilemmas but, in fact, one is left with another set of dilemmas (i.e. weighing up the potential costs against the potential benefits).	In Milgram's study some participants said the experience was personally beneficial in order to help them cope better with this kind of inhumane authority, i.e. to be more cautious in future. As a result, it becomes difficult to quantify the 'costs' and 'benefits' of study in the way required by ethical guidelines.
All institutions where research takes place have an ethical committee which must approve any study before it begins. They look at all possible ethical issues and at how they have been dealt with, weighing up the value of the research against the possible costs in ethical terms.	Although professional bodies and ethical committees provide guidelines for acceptable conduct in research, their regulatory powers are limited. Unlike other professions, there is no obligation to take up membership and the sanctions of exclusion are fairly weak. As a result, although ethical guidelines threaten sanctions for ethical infringements, in reality they have no teeth.	Ethical guidelines and committees may protect the immediate needs of research participants, but may not deal with all the possible ways in which research may inflict harm. If we judge costs and benefits in terms of society at large, we can consider the value in improving people's lives versus the possibility that individuals may be desensitised toward destructive obedience or unthinking conformity.

End of section review

Note that this entire question has been drawn from *different* sections of the module on social influence. This is acceptable. It is also acceptable to set an entire question on one section only.

Sample exam question

a. Describe the procedures and conclusions of **one** study that has explored minority influence. *(6 marks)*

b. Describe **two** ethical issues that were a feature of the study you described in (a). *(3 marks + 3 marks)*

c. Consider whether the findings from obedience research (theories **and/or** studies) can justify the methods used to obtain such findings. *(18 marks)*

See page viii for an explanation of how questions are marked.

Student answer	Examiner's comments
(a) Moscovici is a psychologist who studied minority influence. He did this in an experiment using slides. He got a number of naive participants and two confederates and placed them in a room. He placed, on a screen, a number of blue-coloured slides and instructed the participants to say whether they were blue or green. The two confederates went first. Moscovici found that in the experiment when the confederates were consistent there was over 8% conformity of the majority to this view. This dropped to 1% when the confederates were not consistent. This shows that people are influenced by a minority under certain conditions.	The procedures are 'generally accurate' but there are some important details missing (e.g. how many naive participants). The findings are not creditworthy in this question, though they have been used to produce the conclusions, providing some detail for them. The conclusions are not as good as the procedures, but you are not required to produce the two in balance. Overall a slightly generous **4/6 marks.**
(b) One ethical issue in this study was deception. Participants were not told the true purpose of the study and therefore could not provide truly informed consent. A second ethical issue is protection from psychological harm. Participants might have been distressed by the pressure they were put under.	The first answer is brief but sufficiently detailed for full marks. An ethical issue is named and described and an explanation provided as to why this is an issue. The second answer is of similar length but fails to provide an explanation, such as ignoring an individual's rights. **3/3 + 2/3 marks.**
(c) Obedience research can be justified because it is important and shows insight into human behaviour. This importance can justify the findings and methods used when conducting studies that are distressing and harsh, though sometimes this isn't true. Milgram's experiment caused severe distress to his participants, who thought that they were potentially killing or seriously hurting another participant; at least two participants had seizures. Zimbardo's study was humiliating for participants and it was considered highly unethical the way that they were treated. The findings go a long way to showing that the methods were necessary. Zimbardo became too involved with the study, which meant that he couldn't see the ethical problems that had arisen. Only one participant in Milgram's study regretted having taken part, and all the others felt they had learned something valuable about themselves. However, Zimbardo's study had to be finished early after 6 days, rather than the planned 14 days, because of the distress caused to participants. In Hofling's study the nurses were not distressed even though they were deceived. They said that they behaved as they did because they would normally get in a lot of trouble. However, it is possible that the study harmed their professional relationships. The methods used can be extreme but as long as they don't distress the participants in the long term it is okay. Milgram's research was more acceptable than Zimbardo's, and Hofling's study may have caused long-term harm. [242 words]	This question is similar to the sample on page 88, but this time it involves obedience research. The AO1 content is again description of any theory or study. It appears that this candidate has not thought about what is required for AO1 here and has given only minimal descriptions of the research, thus **2/6 marks for AO1.** The essay is mainly commentary, covering a range of points that are not always effective. For example, 'the findings go a long way to showing that the methods were necessary' needs some explanation, such as suggesting that the findings were useful in changing prison conditions. The final paragraph is not very effective as it repeats previous points. So, despite the range of commentary (slightly limited), the lack of effectiveness means **8/12 marks for AO2, a total of 10/18 marks.**
	Total for whole question is **19/30 marks,** equivalent to a Grade A, possibly a Grade B.

Research methods are the techniques that scientists use in order to conduct systematic studies and produce facts about the world. The research methods used by psychologists have been discussed throughout this book. In this section we offer a summary of the key points and a collation of all you need to know to answer the compulsory research methods question.

In this section there are five exam-style questions, each provided with model answers.

This module is divided into

Questions

Question 1: Based on a field experiment

Question 2: Based on a naturalistic observation

Question 3: Based on a correlational analysis

Question 4: Based on the interview method

Question 5: Based on the natural experiment

COGNITIVE PSYCHOLOGY: HUMAN MEMORY

DEVELOPMENTAL PSYCHOLOGY: ATTACHMENTS IN DEVELOPMENT

PHYSIOLOGICAL PSYCHOLOGY: STRESS

INDIVIDUAL DIFFERENCES: ABNORMALITY

SOCIAL PSYCHOLOGY: SOCIAL INFLUENCE

RESEARCH METHODS

Question 1

A psychological study set out to test the principle that rewards are an effective means of encouraging desirable behaviours. In this study, 20 children were used as participants. All of the children were given a short memory test that involved looking at a picture and then answering questions about items in the picture.

A week later all the children were retested using a second memory test. This time half the group were given a different set of instructions. Group A were told they would receive a reward if they did really well on the test. Group B were given the same instructions but with no mention of a reward.

After the children did the test, they all received a reward. The findings are shown in Table 1.

Table 1: Mean scores on memory test (out of 20) for both groups of participants

	Test 1	Test 2
Group A	13	17
Group B	14	15

You may be asked to justify why a directional or non-directional hypothesis has been chosen. The answer is not to say 'I chose a directional hypothesis because I thought Group A would do better'. This is simply restating the hypothesis. The reason for choosing a directional hypothesis is because you thought the findings would go in that direction, probably because theory or past studies have found this. Alternatively, if past research is unclear about what the likely outcome is going to be, then you would choose a non-directional hypothesis.

Sometimes questions such as this say 'in this study'. Then you would not gain full marks unless you contextualised your answer (i.e. gave an advantage/disadvantage in the context of this study).

You are only asked for **one** advantage of the mean. If you give more than one advantage, only the first answer will be marked, no matter how good the other answers. On this part of the examination, positive marking is not used (positive marking means marks are awarded for the best answer as opposed to the first answer).

Elaborate each conclusion you provide, and do try to find *two* conclusions, otherwise you are throwing away marks. But don't describe the findings; that would earn no marks. Conclusions are an *interpretation* of the findings.

a. Give a directional hypothesis for this study. (2 marks)

b. Give **one** reason why a directional hypothesis might have been chosen in this study. (2 marks)

c. What was the independent variable in this investigation? (1 mark)

d. Explain **one** advantage and **one** weakness of field experiments such as this. (2 marks + 2 marks)

e. In the second half of the experiment, the participants were divided into two groups. Explain how you might divide the participants into two groups. (3 marks)

f. In this experiment the scores were represented by the mean.

 i   Give **one** advantage of using the mean. (2 marks)

 ii Under what conditions would it be preferable to use the median? (2 marks)

g. Describe **one** way in which you could minimise the chance that the participants would guess the aim of the study. (3 marks)

h. Explain why the researchers gave a reward to all of the children at the end of the study. (3 marks)

i. Describe **two** conclusions that can be drawn from the findings of this study. (2 marks + 2 marks)

j. Explain what is meant by the term 'validity' and outline **one** threat to validity in this study. (2 marks + 2 marks)

a Participants do better on a memory test when given the incentive of a promised reward rather than when tested without the incentive of a reward.

> *This would receive full marks because the IV and DV have been operationalised.*

b A directional hypothesis might be chosen because it is testing the established principle that rewards are an effective means of encouraging desirable behaviours.

c The incentive of a promised reward.

d **Advantage:** Because participants are unaware of their participation in an experiment, they are less likely to display demand characteristics.
Disadvantage: The experimenter has less control over the effect of extraneous variables, which might interfere with the purity of the cause–effect relationship.

e The names of all 20 children could be put into a hat. They could then be randomly allocated to the two conditions by pulling the first 10 names out and putting them into condition 1 and the next 10 names into condition 2.

> *Simply saying 'putting their names in a hat' would not be sufficient for full marks because this doesn't offer a full explanation. It doesn't explain how you work out which participants would be in which condition.*

f **i** One advantage is that the mean uses all of the values.
ii It would be preferable to use the median rather than the mean if there were some extreme scores in the data or if the data were ordinal rather than interval.

> *Note that the mean doesn't simply use all of the scores (all measures of central tendency use all of the scores). The mean uses all of the values. This answer is brief but perfectly accurate for the full 2 marks.*

g The researchers could have used a single blind technique; this would involve using a cover story to prevent the participants knowing the purpose of the experiment.

h Researchers would have given all the children a reward at the end of the study for ethical reasons. It would not be fair on the children who were in Group B if they performed the same test and yet did not receive the same reward.

i Both groups performed better on Test 2 than they did on Test 1, suggesting some improvement due to the order in which the tests were taken.
Children in Group A performed better than Group B on Test 2, suggesting that the incentive of a promised reward had motivated them to improve their performance compared to those without that incentive.

> *Notice how each time the findings have been used as a springboard for supplying a conclusion. The term 'suggesting' leads on to a conclusion.*

j Validity refers to the extent that findings can be applied to real life. One possible problem in this study might be that the children guessed what the study was about.

Question 2

A psychological study found that children playing in a park are unlikely to wander very far from their mothers. In fact, they stayed rather close, almost as if they were attached by a piece of string. A group of three psychology students decided to investigate play behaviour in toddlers playing in a park to see how close they stayed to their mothers.

The students sat on a bench in a large open park. The only objects visible were other benches, trees and a path through the park. They recorded observations on a number of different days. The procedure of their study was to identify a mother (or mother substitute) with a young child. Then each student kept a record of the child's play behaviour over a period of 20 minutes. Every 30 seconds they wrote down the distance between mother and child.

Table 1: Record of observations

	Child 1	Child 2	Child 3	Child 4
Touching mother	11	28	5	15
1–2 metres from mother	12	12	29	25
More than 2 metres	17	0	6	0
Number of observations	40	40	40	40

There is no requirement to contextualise the advantage and disadvantage but doing so may provide your answer with detail.

There is no requirement to contextualise the limitation here.

Make sure you present a reasonably detailed account of the steps to be taken as this question is worth 3 marks.

Validity concerns the extent to which the findings of a study are legitimate. What aspects of this study may bias the findings? For example, you might consider the type of parents who take children to parks. Can we generalise from this to all parents?

Note that debriefing is *not* an ethical issue.

a. Describe **one** aim of this study. *(2 marks)*

b. Identify the research method used and give **one** advantage and **one** disadvantage of this method. *(1 mark + 2 marks + 2 marks)*

c. Identify **one** sampling method and explain **one** limitation of this method of sampling. *(1 mark + 2 marks)*

d. Explain how you would ensure reliability among the different observers. *(3 marks)*

e. Describe **one** way in which you could minimise the intrusive nature of your observations. *(3 marks)*

f. Explain **two** features of the study that might affect the validity of the data being collected. *(2 marks + 2 marks)*

g. Identify **one** ethical issue that the researchers should have considered. Explain how this ethical issue could have been dealt with. *(1 mark + 2 marks)*

h. Describe **two** conclusions that can be drawn from the findings of this study. *(2 marks + 2 marks)*

i. The students decided to extend their study to make other observations of children with their mothers. Suggest **one** other observational category they could use, besides distance from mother, and suggest how you would measure this category. *(1 mark + 2 marks)*

a The aim of this study is to see how close children stay to their mothers during play.

An answer that just said 'observing children during play' would only receive 1 mark.

b Naturalistic observation. An advantage of this method is that it is possible to study behaviour in situations (such as the behaviour of a child at play) where the variables cannot be manipulated. A disadvantage is that the researchers cannot control extraneous variables, such as the strength of the attachment bond between the mother and child.

If you are asked to name the research method, it must be one of those named in the specification: laboratory experiment, field experiment, natural experiment, investigation using a correlational analysis, naturalistic observation, questionnaire survey or an interview. Take care not to get muddled about a research 'method' and a research 'design'.

c One sampling method is an opportunity sample. A limitation of this sampling method is that it can be biased towards a particular cross section or type of participants who are available at that time and in that location.

Be careful not to simply label everything as a 'random' sample.

d One way of ensuring reliability among the different observers is by using a pilot study to check that each observer was using the behavioural categories in the same way. Any discrepancies can then be dealt with before the study proper is carried out.

It is important to provide enough detail of what you would do to gain 3 marks. Simply saying 'try out the behavioural categories' would be worth only 1 mark because there is no detail included to demonstrate your knowledge and understanding of how such research is conducted.

e It would be possible to visit the park on a number of occasions prior to the study, so that the children get used to the observers' presence, and do not react differently as a result.

Many candidates write something about disguising themselves so they are not noticed. The answer provided here shows you that there are other ways to reduce intrusion when conducting a naturalistic observation.

f i. There may be a problem with the population validity of this study in that mothers who take their children to the park on a regular basis may not be representative of all mothers, giving a biased view of the behaviour being studied.
ii. This study may not have ecological validity in that the behaviour of children towards their mothers in a play setting may differ from their behaviour in other settings.

For 2 marks you need to identify the problem and also say why this would lower validity (e.g. 'it would give a biased view of the behaviour being studied').

g One appropriate ethical issue is confidentiality. The researchers should ensure that no details are taken of the mothers or their children (e.g. names or photographs) that would in any way compromise their anonymity.

For full marks it would not be sufficient to say 'no details would be taken'. You need to offer some further elaboration of what you would do.

h One conclusion is that children tend to stay close to their mothers during play: children tend to wander no further than 2 metres from their mother. A second conclusion is that there are individual differences between the children studied, with some being more confident to leave their mother's side than others.

These are conclusions rather than findings because they describe how people behave rather than describing how the participants in the study behaved.

i A further observational category could be noting how the child behaves when another person is nearby. The observers could record whether the child is more likely to return to the mother, approach the other person or ignore the other person.

Some candidates don't notice when there are two parts to a question, as here. You must make sure you provide all the detail required by the question.

Question 3

Many students say they feel very stressed when taking exams whereas others say they don't feel stressed at all. Optimum levels of stress are said to be good for high performance, so we might expect a relationship between stress and performance. In order to test this, a psychologist assessed stress and GCSE performance using a random sample of 20 student participants taken from Years 12 and 13 of a large comprehensive school.

Stress was measured using the galvanic stress response (GSR), a measure of ANS activity. A reading was taken just before the student took each GCSE exam, and then an average score was calculated over all of the exams. The higher the score, the greater the ANS activity. An average score was also calculated for GCSE performance by assigning a score of 10 to a Grade A, 8 to a Grade B and so on, so that Grade E scored 2 points. An average for the GCSE scores was calculated by dividing the total by the number of GCSEs taken. Thus, for each student there were two scores: a stress score and a GCSE score.

The graph below shows the findings from the study. The correlation coefficient was −0.73.

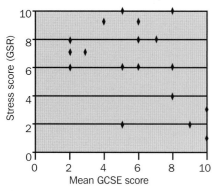

Graph to show the relationship between levels of stress and exam perfomance

Figure 1

> There is no requirement to contextualise your answer here.

> Note that you must contextualise your answer to this question. You could start by explaining what a pilot study is and then use this to explain why a pilot study would be useful here.

> Both the correlation coefficient and the graph should inform your answer.

> There are a lot of marks in this part of the question, so be sure to spend adequate time answering it.

a. Identify the covariables in this study. *(2 marks)*

b. i Explain how the psychologist might have selected the 'random sample' of participants. *(2 marks)*

ii Identify **one** other method of selecting participants and state how you would do this. *(2 marks)*

c. Give **one** strength and **one** limitation of using random sampling to obtain participants. *(2 marks + 2 marks)*

d. Explain what is meant by a pilot study and give **one** reason why it might be appropriate to use a pilot study as part of this investigation. *(1 mark + 2 marks)*

e. Identify the graphical method used to represent the findings. *(1 mark)*

f. Using the information from the graph, describe the relationship between stress and exam performance. *(2 marks)*

g. Explain **two** features of this study that might have affected the validity of the data being collected. *(2 marks + 2 marks)*

h. i Explain what is meant by informed consent. *(2 marks)*

ii Why is it important to gain informed consent from participants? *(2 marks)*

i. The psychologist also decided to ask students about how much stress they experienced during exams to assess their subjective experience. To do this he designed a short questionnaire.

i Describe **two** features he should consider when writing questions for a questionnaire. *(2 marks + 2 marks)*

ii Write **one** appropriate question for this questionnaire. *(2 marks)*

a The covariables are stress score and GCSE score.

b **i** Each member of Years 12 and 13 could have been given a number, and a computer used to generate 20 numbers randomly. This would then be the sample.
ii Another method would have been to use an opportunity sample. You would do this by just asking the first 20 people you come across.

It would be equally acceptable to say 'put all the names of the sixth-formers in a hat and draw out the required number'. You would not, however, get full marks for just saying 'use a computer' or 'put the names in a hat' because not enough detail has been included.

Volunteer sampling is also named in the specification so you might have described this – though any sampling method would be acceptable. But you must describe what you would do; a description of what it is would not be creditworthy.

c A strength of random sampling is that it is potentially unbiased because participants have been selected so that everyone in the population has an equal chance of being selected.
A limitation is that it does not guarantee that the sample is representative of the population – a large sample would be needed to ensure this.

d A pilot study is a small-scale trial run of a study to test the design, with a view to making improvements. It is appropriate to use one here in order to see how easy it will be to get measures of GSR before each exam. If it proves to be difficult then an alternative method will have to be used.

Pilot studies do two things: check your procedures and then lead you to correct any flaws. Make sure you cover both these points when answering questions on pilot studies.

e Scattergraph.

f The scattergraph shows that there is a negative relationship between stress and GCSE performance: as stress increases, GCSE performance goes down. The correlation coefficient of -0.73 suggests there is a strong relationship between these two variables.

The correlation coefficient has been provided to give you an idea on how strong the correlation is between the two variables. This candidate has used the information wisely to provide plenty of detail in the answer. A candidate who just said 'There is a negative correlation' would receive 1 mark.

g There may have been a threat to the internal validity of this study in that the amount of revision could affect both stress scores and GCSE performance. This would mean that the study is not measuring what it intends to measure.
It is possible that students from this particular school have learned to harness their stress in a positive way, whereas this may not be the case for students from other schools, thus the study may lack population validity.

h **i** Informed consent entails a researcher explaining all aspects of a study to participants, including any risks involved in participation, and asking participants to sign an informed consent form.
ii This is important because it is a right for all participants, and the BPS ethical guidelines suggest that it must be given in all studies unless there are good reasons for using deception.

If you simply said 'gaining consent' you would receive no marks because this is a circular answer. What is it that participants are consenting to?

i **i** The researcher should ensure that questions do not prompt the respondents to answer in a certain way (i.e. they should be unbiased). Questions should also be sufficiently clear so that respondents understand the question and can respond accordingly.
ii How stressed do you feel during exams?
(a) extremely stressed (b) moderately stressed
(c) neither stressed nor relaxed (d) moderately relaxed
(e) extremely relaxed

There are other answers that could have been given in (i) such as considering whether questions are closed (for quantitative analysis) or open (for qualitative analysis).

Question 4

An agency involved with young people decides to find out more about attitudes towards dieting in young people from different backgrounds. Staff at the agency have noticed that dieting is rare among certain groups of adolescents. They employ a psychologist to conduct research for them. As a starting point the psychologist decides to interview young people about their eating and dieting habits. He intends to have a set of 10 questions, such as: What did you eat yesterday?, Is this a typical amount of food for one day?, Would you like to lose weight? Then he will ask questions that arise out of the answers given by the participants.

An extract from one interview is given below:

Interviewer: *So what would you describe as the ideal body shape?*

Young girl: *I think most people want to have no tummy and no fat, and to fit into small-sized clothes.*

Interviewer: *It looks to me like you are quite slim. Do you have to watch what you eat to stay so slim?*

Young girl: *I try not to eat anything except an orange for breakfast and to go without lunch.*

Interviewer: *Are your friends the same?*

Young girl: *Most of them.*

You are required to provide *two* weaknesses and no advantages.

Note that there are two parts to this question, as reflected in the marks allocated. You need to provide enough detail of how you would collect your sample to attract the full 2 marks.

As the phrase 'in this study' has been included, your answer should contain some reference to the study rather than offering a more general explanation of how interviewer behaviour may affect a respondent's answers.

There are two parts to this question, so make sure you answer both clearly and give some elaboration in the second part, which is worth 2 marks.

There are 3 marks for both the advantage and disadvantage which means it is important to include a reasonable amount of detail, which you can do by contextualising your answer.

Almost anything could be acceptable here as long as your answer is related to the study and you offer some elaboration of the improvement (rather than just saying, for example, 'more participants').

a. Describe **one** aim of this study. *(2 marks)*

b. Identify the research method used in this study and give **two** weaknesses of using this method. *(1 mark + 2 marks + 2 marks)*

c. Identify **one** way the psychologist might select the sample to be interviewed and explain how he could put this method into practice. *(1 mark + 2 marks)*

d. Give **one** limitation of the sampling method that you selected in (c). *(2 marks)*

e. Explain **one** way in which the relationship between interviewer and participant might have influenced the results obtained in this study. *(2 marks)*

f. Identify **one** ethical issue that the psychologist might have to consider and explain how he might overcome it. *(1 mark + 2 marks)*

g. i The data collected in this study is qualitative. Explain the difference between qualitative and quantitative data. *(3 marks)*

ii Give **one** advantage and **one** disadvantage of qualitative data in the context of this study. *(3 marks + 3 marks)*

h. Explain **two** ways in which the design of this study might have been improved. *(2 marks + 2 marks)*

a An aim of this study is to investigate the relationship between young people's background and their attitude toward eating and dieting.

b This is the interview method.
One weakness of this method is that the interviewer may unintentionally lead the interviewee to respond in a certain way by how they ask a question.
Another weakness is that interviewees may 'fake good', in that they give responses to questions that they feel are socially desirable.

It is, in fact, a mixture of a structured and unstructured interview but such a detailed answer is not required for this part of the question.

c A volunteer sample could be used. A notice could be put on the noticeboard of the agency, giving brief details of the study and asking for volunteers to take part.

d One limitation of a volunteer sample is that it is biased because only certain kinds of people are likely to volunteer – those who are highly motivated.

An answer that simply said 'biased' would barely be worth 1 mark. You must explain why the method would be biased in order to begin earning marks as all sampling methods are biased in some way.

e The interviewer might cause the respondent to answer in a certain way by reinforcing particular responses (e.g. 'It looks to me like you are quite slim').

In this case 'context' is given by providing an example linked to this study.

f An ethical issue in this study would be confidentiality. The researcher would have to ensure anonymity by giving each respondent a number, and not recording any details that could identify a particular respondent.

g **i** Qualitative research stresses the interpretation of language (e.g. an interpretation of interviews) rather than attempting to simply transform it into numbers (e.g. measures of central tendency which would be an example of quantitative data).

This may seem brief for 3 marks but it is both accurate and detailed. A less detailed answer might have said 'Qualitative data is concerned with how people think and feel whereas quantitative data is concerned with how much'.

 ii One advantage is that you collect rich data so you would have lots of detailed information about why different people diet instead of this being restricted by the answers you would expect to get if you used more quantitative questions.
One disadvantage is that it is more difficult to analyse such data; for example, you might get a slightly different answer about why people diet from each respondent and then this could be difficult to summarise.

Notice how clearly each advantage/disadvantage is contextualised to provide enough information to be worth 3 marks each.

h The design of this study might have been improved by interviewing young people from different parts of the city, or even different parts of the country, as this study currently focuses on a fairly narrow cross section of the population.
It could also be improved by gathering other data (e.g. from parents or friends) to substantiate the answers given by the respondents to the interview questions on their actual eating and dieting habits.

These answers are extremely clear and lots of elaboration has been provided.

Question 5

Two female psychology students were intrigued by the idea that women may be more conformist than men, a finding from previous research. They decided to conduct a study to investigate this topic. To assess conformity, they wrote five questions which did not have a right or wrong answer. For example, 'In a survey of 100 students, what percentage said they smoked 10 or more cigarettes a day?'. All the questions required a numerical answer.

The 'researchers' also constructed an answer sheet with space for four answers to each question. Three answers for each question were already filled in, apparently by previous participants. All of the answers were quite similar.

They gave the questions to 20 participants (10 males and 10 females) and asked them to fill in their answers on the prepared answer sheet. If a participant gave an answer which was close to the previous answers, this was counted as conforming.

Each participant received a conformity score indicating the number of times he or she had conformed out of 10 questions.

The findings are shown in the graph and table below.

Table 1	
Male conformity scores 2 4 3 1 0 2 1 3 1 1	Mean **1.8**
Female conformity scores 3 3 5 3 4 2 5 3 4 4	Mean **3.6**

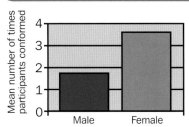

Figure 1

> Candidates often have no idea what is meant by 'experimental design'. There are three possible answers: repeated measures, independent groups or matched pairs (RIM, the letters in the middle of 'experiment'). You have also studied ways of designing observational studies, interviews, questionnaires, and so on.

> For part (iii) you must make sure that you only give one answer. Only your first answer will be marked. However, this doesn't mean that you can only write one sentence, as long as the second sentence is an elaboration of the first one.

> Don't explain what demand characteristics are. *Use* this knowledge to describe how they may occur in this study.

questions

a. Explain why this might be considered to be a natural experiment. *(2 marks)*

b. i What experimental design has been used in this study? *(1 mark)*

   ii Give **one** advantage and **one** disadvantage of this design. *(2 marks + 2 marks)*

c. Identify **one** ethical issue that you would have to consider when conducting this study and explain how you would deal with this. *(1 mark + 2 marks)*

d. i What is the difference between a histogram and a bar chart? *(2 marks)*

   ii Identify the type of graph used to describe the data. *(1 mark)*

   iii Describe **one** reason for using a graph to display the findings of a study. *(2 marks)*

e. Name **one** way that investigator effects might threaten the validity of this study and suggest a way to overcome this problem. *(1 mark +2 marks)*

f. Describe **one** way that demand characteristics might influence your findings. *(2 marks)*

g. i Explain what is meant by reliability. *(2 marks)*

   ii Explain **one** way that the students could check the reliability of the data collected in this study. *(2 marks)*

h. What measure of dispersion would be most suitable to describe the data in Table 1? Explain your choice of measure of dispersion. *(2 marks)*

i. i Write a suitable title for the graph. *(1 mark)*

   ii What is represented by the blue column? *(1 mark)*

j. Describe **one** conclusion that could be drawn from the data in Table 1 and the graph about the relationship between gender and conformity. *(2 marks)*

a This might be considered a natural experiment because the researchers are interested in the difference between males and females with respect to conformity, but they have not manipulated the variable under study (gender).

b **i** Independent groups design.
ii One advantage is that there are no order effects because participants take part in only one condition of the study.
One disadvantage is that participant variables may affect the findings because different participants are used for the two conditions.

There is no requirement to contextualise this answer but you do need to provide detail for 2 marks. An answer that simply said 'One advantage is there are no order effects' would only receive 1 mark because it lacks detail. Always provide a further explanation.
A candidate who got part (i) wrong would get zero marks for the rest of the question.

c An ethical issue in this study is deception, in that participants are led to believe that other people have already given their answers. This could be dealt with through debriefing, where participants have the purpose of the study explained to them, and are able to ask any questions or voice any concerns.

Debriefing would not receive credit as an ethical issue but it is a way of dealing with ethical issues. For full marks you need to say what would happen during debriefing, as has been done in this answer.

d **i** A histogram shows continuous data with a true zero point, whereas a bar chart does not show continuous data.
ii This is a bar chart.
iii The reason for using a graph to display data is so that you can easily compare the findings between the two groups. It is easier than looking at the numbers.

The answer for part (iii) counts as one answer rather than two separate points. If the candidate had written 'One reason is to easily compare the findings and it is a way of summarising data' then this would count as two answers and only the first answer would receive credit.

e There may be a gender interaction effect, in that males may respond differently to females, and vice versa. In order to overcome this problem, half of the female participants could be tested by a male experimenter, and half by a female experimenter. The same arrangement could then be used for the male participants. In this way, the gender interaction effect should balance out across males and females.

You could provide a less detailed response than this and still get full marks but try, as far as possible, always to clearly explain the point you are making.
It would have been acceptable to say 'One problem would be a gender interaction effect. To overcome this one could have a male and female experimenter who each tested half the males and half the females.' Such an answer would just about get full marks. Better to be safe and give a bit more elaboration.

f Because the participants know they are taking part in a study, they may be more likely to give a conforming response simply because they do not want to mess up what they perceive to be a consistent set of results.

If you find it easier to answer this question by stating the definition of demand characteristics first and then using your definition, this is perfectly acceptable. Here is one way to do it: 'Demand characteristics occur when participants respond in predictable ways to experimental cues; for example, in this study participants may have realised the previous answers were fake and either deliberately conformed or not.'

g **i** Reliability refers to whether a measurement or the findings from a study can be repeated if conducted at a later date.
ii Reliability could be checked by comparing responses with the same participants' responses one month later. A high correlation would indicate that participants are responding consistently over time.

h The standard deviation is the best measure to use for this data. It uses all the data, and therefore gives an accurate representation of male–female differences. As there are some extreme scores in the sets of data, other measures of dispersion (e.g. the range) would give an inappropriate indication of the spread of data.

The range would not be suitable to use with this data, so it would get zero marks.

i **i** Graph showing male and female conformity rates.
ii The male conformity rates.

j Females have a greater tendency to give conforming responses whereas males appear to be significantly less conforming.

Notice that the conclusion refers to females in general rather than the participants of this experiment. It is also written in the present rather than past tense. Both of these are characteristics of conclusions, whereas findings refer to participants and are often written in the past tense (because it is what the participants did).